Putting Women Up

The **ISEAS – Yusof Ishak Institute** (formerly Institute of Southeast Asian Studies) is an autonomous organization established in 1968. It is a regional centre dedicated to the study of socio-political, security, and economic trends and developments in Southeast Asia and its wider geostrategic and economic environment. The Institute's research programmes are grouped under Regional Economic Studies (RES), Regional Strategic and Political Studies (RSPS), and Regional Social and Cultural Studies (RSCS). The Institute is also home to the ASEAN Studies Centre (ASC), the Singapore APEC Study Centre, and the Temasek History Research Centre (THRC).

ISEAS Publishing, an established academic press, has issued more than 2,000 books and journals. It is the largest scholarly publisher of research about Southeast Asia from within the region. ISEAS Publishing works with many other academic and trade publishers and distributors to disseminate important research and analyses from and about Southeast Asia to the rest of the world.

Putting Women Up

Gender Equality and Politics in Myanmar

EDITED BY
NETINA TAN • MEREDITH L. WEISS

ISEAS YUSOF ISHAK INSTITUTE

First published in Singapore in 2024 by
ISEAS Publishing
30 Heng Mui Keng Terrace
Singapore 119614

E-mail: publish@iseas.edu.sg
Website: <http://bookshop.iseas.edu.sg>

All rights reserved. No part of this publication may be reproduced, stored in a retrieval system, or transmitted in any form or by any means, electronic, mechanical, photocopying, recording or otherwise, without the prior permission of the ISEAS – Yusof Ishak Institute.

© 2024 ISEAS – Yusof Ishak Institute, Singapore

The responsibility for facts and opinions in this publication rests exclusively with the authors and their interpretations do not necessarily reflect the views or the policy of the publisher or its supporters.

ISEAS Library Cataloguing-in-Publication Data

Name(s): Tan, Netina, editor. | Weiss, Meredith L. (Meredith Leigh), 1972-, editor.
Title: Putting women up : gender equality and politics in Myanmar / edited by Netina Tan and Meredith L. Weiss.
Description: Singapore : ISEAS-Yusof Ishak Institute, 2024. | Includes bibliographical references and index.
Identifiers: ISBN 978-981-5104-41-7 (soft cover) | ISBN 978-981-5104-42-4 (PDF) | ISBN 9789815104431 (epub)
Subjects: LCSH: Women—Political activity—Myanmar.
Classification: LCC HQ1236.5 B9P99

Cover design by Lee Meng Hui
Index compiled by DiacriTech Technologies Private Limited
Typesetting by International Typesetters Pte Ltd
Printed in Singapore by Markono Print Media Pte Ltd

CONTENTS

List of Tables	*vii*
List of Figures	*viii*
Acronyms and Glossary	*ix*
Acknowledgements	*xi*
About the Contributors	*xii*

1. Putting Women Up: Promoting Gender Equality in Myanmar Politics 1
   Netina Tan and Meredith L. Weiss

2. The Secret Garden of Candidate Selection and Women's Political Participation 32
   Aye Lei Tun and Netina Tan

3. Ethnic Parties, Representation, and Female Candidate Recruitment in Myanmar 57
   Jangai Jap and Cassandra Preece

4. Attitudes Towards Women and Political Leadership 88
   Anor Mu, Paul Minoletti, Guillem Riambau, and Michelle Dion

5. Violence, Gender, and Politics   119
   Elin Bjarnegård (and anonymous co-author)

6. Navigating Local Politics and Gender   143
   Cassandra Preece, La Ring Pausa and Paul Minoletti

Appendices
Appendix One: Background of Selected Political Parties and   167
   Vote Shares
Appendix Two: Survey Questions   173
Appendix Three: Focus Group Guide for Field Data Collection   185
Appendix Four: Interview Guide Used for Field Data Collection   188
Appendix Five: Samples of Elite Interview Questions   192

Index   198

LIST OF TABLES

Table 1.1:	Total Number of Elected Women MPs in the Different Levels of Government, 2010–20	14
Table 1.2:	Parties, Candidates, and MPs	15
Table 2.1:	Candidate Selection Methods for the Lower House (Pyithu Hluttaw)	37
Table 2.2:	Party Central Executive Committee (CEC) Membership by Gender	38
Table 3.1:	Electoral Performance by Catch-All Versus Ethnic Parties in Myanmar General Elections	62
Table 3.2:	Ethnic Parties (2015) and Their First Election	64
Table 3.3:	2015 GE, Candidates and Winners by Gender and Party (all legislatures)	75
Table 3.4:	2015 Union Assembly, Candidates and Winners by Gender and Institutionalization (ethnic parties in the states only)	79
Table 4.1:	Descriptive Statistics by Region/State, 2018	95
Table 5.1:	Internet Users in Myanmar, 2011–16	132

LIST OF FIGURES

Figure 1.1:	Administrative Geography of Myanmar	12
Figure 2.1:	Inclusivity and Centralization of Candidate Selection Method	36
Figure 4.1:	Support for Gender Equality Among Men and Women in Myanmar, 2018	97
Figure 4.2:	Political Efficacy, Life Experiences, and Perceptions of Trust, Safety, and Democracy Among Men and Women in Myanmar, 2018	99
Figure 4.3:	Support for Women's Participation in Politics and Political Interest and Knowledge Among Men and Women in Myanmar, 2018	101
Figure 4.4:	Factors Associated with Gender Equality in Myanmar, 2018	104
Figure 4.5:	Factors Associated with Internal Political Efficacy by Gender in Myanmar, 2018	107

ACRONYMS AND GLOSSARY

Amyotha Hluttaw	House of Nationalities (upper house)
ANP	Arakan National Party
CC	Central Committee
CEC	Central Executive Committee
CRPH	Committee Representing the Pyidaungsu Hluttaw
EAO	Ethnic armed organisation
GAD	General Administrative Department
GE	General election
HH	Household Heads (e.g. 100- or 10-HH)
Hluttaw	Legislative chamber
KSDP	Kachin State Democracy Party
LNDP	Lisu National Development Party
MNP	Mon National Party
MP	Member of Parliament
NCDDP	National Community Driven Development Programme
NLD	National League for Democracy
NUCC	National Unity Consultative Council
NUG	National Unity Government
PNO	Pa-O National Organization
PR	Proportional representation
Pyidaungsu Hluttaw	Myanmar's national legislature
Pyithu Hluttaw	House of Representatives (lower house)
SMD	Single-member district
SNLD	Shan Nationalities League for Democracy

Tatmadaw	Myanmar military
TDAC	Township Development Affairs Committee
TEC	Township Executive Committee
TC	Township Chairman
TNP	Ta'Ang National Party
USDP	Union Solidarity and Development Party
W/VTA	Ward/Village tract administrator

ACKNOWLEDGEMENTS

All the authors are grateful to all the participants and interviewees who gave up their time to share their experiences for this research project that started in 2017. We would also like to thank our Enlightened Myanmar Research Foundation (EMReF) colleagues for collecting and translating the data and assisting us with our analysis. While we wish to acknowledge each of them by name, it is not possible given the current climate of repression in Myanmar. Finally, we would like to acknowledge International Development Research Council (IDRC) of Canada for their generous funding of the research project and the writing of this book. And especial thanks to Dr Edgard Rodriguez for his encouragement and unwavering support of us and Myanmar's democracy.

ABOUT THE CONTRIBUTORS

Elin Bjarnegård is Associate Professor in Political Science at Uppsala University, Sweden. In the year 2020–21, she was a Fellow at the Netherlands Institute for Advanced Study in the Humanities and Social Sciences, where she worked on a book about gender politics in authoritarian states. Her research focuses on gender, political parties and conflict and has been published in journals such as *Comparative Politics, Party Politics, Government & Opposition, Politics & Gender* and *Journal of Peace Research*. She is the author of the book *Gender, Informal Institutions and Political Recruitment: Explaining Male Dominance in Parliamentary Representation* (2013).

Michelle Dion is a Professor of Political Science at McMaster University, Canada. Her research interests include three broad themes: the political economy of social policy in Latin America; sexuality, attitudes, and policy; and diversity, methodology, and the profession of political science. She is the author of *Workers & Welfare* (2010) and articles appearing in journals, including *PLOS-One, Comparative Politics*, and *International Studies Quarterly*, among others. She is also a co-editor of the *American Political Science Review* (2020–24).

Paul Minoletti completed a doctorate in Economic and Social History from the University of Oxford in 2011, and since 2012 has worked as a policy researcher in Myanmar. Paul has published on a range of political and economic topics in Myanmar, including gender and political participation, gender and budgeting, economics and conflict, fiscal decentralization and federalism, and public financial management.

Jangai Jap is an Early Career Provost Fellow at the University of Texas at Austin in the Department of Government and a Post-Doctoral Fellow in the Politics of Race and Ethnicity Lab. Her research interests focus on ethnic politics, nationalism, minority-state relations, civil war and Burma/Myanmar politics.

Cassandra Preece is a PhD candidate in Political Science (Comparative Public Policy) at McMaster University. She is a doctoral research fellow for McMaster's Ethnic Quota and Political Representation research project and is a 2020 SSHRC doctoral fellow. Her research interests include elections, ethnic minority representation, ethnic conflict, and political parties in the Asia Pacific.

La Ring Pausa was a Program Officer and researcher at Enlightened Myanmar Research Foundation (EMReF) in Yangon, Myanmar. La Ring has conducted research as a research project manager in the fields of socioeconomics, gender equality and media audiences across the country. He holds a Bachelor of Social Work from Martin Luther Christian University, MLCU Shillong, Northeast India, and Master of Arts in Social Science (Development Studies) from Chiang Mai University, Thailand.

Guillem Riambau is an Assistant Professor of Economics at Universitat de Barcelona, and member of the Barcelona Institute of Economics (IEB) and the Institute and Political Economy Research Center (IPERC). He received his PhD in Economics from Boston University in 2012 and holds a BA in Political Science (2001) and a BA in Economics (2005) from the Universitat Autònoma de Barcelona.

Netina Tan is a University Fellow and Associate Professor of Political Science at McMaster University, Canada. Her work focuses on authoritarian resilience, digital democracy and political representation of women and ethnic minorities. Her work has appeared in *Democratization, Election Law Journal, Electoral Studies, Politics and Gender, Representation, Pacific Affairs*, among others.

Aye Lei Tun is a PhD student in Political Science (Comparative Public Policy) at McMaster University, Canada. She holds a Master of Development Practices degree (2015) from the University of Queensland in Australia and a Master of Gender, Human Rights and Conflict Studies degree (2016) from the International Institute of Social Studies. She was the Senior Gender Program Manager with the Enlightened Myanmar Research Foundation in Yangon.

Anor Mu is a national research consultant working for national and international bodies in Myanmar. She was awarded her bachelor's degree in Population Studies from Yangon University of Economics in 2005 and her master's degree in 2007.

Meredith Weiss is Professor of Political Science in the Rockefeller College of Public Affairs and Policy at the University at Albany, State University of New York, U.S.A. Her research addresses social mobilization and civil society, the politics of identity and development, parties and elections, institutional reform, and subnational governance in Southeast Asia, with particular focus on Malaysia and Singapore.

1

PUTTING WOMEN UP: PROMOTING GENDER EQUALITY IN MYANMAR POLITICS

Netina Tan and Meredith Weiss

The coup that overturned Myanmar's elected government in early 2021 clearly upended the roadmap to democracy the country had been following, however haltingly, for over a decade. As of this writing, Myanmar's political future is uncertain; the military (called the Tatmadaw) has shown no sign of relenting in its assault on the prior elected government and the broad resistance the coup triggered. One might question the utility of exploring the status quo ante in light of the desperate situation now. We contend that understanding how, and how well, aspects of democracy worked during Myanmar's ill-fated experiment is, in fact, essential. Not only might we still hope for restoration of civilian, elected government, under the National Unity Government (NUG) currently contesting the military junta or otherwise, but the underlying sociopolitical patterns evident in the recent past, reflecting societal attitudes and priorities, remain germane. Especially salient in this vein are attitudes towards women's leadership: while neither women nor men can currently seek or hold elected office, institutional features alone were hardly the only arbiters of women's political standing when they could do so.

This book investigates the extent to which men and women have faced different opportunities and challenges in securing election, especially as members of parliament (MPs), but also at subnational tiers, in Myanmar, and why. For instance, have the relevant hurdles been more at the local or national level, in society or in political parties, and structured largely by gender or more by class or other attributes? Understanding these patterns is essential to knowing the extent to which a return to civilian government will likely empower women, or what attitudinal changes, beyond structural ones, would be necessary. Moreover, this investigation allows us to consider Myanmar in comparative context, to see how sociopolitical attitudes and constraints here align with those elsewhere in the region, coup aside.

To answer these questions, we set out to examine women's political representation and opportunities to participate in party politics in Myanmar. Our findings are based on a three-year (2017–20) project funded by the Canadian International Development Research Centre (IDRC) on "Engendering Political Recruitment and Participation at the Party, Local and National Level in Myanmar". The project brought together an international academic team of five members, led by Netina Tan of McMaster University, working in collaboration with Enlightened Myanmar Research Foundation (EMReF), a local non-governmental organization in Myanmar, to examine political parties' and community members' attitudes towards and practices regarding women's political leadership. The qualitative and quantitative data the team gathered allow us to assess men's and women's relative opportunities to participate in both local and national politics in Myanmar, through different political parties. Here we draw together those findings.

We launched the project with a focus on capacity-building, with research-training workshops for the EMReF team members, as well as collective brainstorming as we developed our research methods and approach. We then embarked on two years of extensive primary data collection across Myanmar, as detailed below. Researchers from EMReF conducted the field research, with support from locally based and external team members. We were unable to complete one planned-for component due to the pandemic then ramping up: a visit to Indonesia and Malaysia for comparative research. We then worked together to analyse the data and write up our findings, even as a coup (discussed further below) upended politics—and life broadly—in Myanmar. Enough of our research team, however scattered, stayed with the project for us to complete this volume, as the culmination of our multi-year, collaborative effort.

Much of the existing literature on Myanmar (and on other transitional democracies and/or postcolonial, developing states) typically adopts a historical or culturalist perspective to detail the barriers to women's political access. Our book takes a different approach: it is the first effort of which we are aware to study systematically the key political parties, their candidate selection methods, and how party organization and leadership affect women's political participation at the local and national levels. Our collaborative approach to the work, as well as our original primary data, are rare in Myanmar studies and Southeast Asian comparative work, especially in English (though we know of little that comes close in local languages, either). We provide unparalleled glimpses into the "secret gardens" of candidate selection and internal politics of even less-known parties in Myanmar. Our findings expand upon insights regarding gender inequality in Myanmar politics despite the February 2021 coup.

Yet the coup does loom large, of course, and reinforces how deeply militarization and violence intertwine with politics in Myanmar. Shortly after we completed our field research in Myanmar, Myanmar's military overthrew the National League of Democracy government that had been re-elected the previous year, claiming irregularities, and installed a highly coercive military regime. That coup government remains in place; the country remains in turmoil. The junta has planned provisionally for elections in 2023, but most observers expect these polls not to be meaningful, if they happen at all. We opted to continue with our analysis not only in hopes that the country might soon return to electoral rule, making conclusions about women's access to elected office directly germane again, but also given the extent to which these findings reflect more than just contingent institutional arrangements. Rather, our findings reveal how past institutional structures and rules interact with long-standing socio-cultural practices and attitudes within families and local communities. Those features predated the now-upended democratic regime and will surely outlast the current authoritarian one.

UNDERREPRESENTATION OF WOMEN IN MYANMAR POLITICS

Since liberalization began in Myanmar in 2010, Myanmar has held three nationwide general elections for its national and subnational parliaments. (We sketch these institutions and electoral rules below.) While only 37 parties competed in 2010, in November 2015, many parties that boycotted in 2010 competed and others formed, following changes in the relevant laws, bringing the total contesting to 93, then about 100 in 2020 (Kudo 2011; Oh 2020). In both 2015, the election immediately preceding our research, and 2020, the National League for Democracy (NLD) won a clear majority of both elected and total seats in the national parliament and in most (12 of 14) subnational state/regional parliaments (International Crisis Group 2015, pp. 15–16; Asia Foundation 2020). The party's female leader, Aung San Suu Kyi, is constitutionally barred from becoming president, given a provision aimed specifically at her, disqualifying anyone with foreign immediate family from that office. However, she is widely regarded as the de facto leader of the civilian government. (While detained under trumped-up charges since the coup, she remains the acknowledged leader of the NUG.) The formal position of State Counsellor was created for her, instead.

Notwithstanding the prominence of a charismatic and popular female head of government, other senior elected positions remain extremely male-dominated. Upon her election in 2015, Aung San Suu Kyi, known as Daw Suu, was (and still in the NUG, remains) the only woman in the national-level cabinet, and the vice presidents, speakers, and deputy speakers in the Pyithu Hluttaw and Amyotha Hluttaw, the lower and upper houses of parliament, were all men. Two of the 14 state/region chief ministers were female—they were the first women to hold those positions—as was one state/region hluttaw speaker of the house (also the first woman to hold this position) (Minoletti 2016).

These patterns hold across elected offices. While the proportion of female members of parliament elected in 2015—13.7 percent—was higher than at any time in Myanmar's past, then increased to 16 per cent in 2020, it remained extremely low by international standards. By comparison, the rate globally (as of January 2022) is 26.2 per cent; across Asia, it is 21.1 per cent (IPU Parline 2022). Women's representation in the 14 subnational parliaments was also low, averaging 12.7 per cent of elected MPs in 2015 and even less, 9.7 per cent, when one includes military appointees in that total; women's share of elected state and regional seats increased only to 18 per cent in 2020 (Asia Foundation 2020). States and regions diverged widely in their proportion of female MPs, but that share remained well below parity even in the parliaments with the highest levels of female representation: women were just 26 per cent of elected MPs in Mon State and 30 per cent in Yangon Region in 2020. Three state parliaments included no female MPs at all in 2015 (Minoletti 2016). (We delve more deeply into these data below.)

Political parties vary considerably, too, in the proportion of their MPs who were female. Nevertheless, among the parties that won five or more seats across Myanmar's national and subnational hluttaws in 2015, the highest proportion of female MPs was 16.7 per cent, in both the Shan Nationalities League for Democracy (seven women out of 42 MPs) and the Zomi League for Democracy (one woman out of six MPs). The NLD's rate was slightly lower, at 15.1 per cent. Women were particularly poorly represented in parties such as the Arakan National Party (4.4 per cent of MPs), the Union Solidarity and Development Party (2.6 per cent), and the Pa'O National Organisation (0 per cent) (Minoletti 2017).

This imbalance extends throughout administrative tiers. Only 88 of Myanmar's 16,785 ward/village tract administrators are women (i.e., around 0.5 per cent). We lack research thus far into the extent to which experience of local leadership in Myanmar can lead to political participation at state/regional and national levels; elsewhere, such a progression through levels of government is common, as lower-level office, whether elected or appointed, trains politicians for higher-level positions. Since 2012, the position of ward/village tract administrator has been an elected one in Myanmar. However, these elections are indirect. Each household has a single vote, cast by the head of household, for a "ten-household head", then these ten-household heads elect the ward/village tract administrator.

Most heads of Myanmar households are men, which creates a highly gender-unequal electorate. This imbalance perhaps contributes to the very low number of female ward/village tract administrators. Other key issues related to local-level participation that previous research identifies include the fact that since 2012, there has been no officially recognized position of "village head" and that there are no requirements for ward/village tract administrators to hold public meetings or distribute information (Minoletti 2016). However, the lack of detailed research into local-level political participation, especially from a gender perspective, limits the scope of academic insight into local political processes, as well as how these scale up to the state/regional and national levels. Further study is needed, presumably once the current impasse is resolved, to understand key issues and dynamics. In the meantime, our research—detailed in the chapters to come—represents a step in that direction.

SITUATING MYANMAR IN TERMS OF GENDER AND PARTY POLITICS

The problem of the paucity of women in elected office is not unique to Myanmar. In 1995, the UN World Conference on Women in Beijing, China spurred a global push for gender equality and highlighted women's persistent political underrepresentation as a democratic problem as well as a hurdle for economic and human development. The Beijing Declaration and Platform for Action noted that women were underrepresented despite making up half of the electorate, and notwithstanding political liberalization in many countries (UN Women 1995, p. 79). In 1995, women comprised about 10 per cent of the world's parliamentarians. Today, even after the adoption of gender quotas for elections in more than 130 countries, women still comprise only 26 per cent (IPU Parline 2022).

Women's low level of representation in Myanmar's parliaments is a concern for many reasons. First, representation in governance bodies has symbolic importance, and more gender-equal representation can help foster a greater sense of institutional legitimacy among female citizens—an especially salient consideration when these institutions are still new, as was the case in Myanmar (Mansbridge 1999). Men and women tend to have different preferences and priorities for policy-making and budgetary allocations, and female representatives tend to be more responsive than male representatives to women's preferences (Chattopadhyay and Duflo 2004; Franceschet and Piscopo 2008; Lawless 2015; Tinker 2004).[1] More inclusive and gender-equal participation in governance bodies can thus result in more efficient and effective policy-making—again, a concern in a context of transitional government and resource-scarcity (Agarwal 2009; Beaman et al. 2009; Janssens 2010).

Lastly, changing the gender composition of representation can affect styles of governance. For example, research on the United States has found that female mayors are more likely to acknowledge and address fiscal problems their cities face, and female chairpersons of government committees tend to do more to facilitate discussion among other members (Lawless 2015). While we may see cross-cultural differences in governing styles, which institutional variations may accentuate, it is reasonable to expect similar divergence between male and female styles in Myanmar and elsewhere, as well.

The rise in women's representation worldwide has been largely a consequence of advocacy from the UN system, women's movements, democracy activists, and donors. A surge in research on how women come to power and their substantive impact when in office, focused especially on political parties as mediating institutions, has underpinned this push. Party strategists commonly attribute women's political under-representation to women themselves. When asked about the lack of female candidates, they often lament that no women are willing to step forward, or that there are too few qualified women. This explanation, sometimes labelled as "supply-side", blames women's under-representation on a perceived lack of supply of eligible or qualified women (Bjarnegård 2013; Norris and Lovenduski 1993). Other observers suggested that more emphasis should be placed on "demand-side" explanations, focusing instead on the kind of candidates parties are looking for and the formal and informal criteria they use when selecting candidates to compete in elections (Bjarnegård and Zetterberg 2019; Hennings and Urbatsch 2016).

Increasingly, analysts have realized that supply and demand factors interact: when parties want to recruit women, they also motivate and shape women's ambition, leading more women to step forward (Verge 2015). Programmes that focus solely on raising the skills of potential female candidates, rather than reforming parties in a more gender-equal way, hence miss their mark (Geha 2019). Our starting point is, thus, the assumption that we need to view political parties as male-dominated institutions as well as considering women's sociological position, to understand the ways in which women as a category enter party politics, secure nomination as candidates, and compete in elections.

With few exceptions, academic research has found political parties to play pivotal roles in ensuring or hindering political gender equality

(Kunovich and Paxton 2005). Political parties are the gatekeepers to women's political representation; the manner in which they select candidates for elections is key to understanding the lack of diversity in the ensuing legislature or other elected offices (Lovenduski 2005; Caul 1999; Dahlerup 2007; Gallagher and Marsh 1988). Previous research to explain women's low parliamentary representation in Myanmar, however, has tended to focus less on parties as institutions, leaning more towards supply-side explanations. These studies have found the following factors to be especially important:

- Cultural biases that lead most citizens to prefer male political leaders and women to have less confidence and ambition to try to become parliamentarians.
- Cultural norms that make it harder for women to travel to remote areas and/or overnight (e.g. to campaign), or to avoid harassment. (Although male and female parliamentary candidates both frequently face forms of harassment, harassment of public figures is often gendered, making this more commonly a problem for women than men.)
- The difficulty of balancing family and household responsibilities that women are typically expected to perform with participating in public life.
- That men dominate key leadership positions within parties at both national and local levels (GEN 2013, 2015; Asia Foundation 2014).

The few years preceding the coup saw an increasing amount of research on gender in politics in Myanmar (Zin Mar Aung 2015; Maber and Tregoning 2016; Shwe Shwe Sein Latt et al. 2017; Minoletti 2014). We thus have reasonably good information on certain factors salient to explaining gender differences in political participation and can rule out for Myanmar some explanations that apply elsewhere. For example, while often assumed an explanatory factor, education does not seem to be so in Myanmar. Among those aged over 25, men are more likely than women to be literate and are slightly more likely than women to have completed high school (15.1 per cent of the male population vs. 13.7 per cent of the female population). However, women are slightly more likely than men to have completed tertiary education (9.3 per cent vs. 8.8 per cent), and are noticeably more likely than males to have completed an undergraduate degree (7.6 per cent vs. 6.1 per cent), a master's degree (0.3 per cent vs. 0.2 per cent), or a PhD (0.1 per cent vs. 0.0 per cent) (Government of Myanmar, Department of Population 2017). Thus, gender differences in educational attainment explain little or none of the difference we observe in parliamentary representation.

Nor does labour-force participation seem to matter in the same way it does in some other countries. Although women have a lower labour-force participation rate than men in Myanmar, the gender gap is lower (and in some cases reversed) for many of the occupations from which parliamentarians are most commonly drawn (Minoletti 2017, pp. 26–29). Specifically, the 2015 Labour Force Survey found 80.2 per cent of the male population aged 15 and above to be active in the labour force; the equivalent figure for women was only 51.6 per cent (MOLES, CSO, and ILO 2017). This gender gap in labour-force participation is significant and above that found in many other ASEAN countries. Nevertheless, women are both relatively and absolutely more prevalent than men in occupations classified as "professional": for instance, teachers, lawyers, veterinarians, and medical staff (ILO 2017). Hence, analyst Paul Minoletti (2017, p. 29) concludes: "Overall [in Myanmar], it does not seem that gender differences in occupation are a major factor driving the gender differences we see in women's and men's likelihood to seek or win elected office".

Some explanations relevant in other contexts are germane to Myanmar, but with a twist. For instance, here, as elsewhere, the cost of campaigns may be a particular impediment for women. Political campaigning is expensive. Many parliamentary candidates have to use their own funds to cover some or all of their costs. This requirement may pose a bigger barrier for women than men. However, research by the Gender Equality Network (GEN) found that in Myanmar, party matters more than gender. That is, a party's financial capacity to support their candidates affects their abilities to campaign effectively, regardless of personal resources (Minoletti 2017, p. 40).

Yet an especially debilitating feature of the system, when it comes to gender equity, is the enduring role of the armed forces in government, even prior to the coup. The military ruled Myanmar from 1962 to 2010. Even with the advent of an elected government, the military-drafted 2008 constitution still reserves at least 25 per cent of parliamentary seats for military appointees and ensures that the military appoints several key government ministers (i.e., Defence, Home Affairs, and Border Affairs). The militarization of Myanmar politics and reservation of legislative seats for the military has a significant impact in depressing the number of women in the Pyithu Hluttaws (Harriden 2012, pp. 175–79; Zin Mar Aung 2015). The military appoints very few women to parliament, so the reservation of seats has meant fewer seats for women. Further, the constitution can only be changed with the military's approval.[2] Moreover, the Tatmadaw's long and intimate involvement in Myanmar's politics has had a broader impact on political participation by reinforcing traditional concepts of male authority and superiority as part of a militarization of public space (Hedström, Olivius, and Kay Soe 2021; Hedström and Olivius 2022). As we explore in later chapters, violence in different forms, starting at the level of the family, has pervasive effects on attitudes about women and gender roles; the looming public, and highly masculine, face of Myanmar's military surely amplifies those effects.

Importantly, cultural norms are not static, nor are citizens' voting preferences, when citizens have the opportunity to express them. Although a majority of Myanmar citizens share a preference for male leaders, in the 2015 elections, vote choice was largely based on party allegiance rather than on candidates' characteristics (Minoletti 2017, p. 42). This pattern means whom the parties nominate matters. Consequently, whom the parties recruit and how, and the extent to which this process disadvantages women relative to men, is critical. It is especially these questions, at the intersection of supply- and demand-side explanations for women's political underrepresentation, that our study seeks to address (Minoletti 2017, pp. 36–37).

Recruitment and promotion dynamics within parties are important factors in explaining women's low level of participation (Niven 1998; Lawless and Fox 2010; Bjarnegård and Kenny 2015; Crowder-Meyer 2013). This salience is evident as women are noticeably absent in key party-level decision-making committees and councils. However, we lack detailed insight into how these dynamics operate in Myanmar—for instance, of selection criteria and processes that local bodies, including political parties, use to choose legislative candidates (Barnea and Rahat 2007; Gallagher and Marsh 1988).

To explain the low descriptive representation and participation of women in political parties and in elected offices at all tiers, from village leadership to the national parliament, we organize this book broadly around four key themes:

i. Intra-party dynamics and parties' candidate selection methods (Chapters Two and Three);
ii. Public attitudes towards women's political participation (Chapter Four);
iii. How exposure to gendered violence in the private sphere shapes attitudes towards women's participation in the public sphere (Chapter Five); and
iv. Local governance institutions and processes (Chapter Six).

Intra-party politics has largely been a black box for gender researchers in Myanmar.[3] Existing research tells us little about whether what inhibits women's political advancement is primarily a supply or demand problem, or whether institutional, cultural, or resource factors affect women's more than men's political participation (Minoletti 2017, p. 6; Norris 2012). Nor does it offer substantial insight into the extent to which political parties are bureaucratized or what formal or informal selection criteria guide candidate selection. Similarly, extant scholarship regarding socio-cultural norms and gendered attitudes towards political participation is limited, both in terms of *which* factors matter most for political socialization, and, especially, the effect of these leanings at the grassroots level, where popular attitudes may be less mediated by party or other mechanisms, and where political careers so often begin. The chapters to come shed light on these important questions—not just for knowledge's sake, but also to better prepare the ground for Myanmar's hoped-for return before long to elected, civilian-led governance.

ELECTORAL AND PARTY SYSTEMS IN PRE-COUP MYANMAR

Myanmar's 2008 constitution substantially restructured the preceding military-authoritarian system. One feature that remained constant: ethnicity as a core defining feature of, and fault-line in, the polity. Since 2008, ethnic identities have been institutionally represented in four different forms: ethnic states, self-administered areas, ethnic affairs ministers, and constituencies won by ethnic parties. Geographically, the

FIGURE 1.1
Administrative Geography of Myanmar

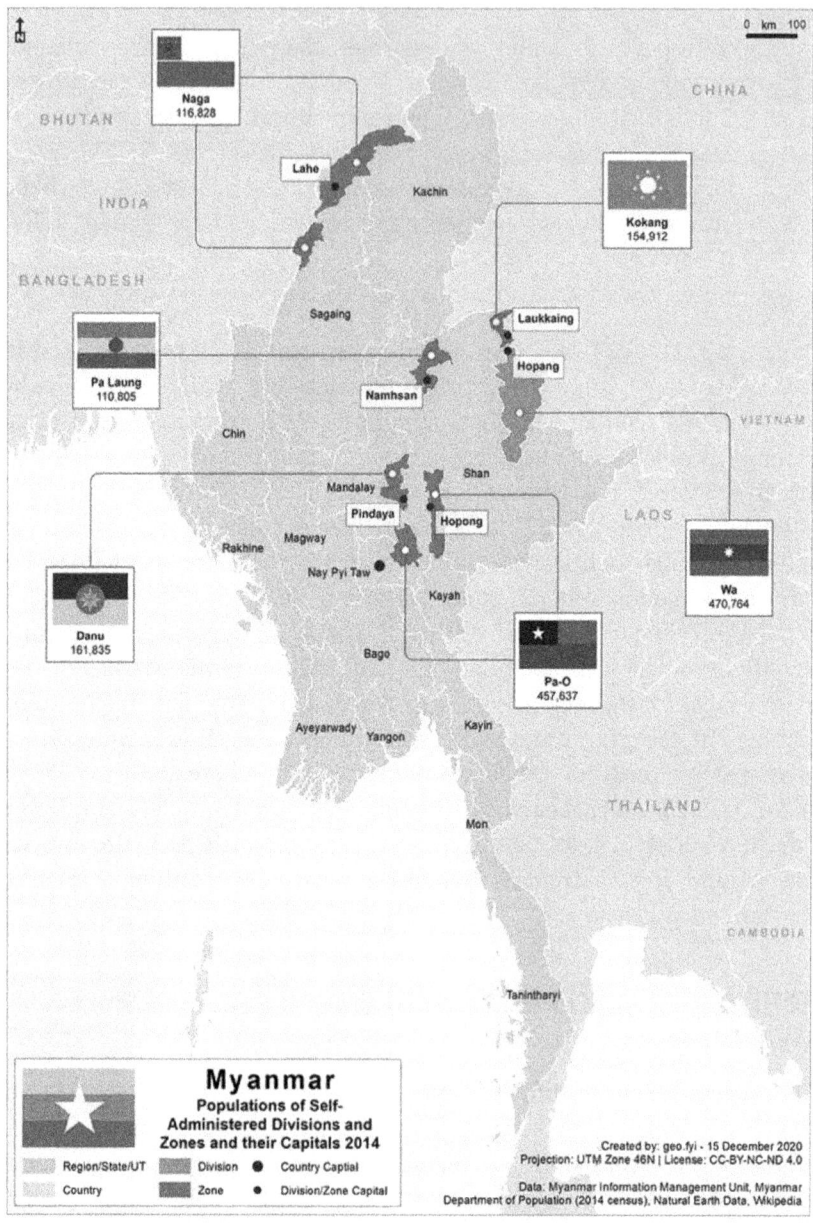

Source: Geo.Fyi (2020).

country is separated into seven regions located in the central area and dominated by the Bamar ethnic-majority population, and seven states within the borderlands, each dominated by ethnic-minority groups. The 2008 constitution also created six self-administered zones and districts (SAZ/SAD) for smaller ethnic groups that comprise minorities within a state or region but are in the majority within a specific township (Jolliffe 2015, p. 32). There are now self-administered zones or districts for the Wa, Kokang, Naga, Pa-O, Palaung, and Danu (Kyi Pyar Chit Saw and Arnold 2014, p. 14). Figure 1.1 maps out this landscape.

Myanmar's bicameral union (national-level) parliament, collectively referred to as the Pyidaungsu Hluttaw, includes the Pyithu Hluttaw and the Amyotha Hluttaw; see Figure 1.2. The Pyithu Hluttaw has 330 elected MPs and 110 MPs appointed by the military.[4] The Amyotha Hluttaw has 168 elected MPs and 56 military-appointed MPs. Myanmar's state and regional parliaments, also called hluttaw, vary dramatically in size, but all also reserve at least 25 per cent of seats for military appointees. In addition to "regular" elected MPs, many states' or regions' hluttaws have elected ethnic affairs representatives, who represent specific ethnic groups residing there.[5]

All of Myanmar's elected MPs are elected via a "first-past-the-post" or majoritarian system. For the Pyithu Hluttaw, each of Myanmar's 330 townships is a single constituency. For the Amyotha Hluttaw, each state or region has 12 constituencies. Since most have more than 12 townships, some townships are grouped together to form single constituencies. However, in other states or regions, the opposite is true, meaning some townships are divided between two constituencies. For state/region hluttaw elections, each township is split into two constituencies.

GENDER BREAKDOWN IN MYANMAR PARLIAMENTS

It is beyond our scope here to detail electoral patterns or parliamentary composition in full across Myanmar's three post-transition, pre-coup elections (2010, 2015, and 2020). Moreover, given the partial nature of the 2010 election—the leading opposition party, the NLD, boycotted—we focus on the presumably more representative 2015 and (to a lesser extent) 2020 elections. Within that ambit, we home in on questions of gender.

Heading into the 2015 elections, women comprised only 6 per cent of MPs in the Pyidaungsu Hluttaw—and that was an increase from a mere 2.7 per cent elected in 2010 (Egreteau 2014; Minoletti 2017). (Intervening by-elections boosted the count.) In 2015, women's share of elected seats increased to a still less-than-impressive 13.7 per cent at the national level. They fared slightly worse at the subnational level: across all state and regional parliaments, women secured 12.7 per cent of seats, though that was a sharp improvement from the 3.8 per cent they held previously, as Table 1.1 indicates.

TABLE 1.1
Total Number of Elected Female MPs in the Different Levels of Government, 2010–20

	Elected MPs No. of Women/Elected MPs (%)			Military-appointed MPs No. of Women/Military MPs (%)			Women as % of All MPs		
	2010–15	2015–20	2020	2010–15	2015–20	2020	2010–15	2015–20	2020
Union Parliament (Pyidaungsu Hluttaw)	28/438 (6%)	67/424 (13.7%)	79/397 (16.6%)	2/164 (1.2%)	2/164 (1.2%)	NA	4.8%	10.5%	NA
Upper House (Amyotha Hluttaw)	4/155 (2.5%)	23/145 (13.7%)	26/135 (15.5%)	0/56 (0%)	0/56 (0%)	NA	1.8%	10.3%	NA
Lower House (Pyithu Hluttaw)	24/28 (7.8%)	44/279 (13.6%)	53/262 (16.8%)	2/108 (1.9%)	2/108 (1.9%)	NA	6.2%	10.6%	NA
State/ Regional Parliaments	25/634 (3.8%)	84/575 (12.7%)	116/641 (18%)	1/221 (0.5%)	2/219 (0.9%)	NA	2.9%	9.7%	NA

Source: Phan Tee Eain and The Gender Equality Network (2014); Shwe Shwe Sein Latt et al. (2017); EMReF (2020).

Women's representation varied considerably among states and regions. In top-performing Mon state, women held nearly 20 per cent of seats in 2015, whereas Chin, Kayah and Rakhine states had yet to elect any women as of the time of our research (Minoletti 2017, p. 12). As we note earlier, that gap persisted in 2020, even as Mon state's share of female MPs edged even higher. The reservation of seats for military appointees notably reduced the proportion of women in office: women secured only 1.2 per cent of military-appointed seats in the Pyidaungsu Hluttaw in 2015, and a paltry 0.9 per cent at the state/regional level (see Table 1.1).

Table 1.2 tallies the proportion of female and male candidates and MPs across all parliaments in the 2015 elections for each of the parties in our study. It is striking that fewer than 20 per cent of candidates in all the parties were women, and only one party had more than 20 per cent female MPs—the Kachin State Democracy Party (KSDP), which only had four MPs in total. The average proportion of female candidates across all parties and independents in the 2015 election was around 13 per cent.[6] Five of our parties exceeded that average, as the table indicates, and four were below average. Women's participation as both candidates and MPs is strikingly low in the Arakan National Party (ANP), Pa-O National Organisation (PNO), and Union Solidarity and Development Party (USDP).

TABLE 1.2
Parties, Candidates, and MPs

Party	Total Candidates	Female Candidates	Women as % of Candidates	Total MPs	Female MPs	Women as % of MPs
MNP	54	10	19%	3	0	0%
SNLD	151	27	18%	42	7	17%
LNDP	28	5	18%	5	1	20%
KSDP	55	8	15%	4	1	25%
NLD	1152	167	14%	886	134	15%
TNP	27	3	11%	12	1	8%
USDP	1151	69	6%	117	3	3%
ANP	79	4	5%	45	2	4%
PNO	24	1	4%	10	0	0%

Source: Extracted from Union Election Commission (UEC) and EMReF (2015).

While this study focuses on gender equality in legislative office, it is worth highlighting also other aspects of political representation. While we do not have exact data on the ethnic composition of MPs or on the total Myanmar population, the proportion of MPs who were Bamar and non-Bamar appeared to correspond roughly to the proportion of the population that is thought to be from these groups (i.e., Bamar comprise around 60–65 per cent). Furthermore, the three probably largest ethnic minority groups accounted for the largest shares of non-Bamar MPs: Shan (6.5 per cent of Pyidaungsu Hluttaw MPs), Rakhine (5.7 per cent), and Kayin (4.7 per cent). In terms of religious groups, the Christian minority were overrepresented among MPs, whereas Muslims were not represented at all, despite being over 4 per cent of Myanmar's population. The share of MPs who were Buddhist roughly corresponded to their share of the general population—close to 90 per cent (Minoletti 2017, pp. 14–15).

Clearly, numerical representation in parliamentary bodies need not entail substantive representation. For example, although ethnic Bamar were not overrepresented among MPs, many ethnic-minority leaders feel that a small Bamar elite that pays insufficient attention to ethnic-minority interests has controlled decision-making within the dominant and highly top-down NLD (TNI 2015, p. 12). Moreover, even prior to the coup, the Tatmadaw continued to wield significant influence over policy-making and implementation in Myanmar and was widely seen to focus on Buddhist and Bamar interests (Stokke 2019b; Fink 2015; South 2018). Clearly, while women's underrepresentation is an important dimension to address, it was not the only area in which Myanmar's pre-coup leadership and democratic praxis fell short of normative ideals.

RESEARCH METHODS AND DATA

Our study draws on two years of extensive primary data collection through a mixed research method. We collected multiple forms of qualitative and quantitative data, including from elite interviews, surveys, focus-group discussions (FGDs), and secondary literature. Samples of our interview protocols and survey and focus-group discussion questions are in the appendices to this book. All told, we conducted 2,889 surveys in four regions to capture variation among voters across the country, 99 focus-group discussions, and 98 semi-structured interviews at the ward and village level across Myanmar in 2018 and 2019. To supplement our focus on ordinary citizens, we also conducted 72 in-depth qualitative interviews with members of nine political parties.

We review each of these methods here; the chapters that follow each draw on one or more of these sets of data.

Interviews with Selected Parties. Since 2010, proliferating parties have risen to advance democracy or (re)claim rights for their respective communities. Broadly, three types of parties have emerged: nationwide multi-ethnic parties such as NLD, ethnic-based parties, and smaller Bamar-dominated parties (Stokke 2019a; TNI 2015). For our research purposes, we chose to focus on nine parties of varied sizes, organizational structures, ages, and ideological platforms:

- Arakan National Party (ANP)
- Kachin State Democracy Party (KSDP)
- Lisu National Development Party (LNDP)
- Mon National Party (MNP)
- National League for Democracy (NLD)
- Pa-O National Organization (PNO)
- Shan Nationalities League for Democracy (SNLD)
- Ta'Ang National Party (TNP)
- Union Solidarity and Development Party (USDP)

Among these parties are the six that won the most seats across all Myanmar's parliaments in 2015 (NLD, USDP, ANP, SNLD, TNP, PNO), as well as the most electorally successful ethnic Kachin, Lisu, and Mon parties (KSDP, LNDP, and MNP).[7] We profile each of the nine parties in Appendix One. The parties in our study include those that:

i   are relatively highly institutionalized and have clear rules that they follow most or all of the time (MNP, NLD);
ii have a low level of institutionalization and frequently perform processes in an ad-hoc manner (KSDP, LNDP, TNP); and
iii fall between these poles (ANP, PNO, SNLD, USDP).

The parties we selected have significantly different histories, political organizations, ideologies, and internal party cultures. For the purposes of this book, we have divided them into three main categories:

i. parties that are "old" by Myanmar standards, having competed in the 1990 elections, then been suppressed by the military government in the 1990s and 2000s (MNP, NLD, SNLD);
ii. newer ethnic-based parties founded since 2010 (KSDP, LNDP, TNP); and
iii. parties with strong connections with the military establishment (PNO, USDP).

The ANP does not fit easily in this schema, as it was formed from the merger of the Arakan League for Democracy (category i) and the Rakhine National Development Party (category ii).

Our findings draw from data collected in 72 interviews our EMReF research team conducted between November 2018 and March 2019 with members of the nine political parties listed above. The EMReF researchers conducted all the interviews in Myanmar language, then translated them into English. One researcher from EMReF and three international researchers then used the English-language data for statistical analysis. Our interviewees included two categories: candidates and gatekeepers. Candidates include respondents who ran for office in 2015, whether or not they won.[8] Gatekeepers are those who did not compete in the 2015 election, but hold positions of authority at the central level (e.g. party chairman, general secretary, central executive committee member, central committee member) or township level (e.g. township chairman or secretary). Also, a few gatekeepers held positions at the state/region or district level of their party. Overall, we interviewed a total of six candidates and four gatekeepers from four larger and electorally successful parties (NLD, USDP, ANP, and SNLD) and four candidates and two gatekeepers from the five smaller parties (TNP, PNO, LNDP, KSDP, MNP).

Broadly, these interviews covered interviewees' personal and political backgrounds; intra-party rules, promotion, and recruitment of candidates for the 2015 elections; and their experiences as politicians. (See Appendix Four for the list of interview questions, translated from Myanmar language into English.) The EMReF research team followed up with telephone calls to senior officials from the central party apparatus if they had questions or missed issues in the original interviews. The data from these party interviews inform both Chapters Two and Three, in which we probe, respectively, candidate selection methods and elite attitudes towards women in politics at the party and state levels, and whether certain types of parties perform better than others in terms of advancing women.

Survey. To assess the perceptions and attitudes of the community towards male and female political leadership, we also conducted a survey in 20 villages with both male and female appointed village or ward leaders. We selected another 40 villages to capture diverse geographical locations—ethnic villages from hilly regions (Shan, Kachin, and Mon state), the dry zone (Magwe Region), and the coastal region (Ayeyarwady Region)—to explore how different cultures, traditions, and livelihoods shape popular attitudes.

For the survey at the community level, we used a randomized sampling method to select townships and villages, but purposive sampling to select states and regions. The questionnaire for the survey required careful preparation, piloting, translation, and back-translation before its launch. Some questions drew upon existing publicly available international survey instruments (e.g., World Values Survey, International Social Survey Program, AsiaBarometer) for ways to capture attitudes towards women in government, perceptions of corruption, and other key social and political characteristics. Other questions were more specific to the Myanmar context and our specific focus. We then developed a coding scheme to enable statistical analysis. See Appendix Two for our survey questions.

Our team conducted quantitative, multi-level regression analysis with these data to understand attitudes and perceptions towards male and female political decision-makers. We analyse the survey's key findings regarding attitudes towards women's political leadership at the local-community level in Chapter Four, and the social roots of those attitudes especially in Chapter Five.

Focus-group Discussions and Community-leader Interviews. Lastly, we probed further into the question of women's ability to participate at the local level by conducting 99 focus-group discussions (FGDs) and 98 semi-structured interviews in wards and villages in Ayeyarwady Region, Mandalay Region, Mon State, and southern Shan State, from September through November 2019. (See Figure 1.1 for the location of these states and regions.) In each state and region, we visited three townships, and in each township, one ward and one village. The three townships in Ayeyarwady Region were Kyaunggone, Ngaputaw, and Nyaungdone; the three in Mandalay Region were Ta-Da-U, Thabeikkyin, and Singu; the three in Mon State were Bilin, Kyaikmaraw, and Kyaikto;

and the three in southern Shan State were Hsi Hseng, Nyaungshwe, and Taunggyi.

We chose the states and regions for our study to reflect a variety of geographical, economic, and cultural features. We took into account where we were able to get access to conduct this qualitative research and the accompanying survey. Due to ongoing conflict, and the difficulty this posed for obtaining access to conduct research safely across multiple randomly selected townships, we did not consider including Kachin State, Rakhine State, or northern Shan State. Once we had chosen our states and regions, we randomly selected townships, ward/village tracts, and villages in each on which to focus. We elaborate on our selection of townships, wards, village tracts, and villages in Chapter Four, which draws upon these data alongside the broader-based survey.

Our team conducted a total of 99 FGDs, with four FGDs in each ward and village—one each with "old" women, "old" men, "young" women, and "young" men. Our final sample consisted of twenty-three Ward/Village Tracts Administrators (W/VTAs), thirty-seven 100 Household Heads (100 HHs), fourteen 10 Household Heads (10 HHs), nine elders and fifteen other community leaders. "Young" refers to age 18–34, and "old" means age 35 and above.[9] 75 per cent of our FGDs had between five and seven participants—our target number. Nine per cent had fewer than five participants, and 16 per cent had more than seven.[10] The FGD discussion topics covered how decisions are made at local levels, what local leaders do for their communities, what opportunities residents have to participate in decision making, and residents' views on female leaders and on desired qualities in leaders more broadly. While our research design originally aimed for gender parity among interviewees, the extent of male dominance among these positions made that difficult to achieve. Only 28 per cent of respondents were women, spread unevenly across categories.

In each ward/village in our study, in addition to the FGDs, our team also conducted semi-structured interviews with four community leaders—98 in all.[11] No accurate data are available on the ethnic composition of Myanmar's population, but it is commonly suggested that Bamar are around 60–65 per cent of the population, meaning the composition of our interviewees and FGDs is broadly representative of the national population in terms of ethnicity. 58 per cent of our FGDs included Bamar participants only; 27 per cent included participants who were all members of a single non-Bamar ethnic group (Mon, Pa-O, Shan, etc.); and the rest included participants of more than one ethnicity.

All the FGDs and interviews followed guides that we wrote first in English and then translated into Myanmar language. The FGDs were organized as group interviews guided by a facilitator and a pre-prepared FGD guide. The FGD and interview guides are available in Appendices Three and Four. The questions in the FGD guide encouraged discussion as a group and focused on collecting information about de facto decision-making as well as on identifying opportunities and hurdles for participation in local politics. Chapter Six in particular draws upon these findings in exploring local-level political participation and distribution of authority.

KEY FINDINGS AND IMPLICATIONS

The chapters to come present and assess our research findings in detail. Here, we offer a bird's-eye overview of what we have learned and where that insight leaves us. Given the circumstances in which Myanmar now finds itself, we offer, too, key takeaways on the trajectory and prospects of this project. The research posed special challenges, both in the process and, of course, in the aftermath.

Our research finds a mixture of institutional, cultural, and individual-level factors that together shape women's chances of pursuing and securing elected office. Institutionally, we find that party type does matter: the more personalized and less institutionalized parties are, the less prone they are to nominate candidates *not* from within gatekeepers' personal networks. Such network-related constraints especially hinder women. Ideology matters, too, precisely in the way one might expect, as those parties inclined towards progressivism are more likely to advance women. That said, ethnic parties are no more likely than catch-all national ones to nominate women to stand for the national parliament—the quest for descriptive representation on one axis need not translate to pursuit of the same goal across axes. Regardless, our findings thus far suggest the need for more work to study the intersections of gender, ethnicity, and religion on women's political pursuit at both the local and national levels.

Compounding these factors are cultural and normative attributes—and while a hoped-for eventual return to elections and civilian leadership may bring a change of parties, perhaps with different internal processes, these cultural factors are likely to persist. Most importantly, men and women experience political agency differently: everything from childhood experiences to marital status play out differently in terms of their effects on the likelihood of candidacy for women and for men. For example, in Chapter 5, Bjarnegård discusses the extent to which one's early childhood experiences with domestic violence can have long-lasting, gendered impacts on attitudes towards politics.

Social norms do (still) favour men as political leaders, in line with a general pattern of overall conservativism. Those attitudes have rarely extended to overtly violent campaign (or counter-campaigning) strategies, at least in recent elections—unless we read the coup as a spectacularly aggressive form of electoral violence—but gendered patterns of verbal harassment, especially online, have marred polls. More broadly, voters in Myanmar tend to associate even local-level political leadership with qualities understood as male, and to consider women as less suited for such empowerment. The experience of having had a female head of government has not shifted the needle on those perceptions, nor—especially in light of the gendering also of violence—is there reason to expect the current interregnum to incline voters towards putting their trust in female politicians.

The process of the research itself warrants discussion. At the time of our survey and field research, Myanmar remained in its comparatively democratic phase. Another election was in the offing—and took place as planned in 2020—and while the polity was some way off from liberal democracy, citizens enjoyed a civilian-led government, a degree of civil liberties, and avenues for political participation. Even under these circumstances, survey and field research posed real challenges. Most notably, some areas remained sites of active, armed ethnic conflict, or "black areas" with limited access. Given our aspirations for both nationwide and sub-nationally representative research, these constraints posed methodological and logistical hurdles. Moreover, legacies of mistrust compounded more basic hassles of gaining ethics approval from relevant government agencies and poor infrastructure at times confounded our team as we moved through the country for interviews and to implement our face-to-face survey.

Of course, our multiyear initiative ended on a decidedly low note. First, we could not complete the final phase of the research: members of our team from EMReF were set to travel to Indonesia and Malaysia in April 2020 to learn more about the experience of a Southeast Asian state with (Indonesia) and without (Malaysia) quotas for female candidates; the pandemic postponed those plans, then the coup cancelled them altogether. Second, we delved into our final analysis and drafting of the chapters assembled here collaborating remotely, adapting to COVID-19 social distancing and travel protocols. But third, and more devastatingly, the coup scattered several of our Myanmar team members and made it impossible for those who remained in Yangon to focus on academic pursuits as their world unraveled. We eventually regrouped, still working remotely, in Myanmar, Canada, the US, and Europe, to make sense of the research findings drawn from what now appears to be a lost era, and on smaller questions than the all-consuming ones Myanmar now confronts, but reflecting a society that *is* still there. The analyses that follow aim not only to detail a past history, but also, more importantly, to reveal and consider underlying fault-lines, frictions, and potentials of enduring relevance.

THE CHAPTERS TO COME

Presently, very few publications on Myanmar politics feature collaborative research findings from both academic and practitioners' perspectives. Our book, and the research project behind it, bring together an exceptional group of Myanmar experts (Aye Lei Tun, Hlat Myat Mon, Khin Myo Wai, La Ring Pausa, Su Su Hlaing, Jangai Jap, and Paul Minoletti) and international academics with expertise in political science (Netina Tan, Meredith Weiss, Michelle Dion, and Elin Bjarngård), economics (Guillem Riambau, Paul Minoletti), gender studies (Netina Tan and Elin Bjarngård), and quantitative survey analysis (Guillem Riambau, Michelle Dion, and Khin Myo Wai).

Chapters Two and Three reveal the "secret garden" of politics: the formal and informal rules governing candidate selection in nine political parties in Myanmar and internal politics in mass-based and ethnic parties. In Chapter Two, Netina Tan and Aye Lei Tun highlight how intra-party politics—the role of selectorate bodies such as central executive committees (CEC) and the selection criteria they use—affected the demand for female candidates in the last two general elections. They find that more organized, institutionalized, and ideologically progressive parties that conduct candidate searches from the local level up are more favourable towards and open to female candidates. In contrast, personalistic and community network-based parties are more arbitrary and likely to turn to personal networks to source for candidates, and to disregard rules and selection criteria. What this contrast implies is that policy recommendations to improve the supply of female candidates ought first to pay attention to party organization, platform, selection rules, and criteria.

We then turn in Chapter Three to the specific orientation of parties, in asking whether ethnic parties facilitate women's representation. Jangai Jap and Cassandra Preece use available qualitative and quantitative data to better understand whether ethnic parties matter for women's political representation at the national level. They investigate candidate selection procedures in ethnic parties and parties' positions on recruiting and supporting female politicians in policy and in practice. Leveraging 2015 election data, this chapter compares ethnic parties with the NLD and the USDP, in terms of their track records in nominating women and their likelihood of winning. They hypothesize that the extent to which ethnic parties put female candidates up for election may be correlated with the degree of party institutionalization. They find, however, that ethnic parties are not more likely than catch-all national parties to recruit or support female politicians.

Looking beyond parties, our survey data allow us to explore societal attitudes—and to confirm that traditional conservative attitudes remain dominant in Myanmar. In Chapter Four, Anor Mu, Paul Minoletti, Guillem Riambau, and Michelle Dion use our survey data to examine mass attitudes towards women and political leadership, including towards women's participation in formal politics. These data allow them to examine which factors affect women and men differently as they contemplate or pursue political careers. The results show that past life experiences, including specifically experience of physical abuse as children, have markedly different effects on women and men in the long run. Formal education, marital status, and perceptions of safety also have divergent effects.

In Chapter Five, Elin Bjarnegård widens the frame, to consider the larger goals of democratic elections in Myanmar, as a presumed important step towards the peaceful resolution of conflict—even as elections themselves carry risk of violence and violations of electoral and personal integrity, especially in a conflict-affected political environment such as Myanmar's. Observers widely lauded the elections of 2015 for being relatively free and fair. But closely following the next polls was the coup d'état, raising questions of how thick the veneer of political peace (at least for central Myanmar) had been during the decade-long period of political liberalization. This chapter investigates the extent to which political candidates or local-level decision-makers in Myanmar's 2015 general elections experienced violence and intimidation as part of campaigns. Recent research suggests that political violence can be gendered in different ways, including in motive, form, and impact.

The second aim of this chapter is to investigate if the extent of violent experiences differs between politically active men and women in Myanmar, and if they face different forms of, or consequences from, violence. The analysis draws on our interviews with gatekeepers and candidates as well as focus group discussions, demonstrating that Myanmar politicians had normalized attacks and abuse as part of politics, even before the 2021 coup. Although most interviewees reported improvements compared to previous political experiences, a majority of our candidate interviewees reported some form of intimidation during their 2015 election campaigns. Verbal or online harassment reported included ethnic or religious aspects. While it is difficult to discern any differences by gender in the *extent* of harassment and verbal abuse, we see discernable differences in the *forms* of harassment that men and women face. Women were more often the victims of personal accusations, often online, including degrading talk directed against family members as well as rumors about their person.

Lastly, in Chapter Six, Cassandra Preece, La Ring Pausa, and Paul Minoletti analyse data on women's and men's political participation and representation at the local level, and perceived gender inequalities in the processes involved. Formal legal, policy-making, and budgetary powers in Myanmar are highly centralized. However, decision-making at ward, village tract, and village levels is central to citizens' lives, especially related to local development, basic administration, security, dispute resolution, and social and religious activities. While women attend local meetings in large numbers, they are less likely than men to participate actively in group settings. Men dominate and speak more in meetings, and leadership positions are highly male-dominated—to the extent that women constitute less than one per cent of ward/village tract administrators in Myanmar. Other key local leadership positions, including 100-household heads and local elders, are likewise extremely male-dominated. Behind this pattern is the reality that women face the downsides to political participation disproportionately more than men, especially in terms of sacrificing time to attend meetings, and do not enjoy the upsides of influencing decision-making and feeling empowered. The pull of masculine leadership stereotypes ensures male dominance of leadership positions and decision-making at the ward and village-tract levels. Feminine stereotypes and expectations that women perform their domestic tasks or stay indoors after dark, in contrast, limit women's participation in local governance.

Taken together, these chapters sketch a landscape not entirely hostile to women's leadership, but still presenting important structural and cultural constraints. Even if elections resume quickly, the playing field in Myanmar will almost certainly remain less than level, unless and until both processes and popular attitudes change.

NOTES

1. Although the quantum of evidence for Myanmar is still limited, research suggests that there, too, men and women have different preferences, and female leaders tend to be more responsive to women's preferences (Minoletti 2014, 2015).
2. Hartery (2019) suggests that the Tatmadaw's constitutional veto is not so secure as assumed. However, this veto is very much de facto in place, and probably applies de jure, as well.
3. Several studies have touched on this issue (e.g. DIPD 2016; Minoletti 2016; Phan Tee Eain 2016). However, none of these studies were able to explore the intraparty level in much detail or depth.
4. In 2015, elections were only held in 323 constituencies; they were cancelled in the other seven due to security concerns. However, two of these constituencies were able to elect MPs in 2017 by-elections.
5. For more on how Ethnic Affairs Representatives are elected, see TNI (2015), p. 7.
6. Note that there is a slight discrepancy between these two sources for how many of the 6,072 candidates were women—Enlightened Myanmar Research Foundation counts 805 (13.3 per cent), whereas the International

Foundation for Electoral Systems gives the number as 800 (13.2 per cent) (EMReF 2015; IFES 2015).
7. UEC database on successful candidates in the 2015 election (hereafter, "UEC database").
8. SNLD had chosen one of our candidate interviewees to run in 2015 in Kyethi Township, but the Union Election Commission (UEC) cancelled elections due to local security concerns. He successfully contested there in the 2017 by-elections. All other candidate interviewees ran in 2015.
9. We also conducted additional FGDs which were (i) with young women in a ward in Singu Township, Mandalay Region; (ii) with older men in a village in Kyaikto Township, Mon State; and (iii) with young men from a ward in Kyaikto Township, Mon State. The extras were a result of our having too many participants.
10. In most of the wards and villages in our study, the ward and village tract administrator (W/VTA), 100-household head (HH), and/or community elders helped us to find FGD participants. However, there were also some instances in which the field researchers walked through the ward/village to find potential participants on the street or in their homes. The FGDs were conducted in W/VTA's offices or homes, monasteries, and community halls.
11. One W/VTA; one village administrator (VA) or 100-HH; one 10-HH or elder; and one other community leader. In practice, we were not always able to interview exactly one from each category in each ward/village. Our final sample consisted of 23 W/VTAs, 37 100-HH, 14 10-HH, 9 elders, and 15 other community leaders. That last category includes not only leaders of community groups (such as women's groups, local development organizations, loan groups, and religious and social groups) but also two members of the local election/voting commission and one village clerk. Of the 98 interviewees, 63 per cent are ethnic Bamar, 34 per cent are non-Bamar, and 3 per cent are mixed Bamar and non-Bamar.

REFERENCES

Agarwal, Bina. 2009. "Gender and Forest Conservation: The Impact of Women's Participation in Community Forestry Governance". *Ecological Economics* 68: 2785–99.

Asia Foundation, The. 2014. "Myanmar 2014: Civic Knowledge and Values in a Changing Society". Yangon: The Asia Foundation.

———. 2020. "2020 General Election: State and Region Hluttaws". Yangon: The Asia Foundation.

Barnea, Shlomit, and Gideon Rahat. 2007. "Reforming Candidate Selection Methods: A Three-Level Approach". *Party Politics* 13, no. 3: 375–94.

Beaman, Lori A., Raghabendra Chattopadhyay, Esther Duflo, Rohini Pande, and Petia Topalova. 2009. "Powerful Women: Does Exposure Reduce Bias?" *The Quarterly Journal of Economics* 124, no. 4: 1497–1540.

Bjarnegård, Elin. 2013. *Gender, Informal Institutions and Political Recruitment: Explaining Male Dominance in Parliamentary Representation*. New York: Palgrave Macmillan.

Bjarnegård, Elin, and Meryl Kenny. 2015. "Revealing the 'Secret Garden': The Informal Dimensions of Political Recruitment". *Politics and Gender* 11, no. 4: 748–53.

Bjarnegård, Elin, and Pär Zetterberg. 2019. "Political Parties, Formal Selection Criteria, and Gendered Parliamentary Representation". *Party Politics* 25, no. 3: 325–35. https://doi.org/10.1177/1354068817715552.

Caul, Miki. 1999. "Women's Representation in Parliament: The Role of Political Parties". *Party Politics* 5, no. 1: 79–98. https://doi.org/10.1177/1354068899005001005.

Chattopadhyay, Raghabendra, and Esther Duflo. 2004. "Women as Policy Makers: Evidence from a Randomized Policy Experiment in India". *Econometrica* 72, no. 5: 1409–43.

Crowder-Meyer, Melody. 2013. "Gendered Recruitment without Trying: How Local Party Recruiters Affect Women's Representation". *Politics & Gender* 9, no. 4: 390–413. https://doi.org/10.1017/S1743923X13000391.

Dahlerup, Drude. 2007. "Electoral Gender Quotas: Between Equality of Opportunity and Equality of Result". *Representation* 43, no. 2: 73–92. https://doi.org/10.1080/00344890701363227.

DIPD. 2016. "Women's Participation in 2015 Election in Myanmar: An Assessment". DIPD.

Egreteau, Renaud. 2014. "Legislators in Myanmar's First 'Post-Junta' National Parliament (2010–2015): A Sociological Analysis". *Journal of Current Southeast Asian Affairs* 33, no. 2: 91–124.

Enlightened Myanmar Research Foundation (EMReF). 2015. "Important Facts About 2015 Election (2015)". Yangon: EMReF. https://merin.org.mm/en/publication/important-facts-about-2015-election-2015.

———. 2020. "17% of Women Were Elected to Parliaments in the 2020 General Election". *Sa Voix Newsletter*, December 2020.

Fink, Christina. 2015. "Myanmar's Proactive National Legislature". *Social Research: An International Quarterly* 82, no. 2: 327–54.

Franceschet, Susan, and Jennifer M. Piscopo. 2008. "Gender Quotas and Women's Substantive Representation: Lessons from Argentina". *Politics and Gender* 4, no. 3: 393–425.

Gallagher, Michael, and Michael Marsh. 1988. *The Secret Garden: Candidate Selection in Comparative Perspective*. London: Sage Publications.

Geha, Carmen. 2019. "The Myth of Women's Political Empowerment within Lebanon's Sectarian Power-Sharing System". *Journal of Women, Politics & Policy* 40, no. 4: 498–521. https://doi.org/10.1080/1554477X.2019.1600965.

Gender Equality Network (GEN). 2013. "Taking the Lead: An Assessment of Women's Leadership Training Needs and Training Initiatives in Myanmar". Yangon: GEN.

———. 2015. "Raising the Curtain: Cultural Norms, Social Practices and Gender Equality in Myanmar". Yangon: GEN.

Geo.Fyi (blog). 2020. "Administrative Geography of Myanmar". 16 December 2020. https://geo.fyi/2020/12/16/administrative-geography-of-myanmar/.

Government of Myanmar, Department of Population. 2017. "The 2014 Myanmar Population and Housing Census: Thematic Report on Gender Dimensions". *Census Report Volume* 4-J. Myanmar: Department of Population, Ministry of Labour, Immigration and Population.

Harriden, Jessica. 2012. *The Authority of Influence: Women and Power in Burmese History*. Copenhagen: NIAS Press.

Hartery, Jesse. 2019. "The NLD Cannot Circumvent the Military's Veto Over Constitutional Amendments". 4 April 2019. https://teacircleoxford.com/2019/04/04/military-seats-in-the-pyithu-hluttaw-the-limits-of-strict-constitutional-construction/.

Hedström, Jenny, and Elisabeth Olivius, eds. 2022. *Waves of Upheaval in Myanmar: Gendered Transformations and Political Transitions*. Copenhagen: NIAS Press.

Hedström, Jenny, Elisabeth Olivius, and Valentina Kay Soe. 2021. "Women's Rights: Change and Continuity". In *Myanmar: Politics, Economy and Society*, edited by Adam Simpson and Nicholas Farelly, pp. 186–203. London and New York: Routledge. http://urn.kb.se/resolve?urn=urn:nbn:se:umu:diva-174695.

Hennings, Valerie M., and R. Urbatsch. 2016. "Gender, Partisanship, and Candidate-Selection Mechanisms". *State Politics & Policy Quarterly* 16, no. 3: 290–312. https://doi.org/10.1177/1532440015604921.

ILO. 2017. "ILOSTAT: Myanmar". UN: ILO. https://ilostat.ilo.org/data/country-profiles/.

International Crisis Group. 2015. "The Myanmar Elections: Results and Implications". Yangon/Brussels: International Crisis Group.

International Foundation for Electoral Systems (IFES). 2015. "Elections in Myanmar: 2015 General Elections – Frequently Asked Questions". Washington, D.C.: IFES.

IPU Parline. 2022. "Global and Regional Averages of Women in National Parliaments". Parline: The IPU's Open Data Platform. https://data.ipu.org/women-averages.

Janssens, Wendy. 2010. "Women's Empowerment and the Creation of Social Capital in Indian Villages". *World Development* 38, no. 7: 974–88.

Jolliffe, Kim. 2015. "Ethnic Armed Conflict and Territorial Administration in Myanmar". San Francisco, United States: The Asia Foundation.https:// asiafoundation.org/resources/pdfs/ConflictTerritorialAdministration fullreportENG.pdf.

Kudo Toshihiro. 2011. "Results of the 2010 Elections in Myanmar: An Analysis". Japan: The Institute of Developing Economies. https://www.ide.go.jp/ English/Research/Region/Asia/20110104.html.

Kunovich, Sheri, and Pamela Paxton. 2005. "Pathways to Power: The Role of Political Parties in Women's National Political Representation". *American Journal of Sociology* (September). http://digitalrepository.smu.edu/hum_ sci_sociology_research/5.

Kyi Pyar Chit Saw, and Matthew Arnold. 2014. "Administering the State in Myanmar". Subnational Governance in Myanmar Discussion Paper Series. Yangon, Myanmar: The Asia Foundation.

Lawless, Jennifer L. 2015. "Female Candidates and Legislators". *Annual Review of Political Science* 18, no. 1: 349–66.

Lawless, Jennifer L., and Richard L. Fox, eds. 2010. "Gender, Party, and Political Recruitment". In *It Still Takes A Candidate: Why Women Don't Run for Office*, pp. 89–111. Cambridge: Cambridge University Press. https://doi. org/10.1017/CBO9780511778797.005.

Lovenduski, Joni. 2005. *Feminizing Politics*. Cambridge: Polity.

Maber, Elizabeth, and Jane Tregoning. 2016. "Finding Feminism, Finding Voice? Mobilising Community Education to Build Women's Participation in Myanmar's Political Transition". *Gender and Education* 28, no. 3: 416–30. https://doi.org/10.1080/09540253.2016.1167175.

Mansbridge, Jane. 1999. "Should Blacks Represent Blacks and Women Represent Women? A Contingent 'Yes'". *The Journal of Politics* 61, no. 3: 628–57.

Minoletti, Paul. 2014. "Women's Participation in the Subnational Governance of Myanmar". Yangon: MDRI-CESD and The Asia Foundation.

———. 2015. "Gender Budgeting in Myanmar". ActionAid, CARE, Oxfam and WON.

———. 2016. "Gender (in)Equality in the Governance of Myanmar: Past, Present, and Potential Strategies for Change". Yangon: The Asia Foundation.

———. 2017. "Gender and Politics in Myanmar: Women and Men Candidates in the 2015 Elections". Yangon: Gender Equality Network.

MOLES, CSO, and ILO. 2017. "Myanmar Labour Force, Child Labour and School-To-Work Transition Survey, 2015: Executive Summary Report". Nay Pyi Taw: MOLES, CSO and ILO.

Niven, David. 1998. *The Missing Majority: The Recruitment of Women as State Legislative Candidates*. Westport, CT: Praeger.

Norris, Pippa. 2012. "Gender Equality in Elected Office in Asia-Pacific: Six Actions to Expand Women's Empowerment". UNDP.

Norris, Pippa, and Joni Lovenduski. 1993. "'If Only More Candidates Came Forward': Supply-Side Explanations of Candidate Selection in Britain". *British Journal of Political Science* 23, no. 3: 373–408. https://doi.org/10.1017/S0007123400006657.

Oh, Su-Ann. 2020. "Parties and Their Significance in the Myanmar 2020 General Election". *ISEAS Perspective*, no. 2020/100, 8 September 2020.

Phan Tee Eain. 2016. "Report on Observing Women's Participation in Myanmar's November 2015 General Election".

Phan Tee Eain, and The Gender Equality Network. 2014. "Myanmar: Women in Parliament 2014". Yangon, Myanmar: Phan Tee Eain (Creative Home) and The Gender Equality Network.

Shwe Shwe Sein Latt, Kim N.B. Ninh, Mi Ki Kyaw Myint, and Susan Lee. 2017. "Women's Political Participation in Myanmar: Experiences of Women Parliamentarians 2011–2016". Yangon, Myanmar: The Asia Foundation. http://asiafoundation.org/publication/womens-political-participation-myanmar-experiences-women-parliamentarians-2011-2016/.

South, Ashley. 2018. "'Hybrid Governance' and the Politics of Legitimacy in the Myanmar Peace Process". *Journal of Contemporary Asia* 48, no. 1: 50–66. https://doi.org/10.1080/00472336.2017.1387280.

Stokke, Kristian. 2019a. "Political Parties and Religion in Myanmar". In *The Routledge Handbook to Religion and Political Parties*, edited by Jeffrey Haynes. London: Routledge.

───. 2019b. "Political Representation by Ethnic Parties? Electoral Performance and Party-Building Processes among Ethnic Parties in Myanmar". *Journal of Current Southeast Asian Affairs* 38, no. 3: 307–36. https://doi.org/10.1177/1868103419893530.

Tinker, Irene. 2004. "Quotas for Women in Elected Legislatures: Do They Really Empower Women?" *Women's Studies International Forum* 27: 531–46.

Transnational Institute (TNI). 2015. "The 2015 General Election in Myanmar: What Now for Ethnic Politics?" *Myanmar Policy Briefing* 17. Amsterdam, Netherlands: TNI. https://www.tni.org/files/publication-downloads/bpb17_web_def.pdf.

UN Women. 1995. "UN Women: Beijing Declaration and Platform for Action". https://www.un.org/womenwatch/daw/beijing/pdf/BDPfA%20E.pdf.

Verge, Tània. 2015. "The Gender Regime of Political Parties: Feedback Effects between 'Supply' and 'Demand'". *Politics & Gender* 11, no. 4: 754–59. https://doi.org/10.1017/S1743923X15000483.

Zin Mar Aung. 2015. "From Military Patriarchy to Gender Equity: Including Women in the Democratic Transition in Burma". *Social Research* 82, no. 2: 531–51.

2

THE SECRET GARDEN OF CANDIDATE SELECTION AND WOMEN'S POLITICAL PARTICIPATION

Aye Lei Tun and Netina Tan[1]

Whom political parties select for elections is key to understanding how women access elected office. In this chapter, we investigate *whom* parties nominated as candidates and *how* the selection process occurred in Myanmar before the coup in 2021, focusing on the nine political parties identified in Chapter One. During Myanmar's short decade of liberalization, political parties flourished and competed in general elections (GE). In the 2020 elections alone, a total of 93 parties competed, 50 more than in 2010. That independent candidates comprised less than 5 per cent of total candidates in 2020's national and local elections indicates that parties are the primary means through which individuals become politicians.

Parties matter as they provide leadership, organization, resources, and name-recognition for candidates (Kunovich and Paxton 2005a; Aldrich 2011). Literature on electoral politics in Myanmar has largely focused on the dominant role of the military, including its political-party guise as the Union Solidarity and Development Party (USDP), or on political elites such as Aung San Suu Kyi from the National League for Democracy (NLD).[2] Despite the importance of parties and the role they play in selecting candidates for elections, we know very little about these processes—what Gallagher and Marsh (1988) call the "secret garden of politics"—during Myanmar's decade of liberalization.

Intra-party politics in Myanmar are opaque and clouded in mystery. This chapter aims to demystify a core process by comparing the key candidate-selection methods in nine parties and their effects on women's political participation. In Asia, Myanmar has had one of the lowest levels of female representation in legislatures from 2010 to 2020. Typically, respondents cite cultural factors such as patriarchy as key deterrents that affect the supply of female candidates (Zin Mar Aung 2015). Here, we go beyond cultural reasons by revealing other institutional factors, such as the role of the selectorate[3]—the body that selects candidates—and the criteria each party looks for that affect the demand for women in politics.

Parties are gatekeepers that narrow the list of candidates to a small pool from which the voters will choose. *Who* selects and *how* the process is implemented in practice affect not only party cohesion but also its gender and ethnic diversity (Rahat and Hazan 2001; Tan et al. 2020). Typically, parties have a legal or written framework that establishes how they elect or select their candidates. However, in Myanmar, not all parties are institutionalized or have written, clear rules within their party constitution. Besides, candidate selection criteria and processes also differ depending on the level of elections. For example, our post-2015 elections studies and interviews found that while party executives at the local level play an important role in selecting candidates for the lower house (*Pyithu Hluttaw*), the party's Central Executive Committee (CEC) at the national level typically has more influence selecting candidates for the upper house (*Amyotha Hluttaw*).

Despite moves towards more democratic and bottom-up candidate selection methods, most Myanmar parties' CECs are dominated by men. Apart from Aung San Suu Kyi, who has served as the chairperson of the NLD, few women in the CEC have held significant roles. Beyond the CEC, too, women are generally underrepresented in decision-making on township committees and less informed about gender equality policies.

As mentioned in Chapter One, only 13 per cent of candidates for the 2015 general elections, from among all parties and independents, were women.[4] For the nine parties we study, fewer than 20 per cent of all candidates were women. Five of our parties exceeded that average (Mon National Party, MNP; Lisu National Development Party, LNDP; Shan Nationalities League for Democracy, SNLD; NLD; and Kachin State Democracy Party, KSDP), and four were below average (Ta'Ang National Party, TNP; USDP; Arakan National Party, ANP; and Pa-O National Organization, PNO). Female candidates or MPs are especially scarce in the ANP, PNO, and USDP. While a few parties voluntarily introduced 30 per cent gender quotas before 2020 GE to increase their number of female candidates, most failed to meet their own quotas. Regardless, we consider aspirant targets to be positive step forward, as the percentage of female candidates increased from 10.5 per cent in 2015's GE to 17 per cent in 2020.

The findings for this chapter are drawn from data collected in 72 interviews our EMReF research team conducted between November 2018 and March 2019 with members of nine political parties: ANP, KSDP, LNDP, MNP, NLD, PNO, SNLD, TNP, and USDP. See Chapter One for an explanation of our research process, and Appendices One and Four, respectively, for information on these parties and our interview questions.

This chapter begins with a brief introduction of the literature on candidate selection before comparing candidate selection methods for the nine parties before the 2015 GE. The next section then examines the parties' candidate preferences and practices for promoting women's political participation. We summarize the implications of our findings for putting more women up as candidates in post-coup Myanmar in the conclusion.

CANDIDATE SELECTION

Candidate selection is an intra-party process through which parties choose and formally nominate[5] their candidates before a general election. It is part of a wider political recruitment process by which individuals are inducted into high-profile national political and subnational positions, and, hence, a critical link between voters and the policy-making process (Czudnowski 1975, p. 219). How parties decide upon candidates is determined by the respective party's rules and procedures (Bjarnegård and Kenny 2016; Krook 2010). As elsewhere, in Myanmar, the size, age, ideology, and degree of institutionalization of the party's organization affect its candidate selection method. Following Huntington, institutionalization is a "process by which organizations and procedures acquire value and stability" (1965, p. 394). More institutionalized parties are typically more rule-oriented in selecting their candidates, whereas weakly institutionalized parties tend to be more ad hoc (Norris and Lovenduski 1995, p. 21). (Chapter Three delves further into how greater party institutionalization might affect women's political participation, with reference specifically to ethnic parties.)

Candidate selection methods can differ widely in their degree of inclusivity, autonomy, and centralization (Rahat and Hazan 2001). These differences can have direct impacts on the cohesion and gender and ethnic diversity of a party's membership. Typically, more inclusive procedures will involve a larger selectorate and a less centralized, more bottom-up selection process. The autonomy of a very big or inclusive selectorate, or one with little control over the quality of candidates, tends to be low. Typically, decentralized candidate selection tends to be more democratic and encourages more intraparty competition amongst candidates, as they may have to compete with each other in internal elections to succeed (Rahat 2007, p. 159).

On the other hand, parties with more exclusive, centralized processes tend to have smaller selectorates, which have more autonomy in decision-making. Such a selectorate may set requirements for candidacy, exclude external intruders who do not meet its admission requirements, and appoint candidates without interference from outside organizations such as religious groups or unions (Lovenduski and Norris 1993, p. 321). Autonomy also increases with centralization of decision-making power at the national level. Hence, there are trade-offs between the decentralized and inclusive versus the centralized and exclusive models of candidate selection. See Figure 2.1 for a synopsis. For Myanmar's 2015 and 2020 elections, bigger parties such as the NLD and the USDP largely adopted more exclusive, autonomous, and centralized candidate selection procedures. However, the smaller, ethnic-based parties were more decentralized, inclusive, and ad-hoc in their candidate selection methods.

FIGURE 2.1
Inclusivity and Centralization of Candidate Selection Method

Inclusive & decentralized ◄————————————► Exclusive & centralized

Selectorate	General electorate	Party membership	Selected party agency	Non-selected party agency	Single leader
Centralization	Local	Regional			National
Candidacy	All citizens	Party members			Party members & additional requirements
Electoral Method	Voting				Appointment

Source: Extracted from Rahat and Hazan (2001), pp. 301 and 305.

OVERVIEW OF CANDIDATE SELECTION FOR MYANMAR'S 2015 GE

Our study of nine selected parties found that most parties' approach to candidate selection differs by level of government. For example, elections for the lower house (Pyithu Hluttaw) would see more decentralized and inclusive models, whereas selectorates for local township chairman (TC) or township executive committee (TEC) have more autonomy in selecting candidates. On the other hand, procedures for elections for the upper house (Amyotha Hluttaw) would usually be more centralized and exclusive, allowing the party's central executive committee (CEC) more autonomy over the selection of candidates. We return later to the implications of the more decentralized, inclusive approach to candidate selection common for lower house elections.

Typically, for the selection of candidates for the national Pyithu Hluttaw, parties in Myanmar adopt a bottom-up, decentralized candidate selection process. The general practice is for the TC or TEC to compile a list of preliminary nominees for internal election or sometimes directly select the candidates. Then, the names of the candidates are sent to the party's CEC for approval or rejection. But in reality, practices may vary across parties depending on their size, organizational structure, supply of candidates, and degree of institutionalization.

As Table 2.1 shows, the nine parties we examined differ in the candidate selection role played by the selectorate (CEC, TC, or TEC) at different levels and their selection method (internal election, appointment, self-nomination). Broadly, the LNDP, NLD, and ANP adopted the bottom-up candidate nomination process at the local level, while the MNP, PNO, KSDP, and SNLD had the CEC members appoint candidates when townships were unable to identify enough candidates.[6]

TABLE 2.1
Candidate Selection Methods for the Lower House (Pyithu Hluttaw)

Parties	Selectorate	Candidate Selection
ANP	TEC	Internal election + appointment
KSDP	TC + TEC + CEC	Internal election
LNDP	TEC + CEC	Allows self-nomination or appointment
MNP	TC + TEC	Internal election or appointment
NLD	TC + CEC	Internal election and appointment (about 20% of candidates)
PNO	TEC	Internal election + selection
SNLD	TC	Internal election + appointment
TNP	TC	Secret election. No specific rules, allows self-nomination, even non-party members
USDP	TC + TEC + candidate selection team + CEC[49]	Allows self-nomination

Note: Township Chairman (TC); Township Executive Committee (TEC); Central Executive Committee (CEC)

Source: Compiled by the authors.

In our study, the NLD and USDP's CEC retain the most power and autonomy over the candidate selection process, including the right to reject lower house candidates proposed at the township level. However, for the NLD, the TC and TEC play an important role in selecting candidates for the upper house. They are responsible for reviewing candidates' biographies, experience, and submitting their names up to the central level. The NLD appears to have the clearest division of labour in seeking out candidates for different levels of government, compared with other parties such as the TNP or the SNLD. Yet, how even the NLD's CEC ultimately decide and the rules other parties follow for selection remains unclear.[7]

PARTIES' CENTRAL EXECUTIVE COMMITTEES

The most important internal organization for political parties is the CEC. Typically, the CEC, which includes key party elites, ultimately chooses or itself is the selectorate that decides on the list of candidates who compete in elections. It is important to examine who the selectorate is and its preferences, as it determines the demand for female candidates. Despite the limitations of our data, we can confidently assert that the CEC plays a more important role than the Central Committee (CC) in selecting candidates for the ANP, MNP, NLD, TNP, and USDP. As Table 2.2 shows, all nine of our parties' CECs are, unsurprisingly, male-dominated. We contend that this has a direct impact on the gender balance of candidates.

TABLE 2.2
Party Central Executive Committee (CEC) Membership by Gender

Parties	Total CEC members	Women in CEC	Women in CEC (%)
KSDP	36	11	31%
MNP	27	6	22%
NLD	21	4	19%
SNLD	25	4	17%
LNDP	31	5	16%
PNO	48	5	10%
TNP	19	1	5%
ANP	39	2	5%
USDP	45	1	2%

Source: Tan et al. (2020), p. 20.

Party elites tend to recruit members like themselves. Male party leaders tend to choose male candidates. It has been demonstrated in different studies that male gatekeepers will not just select male successors, but that they will also protect the existing internal party culture and existing practices (Verge and Claveria 2018). Previous research also shows that for senior party positions to be primarily held by men tends to reproduce male dominance. First, their dominance sends a symbolic and discouraging signal to aspiring women (Cheng and Tavits 2011). Second, people in senior party positions are the ones who have the most say over who gets in and who gets promoted, and they also exert a great deal of influence over policy priorities and internal party culture (Bjarnegård and Kenny 2013). While the status quo is favourable to insiders who know the rules of the game, it disfavours newcomers, such as women. When there are more women in senior positions, more women are apt to be nominated and selected, and new party priorities are more likely to emerge (Mendelberg, Karpowitz, and Goedert 2014; Catalano Weeks 2019).

Table 2.2 shows that out of the six parties for which we have complete data, KSDP has the highest proportion of women in their CEC (31 per cent), and ANP and TNP have the lowest (5 per cent). Only KSDP and MNP have over 20 per cent female leadership. Even then, the only women holding key senior positions were in NLD, of which Aung San Suu Kyi is the powerful leader, and the ANP and LNDP, in which women serve as vice-chairpersons. Otherwise, most women in the CECs serve in lower-status positions like treasurer and auditor, as in KSDP and SNLD, while men hold the more senior positions. For example, for the PNO and USDP, all senior positions are held by men, with women only being basic members of the CEC.[8] A female candidate we interviewed from PNO explained that women involved in the CEC were often assigned unimportant roles and key positions were given only to men. Hence, if male-dominated CECs tend to choose candidates like themselves or function like an "old boy's network", then this will adversely impact the demand for female candidates.

Previous research indicates that across all the 91 parties that competed in the 2015 election, only three (the Mon Women's Party, the NLD, and the Danu National Organization Party) had a woman in any of the three most senior positions, i.e. leader, deputy-leader, or chairperson (Phan Tee Eain 2016). Of these, only the NLD won seats in the 2015 election. As has been argued elsewhere, Aung San Suu Kyi's position as the leader of the NLD and Myanmar's civilian government was highly unique and unrepresentative of other parties. It is unlikely that she would have reached this position if she were not the daughter of Myanmar independence hero Aung San (Gender Equality Network 2017, p. 34).

Without gender equality in elite party positions such as the CEC, it is difficult for women to access top party leadership positions or be selected as candidates. For example, an interviewee from PNO remarked, "The positions for president, vice president, and secretary, etc. were assigned to men ... The women don't possess those kind of important roles. Women are just members in the CEC and CC".[9]

The prevalence of male-dominated CECs suggests a lack of advocates for female candidates and very few female role models for women who aspire to join party politics. Only Aung San Suu Kyi was widely cited as a female role model by our interviewees. Others typically mentioned male national leaders from history, such as General Aung San, U Nu, Thakhin Than Tun, and Dee Dote U Ba Cho, or, among interviewees from ethnic parties, leaders of armed ethnic movements, such as U Aung Kham Hti (Pa-O/PNO); U Sai Leik (Shan/SNLD); U Naing Ngwe Thein, U Naing Thein Maw, and U Naing Tun Thein (Mon/MNP); and U Aye Thar Aung (Rakhine/ANP). The over-dominance of male leaders in parties' CECs thus affects both the demand for and supply of female candidates.

ROLES OF TOWNSHIP CHAIRMEN AND TOWNSHIP EXECUTIVE COMMITTEES

Aside from the powerful CEC, our interviews also strongly suggest that the TC or TEC play important roles at the local level in vetting and nominating lists of candidates. This is significant, as very few studies have paid attention to party politics at the local level. Further, the decentralized aspect of candidate selection also suggests that efforts to improve gender equality ought to begin from the bottom up and not focus on elites alone. (Chapter Six delves further into local politics.)

To nominate candidates for the lower house, a party's TC and TEC typically collaborate to develop a list of names, then organize an internal election to rank the potential candidates. Aside from getting advice from the TEC, three parties—ANP, MNP, and NLD—also mentioned that their parties have dedicated "candidate selection teams" or "election winning teams" from the central level to help identify good candidates. These bodies are closely linked to but separate from the CEC.[10] The USDP also has candidate selection teams at the township, district, and state/region levels. After conferring with the TEC, the state/region candidate selection team submits their recommendations directly to the CEC.[11]

In all, 39 of the 45 responses (86 per cent) we received from members of parliament (MPs) affirm that the TC plays an important role in nominating and selecting candidates.[12] Candidate selection for the 2015 GE for the ANP, MNP, PNO, SNLD,[13] and TNP was comparatively bottom-up and decentralized, with the TC and TEC playing a big role in identifying and finalizing the list of candidates. Most interviewees from SNLD and TNP agreed that the TC played an important role in deciding upon eligible candidates, while the TC would also consult other senior community leaders. As one TNP interviewee said:

> The township chairman was the most important person in pre-selection of candidates because he knew about the candidates in his township. He checked the lists that were submitted from the village/ward level and then he submitted to CEC. He didn't decide by himself. He discussed with the elder persons in the township.[14]

In other words, the TC and TEC work together to identify potential candidates from the township. For the ANP, the TEC was key in proposing a list of candidates to the CEC, and even played a key role in organizing an internal election to finalize the candidate list. As one ANP interviewee explained, "The TEC is very important in candidate selection for all parliaments. For state and regional level parliament, the TEC and representatives from villages in the constituency vote and decide at the township level."[15]

The discussion of internal elections at the township level of the party suggests a positive development. As Table 2.1 shows, six out of nine parties reported having an internal election or voting process (ANP, KSDP, MNP, NLD, PNO, and SNLD) to finalize their list of candidates at the township level, before sending it to the CEC for confirmation. The fact that there is some form of voting amongst a group to determine the candidates suggests a more inclusive, bottom-up, consensus-based selection process that is not solely dependent on a single leader or a few CEC members who may not know the candidates from the township level.

Regardless, again, not all parties abide by the bottom-up process. Some candidate election processes were more ad-hoc for the 2015 GE. For example, interviewees from the SNLD,[16] TNP,[17] and KSDP complained about the lack of rules and established processes for nominating and finding candidates.[18] The KSDP appeared most disorganized before the elections, with no specific process. Interviews also reported that the party accepted the CEC's directly appointing candidates or candidates' self-nomination.[19] Interviews from the SNLD also expressed frustration with the lack of clear party rules regarding candidate eligibility.

NON-PARTY, RELIGIOUS ORGANIZATIONS, AND ELDERLY MEMBERS

Our study also revealed that non-party members are occasionally involved in parties' candidate selection. About 20 per cent (15 out of 72 respondents) of our total interviewees reported the involvement of non-party members.[20] This is unusual as candidate selection is typically reserved for party members. Yet, non-party members such as religious leaders, retired former party leaders, or experts from non-government organizations were reportedly involved at the township level, especially from the NLD, USDP, LNDP,[21] MNP, ANP, and KSDP. For example, the KSDP reported that, "[T]here were some foreign advisors who made some suggestions and some experts from NGOs got involved too",[22] while NLD said that "law experts" were involved in working with CEC members to examine candidates' profiles.[23] As for the USDP, elderly respected persons, retired party members, and former MPs or military personnel were involved in screening candidates' profiles and work experience.[24] The PNO also included influential people such as monks, abbots, and village track administrators in nominating candidates, although the TEC still filtered their candidates.[25]

In the party politics literature, the involvement of non-party members such as trade union members in candidate selection typically suggests that the party selectorate lacks autonomy in decision-making and is susceptible to external pressures. In Myanmar, in contrast, the involvement of non-party members may indicate that the parties lack local resources. Alternatively, the inclusion of non-party religious or senior ethnic leaders may add legitimacy to the party's selection process, to broaden its support base or simply widen its pool of candidates. The inclusion of senior religious or ethnic leaders, who are mostly males, may disadvantage female candidates given that there are typically more males than females involved in local religious or ethnic community activities.

PREFERRED CANDIDATE TRAITS

Beyond the question of *who* decides on a party's slate of candidates, it also matters what they are looking for. What are a given party's preferred traits for candidates for the lower house? Is gender an important selection criterion?[26] Our study of nine parties found a long list of preferred qualities of ideal candidates. Regardless of the type of party organization, the most preferred trait that we found was party experience. In fact, 80 per cent of our interviewees said that their parties prefer candidates who have held a specific position within the party (e.g. in the CEC, central committee, district committee, or township executive). One USDP interviewee even reported that their party gives preference to candidates with backgrounds in the Tatmadaw, Myanmar's military.[27]

The other qualities that the parties prefer were educational qualifications (36 per cent),[28] followed by youth (22 per cent), being from a certain ethnic group (17 per cent), then popularity or being well-respected by the community (15 per cent). Ten per cent of interviewees highlighted occupational background or political experience as preferred criteria. Among these qualities, the parties' preference for candidates with a high level of education would benefit politically inexperienced women, as there are more highly educated women than men in Myanmar (Crisp and Clementi 2020).

Overall, however, only 8 per cent of interviewees cited gender as a selection criterion. We found no differences between male and female interviewees regarding their party's preferred traits in candidates. This suggests that the interviewees—who include party gatekeepers, party elites, and candidates—do not consider gender an important selection criterion or factor for exclusion. This is somewhat counter-intuitive, especially given that some parties have publicly announced plans to diversify and promote women in politics. For example, in 2013, the NLD announced a diversity policy to recruit and promote women, youth, and ethnic minorities as parliamentary candidates. However, despite these efforts, only five out of ten NLD interviewees mentioned "women" when they were asked the type of candidates their party prefers. In fact, three NLD MPs were unaware of the diversity policy when asked. This lack of awareness implies that, in practice, the diversity policy was not actively enforced in all townships. One female NLD MP supported this interpretation, explaining, "We do have the priority or preferences for women, ethnic people and youth but the rule should be clear and implemented in practice."[29] Altogether, the interviews show that comparatively, other descriptive traits such as ethnicity, religion, and geographical backgrounds matter more than gender.

Aside from direct party experience, our interviewees from MNP, NLD, SNLD, and ANP also report political experience more broadly as an important criterion or profess past political experience as inspiration for them to join politics. Political experience refers broader involvement in one or more of the following: as activists in protest movements such as the U Thant funeral movement,[30] the 1988 uprising,[31] or the Saffron revolution;[32] participating in an ethnic armed group; and participating in the 1990 election.[33] For example, one ANP female candidate explained:

> In 2007, I actively participated in the Saffron Revolution. Actually, my ambition was just for better education, it is not the politics. But I realised that we need to set up a good system. I joined politics since I believe that every citizen should have responsibilities.[34]

Additionally, a number of interviewees mentioned social organization roles or religious backgrounds as important traits, either their having worked as (religious) teachers or as a means through which they had gained experience in public life and trust and respect from their community.[35] Unsurprisingly, interviewees from ethnic-based parties (especially KSDP, LNDP, MNP, SNLD, and TNP) were most likely to describe their experiences in community groups such as ethnic literature and cultural committees, ethnic youth committees, or church-based social groups as sources of their own political ambitions.[36]

The preference for candidates with party or political experience is disadvantageous to aspiring female candidates as there are very few women in higher political or party leadership positions. A way to overcome this barrier is to actively recruit women without political or party experience. For example, while some parties (ANP, MNP, SNLD) require a minimum of six months' party membership for candidacy, others (KSDP, KMDP, NLD, TNP) have reported recruiting non-party members as candidates. One TNP interviewee elaborated, "A person who is not from TNP party also has the chance to be a candidate. In the 2015 election, 3 out of 12 MPs were not from TNP party."[37] The inclusion of non-party members as candidates ought to be extended to apply not only to men, but also to women.

Additionally, ethnicity and geography matter for candidates aspiring to enter electoral politics. In our study, seven out of nine parties —ANP (Rakhine), KSDP (Kachin), LNDP (Lisu), MNP (Mon), PNO (Pa-O), SNLD (Shan), TNP (Ta'ang)—were ethnic-based. All seven mentioned the importance of recruiting ethnic candidates who are representative of the areas from which they come. For example, one KSDP interviewee said the party has a guidebook for selecting "local and ethnically representative candidates" and explained, "if the area is Lisu dominated, the candidate should be Lisu, if that area is dominated by Lachind, the candidate should be Lachind".[38] KDSP's preference for descriptive representation is consistent with those of our other parties, except the SNLD,[39] which announced in 2019 that they intended to broaden their membership base from solely "focused on ethnic Shan people and Shan State" to a "state-oriented or policy-oriented party" (Myat Moe Thu 2019). Whether SNLD will effectively broaden its appeal to voters and candidates from non-Shan ethnic groups in the post-coup years remains to be seen.

In contrast to ethnic-based parties, the two "national" parties in our study, NLD and USDP, both of which have a presence across the country, recruited candidates from different ethnic backgrounds as they attempted to represent all ethnicities from different regions. Electoral geography matters, as the USDP gave preference to recruiting candidates from the predominant ethnic group residing in a particular constituency.[40] Apparently, the NLD also had a policy to give preference to non-Bamar ethnic candidates.[41] See Chapter Three for more analysis of candidate recruitment among ethnic parties.

ARE PARTIES PROMOTING WOMEN'S PARTICIPATION?

The total share of female candidates that parties nominated across central and subnational legislatures did increase from 10.5 per cent in 2015 to 17 per cent for the 2020 GE.[42] But did the parties under study do enough to support gender equality? About 60 per cent of our interviewees reported that their party (KSDP, NLD, and TNP) had some plan or policy to raise the number of female candidates for the 2015 election. However, around 25 per cent said that their party had no such policy while the rest did not know or did not answer. Despite having a stated gender and diversity policy, NLD interviewees, in particular, complained that their party policy was ineffective, and three interviewees did not think that their party had a gender policy. Interestingly, there was no gender difference in the response to the question.

Yet, despite the lack of policy awareness or stated policies, most interviewees expressed the need for more women in politics. For example, while SNLD does not have a gender equality or diversity policy, interviewees said that party leaders at both the central level and in some townships were making ad-hoc efforts to raise the number of female candidates. One female SNLD candidate described her experience of being directly appointed to a winnable constituency, even though she had not sought such a role:

> In my township, I was a township party officer, but I didn't know they nominated me. I did not even say I wanted to be elected. I was so surprised when I received the letter from the CC. I did not get a chance to refuse at that time. I requested to the township party that if I was selected as a candidate, please assign me to Shan State Hluttaw because I have a baby and I can't go to Naypyitaw. However, the township party didn't listen to me. They sent the [candidate] list to the CC. Finally, I was assigned as a Pyithu Hluttaw candidate.[43]

On the other hand, a woman in the USDP reported that her party allocated female candidates to unwinnable seats, just to raise the number of women contesting.[44] This practice is reflected in their electoral results: while 6.1 per cent of the USDP's total candidates were women, only 2.6 per cent of their successful candidates were women in 2015 (Enlightened Myanmar Research Foundation 2015, p. 27). These data contrasted with the aggregate trend for the 2015 election, in which women comprised of 13.6 per cent of *successful* candidates and 13.5 per cent of *total* candidates for both the upper and lower houses (Minoletti 2016, p. 6). This suggests that women who want to increase their chances at candidacy and electability ought to join more democratic oriented parties than militant or traditional parties such as the USDP.

Most parties in our study lacked a strategic plan, or a clear gender equality policy, to increase the number of female candidates and women's political participation. While the NLD has a stated gender and diversity policy, it is not enforced in practice. Further, despite some of the parties' having a women's wing or committee, most of the funding for women's political activities still relies on external NGO or university support. Very few parties offer capacity-building training for female party members or specific policies to promote women's leadership.

Our interviewees stated that most gender-promotion activities at the time were funded or organized by external organizations, with limited effort or financial contributions from the party. Multiple interviewees from KSDP, NLD, and USDP mentioned the positive role they felt their women's committee/wing could play in promoting the number of female candidates and women's increasing participation in the party.[45] However, while these bodies may have an effect, there is also a risk that these bodies could become silos and limit gender equality within the parties.[46]

Finally, parties can work to change patriarchal values and gender relations within the communities they represent. Towards the end, three interviewees from SNLD said that their party was targeting having 30 per cent female candidates for the 2020 election.[47] Similarly, CNLD also reported a 30 per cent target. However, in the 2020 GE, they nominated only 10 per cent female candidates. In practice, if the quota policies were enforced in earnest, they might assert a stronger effect at raising women's participation than providing workshops or training. Recruiting more women to the party's decision-making roles or creating more spaces for women in the community and in key party leadership positions, in which women can exercise leadership power prior to entering elections, would increase the number of female role models and encourage more women to join politics. Overall, parties' histories and political will to make gender equality a priority are more important for women's representation than the persistence of traditional gender relations within the ethnic group(s) they represent.

IMPLICATIONS FOR WOMEN'S POLITICAL PARTICIPATION

It is often assumed that women lack political ambition or capacity (Lawless and Fox 2010). However, our focus on candidate selection processes and criteria aims to show that the problem of women's political underrepresentation in fact lies with the parties themselves (Josefsson 2020; Kunovich and Paxton 2005b). Parties' demand for a certain type of candidate often also creates a supply of that type of candidate, by sending encouraging signals. Parties at both the national and local levels set the tone if they actively seek out and recruit underrepresented women. Further, party organization and the process by which candidates are selected also matter. When parties are guided by a hierarchical organization such as the USDP, patriarchy, or patronage, they tend to field fewer women (Bjarnegård and Kenny 2016). It is much easier for new female candidates to enter an institutionalized party that follows a set of clear, specific rules than to enter a party based on an "old boys' network" or religious ties, or where only insiders know what it takes to be selected as a candidate or a political elite.

Our comparison of candidate selection methods among nine parties of different sizes and orientations also provided some insights on the challenges of, and ways to promote, women's political participation at the local and national levels in the post-coup era. First, the ways in which candidate selection is organized by the central executive or local levels can affect the diversity of candidates. Our chapter, which focuses mostly on candidate selection for the lower house, found that a bottom-up process that includes an internal election at the township level, and deliberation among TEC members are more inclusive, decentralized, and representative. In our study, LNDP, MNP, NLD, and SNLD have fairly bottom-up candidate selection processes and nominated the highest percentage of female candidates in the 2015 elections. In this category, MNP, NLD, and SNLD, that participated in the 1990 elections, could be categorized as highly pro-democracy in their policy positions. In contrast, the two parties in our study most closely linked to military organizations—the PNO (the PNA/People's Militia Force) and USDP (the Tatmadaw)—have a less democratic outlook. Unsurprisingly, these parties have few female candidates, and very low levels of women's participation. This suggests that women have better prospects in becoming politicians if they join more institutionalized and pro-democracy parties.

Second, parties vary considerably in their selectorate—"who" has the most power in selecting candidates. We know the CEC is most important, and more so than the CC, for nominating candidates especially for the ANP, MNP, NLD, TNP, and USDP. However, for the KSDP, LNDP, PNO, and SNLD, the TC or TEC have more say. Some parties have more than one selectorate and not solely dependent on one person or leader. While having more selectorates may be more democratic and less susceptible to nepotism, the lack of clear guidance on "who" ultimately decides may confuse and create internal strife between candidates. Potential female candidates will perform better if they actively seek out and learn who the selectorate is and its selection criteria.

Third, all the CECs and local township leaders in our study are male-dominated; this skew has implications for women's political participation, as earlier mentioned. The lack of female role models compounds the lack of internal advocates to select women as candidates. Efforts to promote women's candidacy and political participation require attention not only from the top-down, CEC level but also from the bottom-up, local level. Gender quotas or setting targets of ensuring at least 30 per cent women in key party bodies is a way to break the historical legacies and structural barriers in those decision-making bodies. As parties that adopt gender quotas are more likely to make headway in raising their percentage of female politicians (Tan 2015, 2021), party leaders need to make concerted efforts to actively encourage, promote, or appoint women to the CEC, CC, and TECs. Also see Chapter Six, which examines the institutional barriers and recommendations for women to participate in male-dominated politics at the local ward and village tract levels.

Fourth, cultural differences between ethnic groups could also explain differences in women's representation within parties. For example, Pa'O and Rakhine cultures tend to be highly patriarchal (Löfving 2011),[48] and the ANP and PNO both have very low levels of women's participation. However, cultural effects may not totally determine women's level of participation. For example Kachin society is traditionally highly patriarchal (Minoletti 2014, pp. 19–20 and 25), but KSDP has higher levels of female participation than other parties in our study.

As we saw, ethnic parties tend to select on ethnicity and geographical background; that practice could disadvantage ethnic-majority, female candidates. Thus far, only SNLD indicated willingness to diversify in their recruitment and campaign strategies. A key issue to watch is if the trend of mergers between ethnic parties helps with the recruitment of more diverse slates of candidates in the post-coup era. In the run-up to the 2020 GE, disaffection with the NLD led to mergers among parties from the same ethnic state. For example, the KSDP formed in August 2017 following the merger of several ethnic-based parties; the Karen National Democratic Party (KNDP) was formed following mergers in February 2018; the Kachin State Party (KSP) in August 2018; and the Mon Party in August 2018 (Aung 2018). These mergers show that the ethnic parties are strategic in pooling their resources to select candidates and avoiding split votes amongst their mutual ethnic-voter base. If these party mergers are sustained in the post-coup period, they may succeed in appealing to voters and attracting more female (ethnic) candidates in future elections.

CONCLUSION

Our findings, based on extensive interviews with 72 party gatekeepers, candidates, and members of parliament from nine selected parties, found significant differences in how parties select candidates for the lower house. While the same actors (CEC, TC, TEC, etc.) tend to be involved, who has the final say varies. Moreover, six out of our nine parties conduct internal local elections prior to consolidating lists of candidates for the CEC. This suggests a more bottom-up, democratic, and inclusive candidate selection process than when decisions are solely made by a single leader or controlled centrally by the CEC.

Despite the religious or socio-ethnic patriarchal values inherent in parties, efforts to diversify and improve gender equality in politics could be enhanced by the administration's political will to introduce gender quotas or targets at the party's central, town, and village levels of governance. Ensuring more women join the CEC would be a critical signal to party members and provide role models for younger aspiring candidates. Women on the CEC could also advocate for more gender-equitable policies. Enforcing gender quotas at the party's lower levels of governance would offer women the practical training and political experience. This training option is better than simply relying on external agencies to sponsor gender training and research capacity-building programmes.

While the military coup on 1 February 2021 has dramatically dampened party politics and women's political participation, there is little doubt that party politics will be back, perhaps with more rigour and strength than before, when national elections are held once again. In fact, the coup has provided an unprecedented opportunity for the various parties to come together, in vehement opposition to military rule. The National Unity Government (NUG), which includes the Committee Representing the Pyidaungsu Hluttaw and some former members of parliament, agitates for political reform and to return to civilian rule. Meanwhile, talks are underway to encourage the NUG to advance gender equality in government and introduce a system of gender quotas. This development bodes well and will likely set a good example for more institutionalized and gender-equal candidate selection processes when civilian rule returns to Myanmar.

NOTES

1. We are grateful to all the interviewees who gave their time to share their experiences for this research project. We are also thankful to our EMReF colleagues Cing Van Kim, Hla Myat Mon, La Ring Pausa, Myo Thant Zaw, Shwe Ye Oo, and Su Su Hlaing for collecting and translating the data on which we draw.
2. For example, see Croissant (2013); Stokke, Khine Win, and Soe Myint Aung (2015).
3. The selectorate could consist of one person or many people, including the whole nation. Typically, the bigger and more diverse the selectorate, the more inclusive and democratic the process (Rahat and Hazan 2001, p. 301).
4. Note that there is a slight discrepancy between these two sources for how many of the 6,072 candidates were women—Enlightened Myanmar Research Foundation counts 805 (13.3 per cent), whereas International Foundation for Electoral Systems gives the number as 800 (13.2 per cent) (EMReF 2015, p. 9; IFES 2015, p. 2).
5. Nomination is the legal process by which election authorities screen the candidates that parties recommend, approve their candidacy, and print their names on the ballot paper.
6. Interviews with HM-MGK01, HM-MGK04, and SS-GKCECM01.
7. Interview with LR-MMP08. NLD interviewees in our study also expressed unhappiness with the lack of transparency in the CEC's candidate selection process.
8. The data on CEC composition provided by MNP to the authors of this chapter only specified who held the position of chairperson and secretary

(both of whom are male), and the data provided by TNP did not specify the positions held by any of the CEC members.
9. Interview with HM-FMP15.
10. Interviews with LR-MMP01, SS-GKCECM01, and SS-GKTECM05.
11. Interview with LR-GKCECM01.
12. See interview Question 14b: Did your Township Chairman play an important role in selecting candidates?
13. SNLD interviewees say that the process for nominating candidates was open. They also have a policy to prevent conflicts of interest, whereby MPs cannot serve as township party chairmen. Interview with HM-FGK03.
14. Interview with HM-MMP03
15. Interview with SS-MMP06.
16. "[T]here were no party rules for it. That's why things were chaotic". Interview with HM-FMP11.
17. TNP does not have specific rules or criteria for selecting candidates and conducts selection based on "secret voting". One respondent complained, "The township chairman and committee's role were not that important. It was not even the case that the township committee selected the candidates and submitted the list to the central level in 2015".
18. Interview with LR-FMP07. The high number of Kachin parties competing could explain the lack of candidates for the KSDP in 2015 GE.
19. Interviews with LR-FMP07, LR-GKCECM04, and LR-MMP11.
20. In response to Question 14c: Were there other individuals who played a key role in the candidate selection process?
21. LNDP respondents identified religious leaders/pastors, respected/ knowledgeable persons, and village representatives as being involved in township-level candidate selection. Interviews with LR-MMP07, LR-MMP09 and LR-GKCECM07
22. Interview with LR-MMP11.
23. Interview with LR-MMP01.
24. Interview with LR-GKCECF01.
25. Interview with HM-MMP10.
26. We draw on survey questions 20 and 23, which we posed to both candidates and gatekeepers: "In your opinion, what kind of candidates does your party prefer? Are there specific criteria or skills your party is looking for?"; and "In the 2015 elections did your party have policies to increase the number of female candidates? If so, how effective do you think these were?"
27. Interview with LR-GKCECM01.
28. Some parties also expressed a preference that candidates be university graduates. Interviews with HM-FMP08, HM-FMP11, and LR-MMP11.
29. Interview with LR-FMP02.

30. Interview with LR-MMP01.
31. Interviews with HM-FGK03, LR-FMP01, LR-GKCECM03, LR-MMP01, LR-MMP03, SS-GKCECM03, SS- GKTECM03, SS-MMP06, and SS-MMP07.
32. Interview with SS-FMP02.
33. Interviews with SS-GKTECM01, SS-FMP03, and SS-MMP02.
34. Interview with SS-FMP02.
35. For example, interviews with HM-MMP05, HM-MMP10, LR-FMP05, LR-FMP06, LR-GKCECM02, LR- MMP04, LR-MMP07, SS-FMP01, and SS-GKCECM03.
36. For example, see Interviews with HM-MMP02, HM-MGK06, HM-MMP07, LR-FMP05, LR-FMP06, LR- MMP06, LR-MMP11, SSGKCECM01, and SS-GKTECM01.
37. Interview with HM-MMP05.
38. Interview with LR-FMP06.
39. In our interviews, one SNLD respondent said that "[T]he party prefers people who act for all ethnic groups in Myanmar, not only for the Shan people. That means the person is not a racist … Moreover, the party prefers people who would listen from all sides". Interview with HM-MGK05.
40. Interview with LR-FMP04.
41. This policy was also stated in the NLD candidate guidebook for the 2015 general elections. Interviews with LR-FMP01, LR-FMP02, LR-GKCECM02, LR-MMP01, and SS-GKTECM03.
42. This analysis draws from Questions 23 and 24: "In the 2015 elections, did your party have policies to increase the number of female candidates? If so, how effective do you think these were?"; and "Does your party have any plans or policies to try and increase the number of female candidates for 2020?"
43. Interview with HM-FMP09.
44. Interview with LR-GKCECM01.
45. Interviews with LR-FMP03, LR-FMP06, LR-GKCECM02, LR-GKCECM06, LR-MMP02, LR-MMP03, SS-GKDM01, SS-GKSM01, and SS-GKTECM01.
46. One of our investigators who has given trainings to many Myanmar political parties highlighted this risk.
47. Interviews with HM-FMP08, HM-FMP11, and HM-MGK01.
48. Interview with HM-FMP15.
49. Interview with LR-GKCECF01.

REFERENCES

Aldrich, John H. 2011. *Why Parties?: A Second Look*. Chicago: University of Chicago Press.

Aung Aung. 2018. "Understanding Ethnic Political Parties in Myanmar: The Cases of Mon and Karen States". *ISEAS Perspective*, no. 2018/57, 20 September 2018.

Bjarnegård, Elin, and Meryl Kenny. 2013. "Gender, Institutions and Political Recruitment: A Research Agenda". *Gender Politics at Edinburgh* (blog). https://genderpoliticsatedinburgh.wordpress.com/2013/06/18/gender-institutions-and-political-recruitment-a-research-agenda/.

———. 2016. "Comparing Candidate Selection: A Feminist Institutionalist Approach". *Government and Opposition* 51, no. 3: 370–92. https://doi.org/10.1017/gov.2016.4.

Catalano Weeks, Ana. 2019. "Quotas and Party Priorities: Direct and Indirect Effects of Quota Laws". *Political Research Quarterly* 72, no. 4: 849–62. https://doi.org/10.1177/1065912918809493.

Cheng, Christine, and Margit Tavits. 2011. "Informal Influences in Selecting Female Political Candidates". *Political Research Quarterly* 64, no. 2: 460–71.

Crisp, Rebecca, and Asha Clementi. 2020. "Reality or Rhetoric: Understanding Gender Inequality and Education in Myanmar". *Australian Institute of International Affairs* (blog). 30 July 2020. https://www.internationalaffairs.org.au/australianoutlook/reality-or-rhetoric-understanding-gender-inequality-and-education-in-myanmar/.

Croissant, Aurel. 2013. "Why Do Military Regimes Institutionalize? Constitution-Making and Elections as Political Survival Strategy in Myanmar". *Asian Journal of Political Science* 21, no. 2: 105–25.

Czudnowski, M. 1975. "Political Recruitment". In *Handbook of Political Science: Volume 2, Micropolitical Theory*, edited by Fred I. Greenstein and Nelson Polsby, pp. 155–242. Reading, MA: Addison-Wesley Educational Publishers Inc.

Enlightened Myanmar Research Foundation (EMReF). 2015. "Important Facts About 2015 Election (2015)". Yangon: EMReF. https://merin.org.mm/en/publication/important-facts-about-2015-election-2015.

Gallagher, Michael, and Michael Marsh, eds. 1988. *Candidate Selection in Comparative Perspective: The Secret Garden of Politics*. Beverely Hills and London: Sage Publications.

Huntington, Samuel P. 1965. "Political Development and Political Decay". *World Politics* 17, no. 3: 386–430. https://doi.org/10.2307/2009286.

International Foundation for Electoral Systems (IFES). 2015. "Elections in Myanmar: 2015 General Elections – Frequently Asked Questions". Washington, D.C: IFES.

Josefsson, Cecilia. 2020. "How Candidate Selection Structures and Genders Political Ambition: Illustrations from Uruguay". Text. February 2020. https://doi.org/info:doi/10.1332/251510819X15693187680761.

Krook, Mona Lena. 2010. "Beyond Supply and Demand: A Feminist-Institutionalist Theory of Candidate Selection". *Political Research Quarterly* 63, no. 4: 707–20. https://doi.org/10.1177/1065912909336275.

Kunovich, Sheri, and Pamela Paxton. 2005a. "Pathways to Power: The Role of Political Parties in Women's National Political Representation". *American Journal of Sociology* 111, no. 2: 505–52. https://doi.org/10.1086/444445.

———. 2005b. "Pathways to Power: The Role of Political Parties in Women's National Political Representation". *American Journal of Sociology*, September 2005. http://digitalrepository.smu.edu/hum_sci_sociology_research/5.

Lawless, Jennifer L., and Richard L. Fox. 2010. *It Still Takes a Candidate: Why Women Don't Run for Office*. New York: Cambridge University Press.

Löfving, Annami. 2011. "Women's Participation in Public Life in Myanmar". Yangon: ActionAid, CARE and Oxfam.

Lovenduski, Joni, and Pippa Norris. 1993. *Gender and Party Politics*. London: Sage Publications Ltd.

Mendelberg, Tali, Christopher F. Karpowitz, and Nicholas Goedert. 2014. "Does Descriptive Representation Facilitate Women's Distinctive Voice? How Gender Composition and Decision Rules Affect Deliberation". *American Journal of Political Science* 58, no. 2: 291–306. https://doi.org/10.1111/ajps.12077.

Minoletti, Paul. 2014. "Women's Participation in the Subnational Governance of Myanmar". Yangon: MDRI-CESD and The Asia Foundation.

———. 2016. "Gender (in)Equality in the Governance of Myanmar: Past, Present, and Potential Strategies for Change". Yangon: The Asia Foundation.

———. 2017. "Gender and Politics in Myanmar: Women and Men Candidates in the 2015 Elections". Yangon: Gender Equality Network.

Myat Moe Thu. 2019. "SNLD to Change Focus from Ethnic- to Policy-Oriented Party". *Myanmar Times*, 1 March 2019. https://www.mmtimes.com/news/snld-change-focus-ethnic-policy-oriented-party.html.

Norris, Pippa, and Joni Lovenduski. 1995. *Political Recruitment: Gender, Race, and Class in the British Parliament*. Cambridge: Cambridge University Press.

Phan Tee Eain. 2016. "Report on Observing Women's Participation in Myanmar's November 2015 General Election".

Rahat, Gideon. 2007. "Candidate Selection: The Choice Before the Choice". *Journal of Democracy* 18, no. 1: 157–70.

Rahat, Gideon, and Reuven Hazan. 2001. "Candidate Selection Methods: An Analytical Framework". *Party Politics* 7, no. 3: 297–322.

Stokke, Kristian, Khine Win, and Soe Myint Aung. 2015. "Political Parties and Popular Representation in Myanmar's Democratisation Process". *Journal of Current Southeast Asian Affairs* 34, no. 3: 3–35.

Tan, Netina. 2015. "Introduction: Quotas and Non-Quota Strategies in East Asia". *Politics & Gender* 11, no. 1: 171–75. https://doi.org/10.1017/S1743923X14000622.

———. 2021. "Gender Quotas, Reserved Seats and Electoral Incentives in Asia". In *Women, Power, and Political Representation: Canadian and Comparative Perspectives*, edited by Roosmajin de Geus, Erin Trolley, Elizabeth Goodyear-Grant, and Peter John Loewen, pp. 108–18. Toronto, Canada: Toronto University Press. https://utorontopress.com/ca/women-in-politics-women-in-leadership-4.

Tan, Netina, Paul Minoletti, Elin Bjarnegård, and Aye Lei Tun. 2020. "Party Building and Candidate Selection – Intraparty Politics and Promoting Gender Equality in Myanmar". Yangon, Myanmar: Enlightened Myanmar Research Foundation.

Verge, Tània, and Sílvia Claveria. 2018. "Gendered Political Resources: The Case of Party Office". *Party Politics* 24, no. 5: 536–48. https://doi.org/10.1177/1354068816663040.

Zin Mar Aung. 2015. "From Military Patriarchy to Gender Equity: Including Women in the Democratic Transition in Burma". *Social Research* 82, no. 2: 531–51.

3

ETHNIC PARTIES, REPRESENTATION, AND FEMALE CANDIDATE RECRUITMENT IN MYANMAR

Jangai Jap and Cassandra Preece

Ethnic parties make up a significant portion of the electoral landscape in Myanmar politics. In fact, 48 per cent of the political parties that competed in the 1990 general election were ethnic parties, 62 per cent in 2010, 60 per cent in 2015, and 59 per cent in 2020.[1] Between 1990 and 2020, the proportion of female candidates in Myanmar elections also increased. Are these two trends linked? Is there something distinctive about ethnic parties as a type, and do they more effectively facilitate women's political representation than their catch-all counterparts?

Existing literature highlights the important role of political parties in explaining varying levels of women's representation around the world (Caul 1999; Pitre 2003). Parties play a critical role in recruiting and selecting candidates, thereby contributing to the gender makeup of legislatures and political bodies (Tan et al. 2020). As we discuss in greater detail below, existing literature finds mixed results regarding the effect of ethnic parties. Broad studies on women's representation have often concluded that electoral rules and circumstances that benefit women can also be applied to other marginalized groups, such as ethnic minorities (Matland and Taylor 1997; Caul 1999). Yet, others find a potential for competition between different under-represented identities (Lien et al. 2007), or express fears over patriarchal attitudes among specific ethnic groups that would disadvantage women candidates (Okin 1999).

Ethnic parties might therefore be less likely than catch-all parties to pay attention to gender inequalities (Goetz 1998; Holmsten, Moser, and Slosar 2010). However, ethnic parties seem to perform differently under different electoral rules. Ethnic parties in single-member districts (SMD), where voters elect a single candidate to represent the constituency by plurality or majority vote, have been found to include more women than their catch-all counterparts. However, ethnic parties appear to exclude women—that is, do not nominate female candidates—at an even higher rate in proportional representation (PR) systems, where parties secure seats in larger constituencies per the share of the popular vote they or their candidates win, without gender quotas (Holmsten, Moser, and Slosar 2010). This is perhaps because the nomination and candidate selection decisions in PR systems are more heavily concentrated among the party elite and provide more opportunity for patriarchal attitudes to dominate (ibid.).

Yet, existing literature also suggests a moderating effect of party institutionalization, rather than just electoral rules. More institutionalized parties are believed to be better able to provide crucial psychological, organizational, and material support to women (Wylie 2020). Formal institutions and the transparency of those institutions provide clearer pathways for the advancement of women's political representation (Kittilson 2006). Institutions surrounding candidate selection procedures are especially critical, with existing studies finding that women fare better in parties whose candidate selection is more institutionalized and formalized (Escobar-Lemmon and Taylor-Robinson 2009; Lovenduski and Norris 1993). Among ethnic parties then, those that are more institutionalized are expected to better facilitate women's representation.

Given low initial levels of women's representation and the prevalence of ethnic parties in its post-transition, pre-coup elections, Myanmar offers an especially useful test case of whether ethnic parties are helpful, neutral, or harmful in increasing women's access to political office. Do ethnic parties contribute to increasing women's representation and political participation? If so, under what conditions? While our data draw specifically from pre-coup Myanmar, we would expect similar patterns to hold elsewhere. Moreover, as parties and other organizations regroup or persist in Myanmar, even absent formal elections, women's representation and voice in their ranks remains no less salient. Questions of what organizational qualities and institutional features are most conducive to advancing women as leaders remain relevant.

While issues related to ethnic minority representation and ethnic parties in Myanmar constitute one of the most robust lines of academic research on Myanmar politics, there is very little scholarly work on women's representation. Rather, this topic has largely been relegated to research by international organizations, local NGOs, and think tanks. The intersection of these lines of inquiry thus presents an unsurprising blind spot: we do not know much about the role of ethnic parties in facilitating women's representation in Myanmar. This chapter aims to fill this gap by examining (1) the extent to which ethnic parties prioritize women's representation, (2) whether ethnic parties are more effective in facilitating women's representation than their catch-all party counterparts, and (3) whether some ethnic parties are more effective at facilitating women's representation than other ethnic parties. Our findings shed light on intra-party dynamics in Myanmar, but also add to our wider understanding of the interplay of dimensions of identity politics and representation.

To investigate whether ethnic parties promote women's representation, we rely on interview data from 50 in-depth interviews conducted from November 2018 to March 2019 with members of parliament (MPs) and party gatekeepers from seven ethnic political parties, as described in Chapter One. Additionally, we leverage data from the 2015 election to compare the track records of ethnic parties in nominating women as candidates and these candidates' success rate compared to those of the two major national parties, the National League for Democracy (NLD) and the Union Solidarity and Development Party (USDP). We also use these data to investigate whether the level of party institutionalization (for which we take party age in part as an indicator), as well as ideological differences across generations of parties—in particular, democratic orientations—explains variation among ethnic parties.

Analysis of these data reveals ambiguous findings. First, while interviewees from ethnic parties expressed concerns related to cultural norms and traditional attitudes that might impact levels of women's representation in Myanmar, there is limited evidence to suggest this sets ethnic parties apart from catch-all parties. We cannot be certain that traditional norms and attitudes were more pervasive among ethnic parties than among catch-all parties. Second, in the 2015 election, ethnic parties fielded more female candidates than catch-all parties (both the NLD and the USDP), but the NLD was more effective than the ethnic parties in getting female candidates elected. Third, regarding variation among ethnic parties, older parties, which were more institutionalized and showed more democratic orientation, did not field more female candidates than newer parties, but a greater proportion of female candidates from older parties were elected. Given these findings, we cannot draw a general conclusion about whether ethnic parties are more effective in facilitating women's representation. However, we may infer that commitment to democratic values makes a difference with respect to supporting female politicians.

This chapter proceeds as follows. We begin with an overview of ethnic parties in Myanmar, followed by a discussion of existing literature and expected findings. Our empirical section consists of three sets of analyses. First, we draw from qualitative interviews to better understand ethnic parties' candidate selection procedures and their stances on recruiting and supporting female politicians, as codified in party policies and in practice. Second, we leverage data from the 2015 election to compare ethnic parties' records to those of the NLD and the USDP regarding whether they fielded women in electoral competitions and whether their female candidates won. Third, we again rely on data from the 2015 election to investigate whether the level of party institutionalization (age) explains variation among ethnic parties. We conclude the chapter by highlighting important areas for future research and further theory-testing, and outlining implications of the recent coup on ethnic parties and women's representation in Myanmar.

BACKGROUND: ETHNIC PARTIES IN MYANMAR

Prior to the 2021 coup, political parties in Myanmar could be divided into three broad categories: catch-all or nationwide parties; parties that represent ethnic minorities' interests; and smaller parties representing the Bamar ethnic majority (Kempel, Chan Myawe Aung Sun, and Aung Tun 2015). The NLD and USDP were the main catch-all parties. Since Myanmar's political transition in 2010, new parties emerged and old parties transformed, producing a dynamic and diverse electoral landscape. For many ethnic parties in Myanmar, ethnicity features prominently in their name (e.g., Mon Unity Party, Kachin State People's Party, Shan Nationalities League for Democracy, etc.).

Broadly, "ethnic" parties can be distinguished from "catch-all" parties by their name, election promises, and leadership profiles (Chandra 2011, p. 155). Unlike catch-all parties, ethnic parties tend to have narrow objectives, aimed exclusively at championing the interests of a particular ethnic group (Gunther and Diamond 2003). Often, ethnic parties possess low levels of ideological or programmatic commitment and low levels of organizational structure. In many cases, ethnic parties are weakly institutionalized and have smaller membership bases and voter bases than mass-based parties (ibid.). Ethnic parties in Myanmar are no exception. In fact, "aside from a general commitment to democracy and federalism, few [ethnic parties in Myanmar] have any apparent ideological underpinnings or developed party platforms" (Pedersen 2008, p. 51). In short, aside from championing specific ethnic interests, ethnic parties are hardly distinguishable ideologically from one another.

There are debates over whether ethnic parties are normatively good or bad. On one hand, the literature that views ethnicity with primordialist assumptions claims that the politicization of ethnicity "infects" the political system and has a destabilizing effect (Rabushka and Shepsle 1972; Horowitz 1985). On the other hand, literature that views ethnicity from a constructivist perspective claims that ethnic parties can, in fact, help to sustain democracy if institutions foster the politicization of multiple dimensions of ethnic identity (Chandra 2005). While sometimes controversial, ethnic parties can play a role in effectively communicating the demands of minority communities and mitigating ethnic tensions in deeply divided societies (Bogaards 2010; Stokke 2019).

While ethnic parties are numerous in Myanmar, they have performed poorly and have offered very little political representation for ethnic minority communities. Given a history of ethnic conflict that has maintained and perhaps even heightened the political salience of ethnic cleavages in Myanmar, ethnic minority communities, the ethnic parties themselves, and country observers expected ethnic parties to prevail over catch-all parties, at least in ethnic-minority areas (TNI 2015). However, ethnic parties have consistently underperformed overall (see Table 3.1), winning just over 18 per cent of seats up for grabs in the 2015 election and 10 per cent of seats in 2020. In the states where ethnic minorities constitute the majority of the local population, they hold just 30 per cent of elected seats (137 of 451) in the state and national legislatures.[2] At the same time, the ethnic-minority population has maintained roughly proportional representation in these legislative chambers. In other words, a substantial share of ethnic-minority MPs have been associated with catch-all rather than ethnic parties. This

TABLE 3.1
Electoral Performance by Catch-All Versus Ethnic Parties in Myanmar General Elections

Party	2010			
	Pyithu Hluttaw	Amyotha Hluttaw	State/Regional Assembly	TOTAL
Union Solidarity and Development Party	259	129	493	881
Ethnic parties	45	29	139	213
2015				
National League for Democracy	225	135	476	836
Union Solidarity and Development Party	30	12	73	115
Ethnic parties	37	19	79	135
2020				
National League for Democracy	258	138	501	897
Union Solidarity and Development Party	26	7	38	71
Ethnic parties	31	15	71	117

Source: Data compiled by the authors from Union Election Commission reports and other sources, including: CPCS (2011); TNI (2015); ICG (2015); Myanmar Times (2015).

phenomenon has challenged the assumption that ethnic-minority voters in Myanmar prefer ethnic parties over catch-all parties, prompting a closer look at party characteristics beyond ethnic commitments.

WAVES OF ETHNIC PARTY ESTABLISHMENT

Existing literature identifies party age as an important characteristic distinguishing ethnic parties that performed well from those that did not (Jap and Ziegfeld 2020). Indeed, the Rakhine and Shan ethnic parties that consistently performed well in the 2010, 2015, and 2020 elections are much older than the majority of ethnic parties that competed in these same elections. That pattern suggests a temporal dimension to ethnic-party success: either that older and newer ethnic parties differ in some salient quality, or that more institutionalized parties have a more general advantage over newer competitors. This section provides a historical overview of the emergence of ethnic parties in Myanmar.

The presence of ethnic parties in Myanmar traces back to the decolonization period. During that period of rapid political development, leaders from various segments of Myanmar society established political organizations to represent their communities. Examples of such organizations included the Kachin National Congress Party and Karen Youth Organization (KYO) (Thawnghmung 2011). The most well-known one at the time was perhaps the Karen National Union (KNU), an umbrella organization of various Karen organizations. (The KNU eventually went underground and became one of the most well-organized non-state armed organizations in Myanmar.) These ethnic parties from the 1940s participated in early elections in Myanmar. In fact, the KYO was the second-best performing party in Myanmar's first general election in 1947.[3]

While dozens of ethnic parties operated during Myanmar's parliamentary period (1948–62), most did not survive the socialist period (1962–88); a few survived in name only. After the coup in 1962, the military leader, General Ne Win, established the Burmese Socialist Programme Party (BSPP) and a single-party regime, outlawing all other political organizations (Taylor 2009). Ethnic-minority political leaders were incorporated into the BSPP structure or stayed out of politics altogether. Eventually, ethnic parties and other political organizations

TABLE 3.2
Ethnic Parties (2015) and Their First Election

2015	2010	1990
1. Ahka National Development Party	1. All Mon Regions Democracy Party	1. Arakan National Party
2. Arakan Patriot Party	2. Chin National Democratic Party	2. Chin League for Democracy
3. Asho Chin National Party	3. Chin Progressive Party	3. Kachin National Democracy Congress Party
4. Danu National Democracy Party	4. Inn National Development Party	4. Karen National Party
5. Danu National Organization Party	5. Kaman National Progressive Party	5. Kokang Democracy and Unity Party
6. Democracy and Human Rights Party	6. Kayan National Party	6. Lahu National Development Party
7. Dynet National Race Development Party	7. Kayin People's Party	7. Mon National Party
8. Inn Ethnic Party	8. Kayin State Democracy and Development Party	8. Mro National Development Party
9. East Shan State Development Democratic Party	9. Khami National Development Party	9. Shan Nationalities League for Democracy
10. Kachin Democratic Party	10. Pa-O National Organization	10. Shan State Kokang Democracy Party
11. Kachin State Democratic Party	11. Phlone-Sgaw Democracy Party	10. Union Pa-O National Organization
12. Kayah Unity Democracy Party	12. Rakhine State National Force Party	12. Zomi Congress for Democracy Party
13. Kayin Democratic Party	13. Shan Nationalities Democratic Party	
14. Khumi National Party	14. Ta'ang National Party	
15. Lhavo National Unity and Development Party	15. Unity and Democracy Party of Kachin State	
16. Lisu National Development Party	16. Wa Democratic Party	
17. Mon Women's Party	17. Wa National Unity Party	
18. Mro National Democracy Party		
19. Mro Nationalities Party		
20. Rakhine Patriotic Party		
21. Red Shan (Tailai) and Northern Shan Ethnics Solidarity Party		
22. Tailai Nationalities Development Party		
23. United Kayin National Democratic Party		
24. Zo Ethnic Regional Development Party		

Source: TNI (2015).

stopped functioning as political parties, though many continued to operate under the umbrella of ethnic self-determination movements or as part of civil society.

As such, the oldest political parties in Myanmar trace their origins to the pro-democracy movement that emerged in the aftermath of the BSPP collapse in 1988 (ibid.).[4] The most prominent party was the National League for Democracy, which was led by Aung San Suu Kyi. Around the same time that the NLD was established, many ethnic-minority communities also established pro-democracy parties with an emphasis on advancing those communities' interests. Examples of such parties included the Shan Nationalities League for Democracy, Arakan League for Democracy, and Chin National League for Democracy. These ethnic parties and the NLD worked together in alliance during the 1990 general elections. In the aftermath of the election, however, the military dictatorship—reconstituted as the State Law and Order Restoration Council—refused to allow a peaceful transfer of power. By early 1993, the junta disbanded the existing political parties, though many persisted underground.

After this wave of ethnic party formation, there were two more waves, prior to the 2010 and 2015 elections. As a result, by the 2015 election, several parties claimed to represent a single ethnic community. Table 3.2 indicates ethnic parties that competed in 2015 by their founding election.[5] As we discuss below, when an ethnic party was established has profound implications for its effectiveness in facilitating women's representation.

WOMEN'S REPRESENTATION AND ETHNIC PARTIES IN MYANMAR

Women in Myanmar have been underrepresented in the country's parliament to a greater extent than in neighbouring countries and the global average. Following the 2010 elections, female MPs accounted for just 3 per cent of the national legislature (Minoletti 2020).[6] Following the 2015 elections, that figure tripled to 10 per cent. In 2015, the global average was 23 per cent, and the Asian average was 19 per cent (GEN 2017), indicating that while there has been an improvement in Myanmar, women still fare poorly. What explains the paltry level of women's political representation in Myanmar?

The empirical literature is divided on whether electoral systems matter more than party-level factors (i.e., whether the party is ethnic or catch-all) for women's representation. Wängnerud (2009) finds that the election of women is generally "favored by electoral systems with party lists [i.e. voters select only the party, which rank-orders its candidates to determine who assumes whatever seats the party wins], proportional representation (PR), and large district magnitudes [number of legislators per constituency]". This is mainly due to the nature of the party-list system—where a woman can be placed farther down on the list and still be elected—and also to the competitive nature of the PR system, since gender equality might become prevalent among all parties once one party emphasizes it (Wängnerud 2009, p. 54; McAllister and Studlar 2002). However, when considered in tandem with the electoral system, party-level factors do also appear to be important in driving the level of women's political representation. For instance, Holmstem et al. (2010) find that in single-member districts (SMD), ethnic parties elect more women than their catch-all counterparts, but not in PR systems without gender quotas.

Given that this study examines a single country (Myanmar), which has utilized the SMD system, the electoral system is a common denominator for all parties. Explanations rooted in the electoral system, which primarily operate at the national or country level, are hardly useful in helping us better understand a subnational-level phenomenon—that is, whether ethnic parties are more effective in promoting women's representation compared to catch-all parties that compete in the same electoral system.

Thus, in this section, we consider two prominent explanations that operate at the party level: gender norms and party institutionalization.[7] Gender norms, we argue, are likely to affect ethnic parties more than catch-all parties. Party institutionalization is the more fine-grained explanation, as it varies among parties, including among ethnic parties. After discussing what each of these theories would lead us to expect, we evaluate the extent to which our evidence supports each of these hypotheses.

(Conditional Effects of) Gender Norms

In addition to the electoral system, existing explanations also emphasize gender norms and expectations as potential barriers to increasing women's representation in Myanmar. Researchers and local activists have found cultural and traditional norms that discriminate against women to be present across all societal cleavages in Myanmar (Peace Support Fund 2016). Besides, Buddhist cultures in Myanmar maintain traditional and patriarchal attitudes related to male power, which lead to socially assigned gendered roles and beliefs that women are inferior (ibid.). Customary laws in ethnic minority communities are thought to provide men with power over their wives and other women through inheritance and marriage laws (Minoletti 2014). These cultural norms and patriarchal attitudes may mitigate both the supply of and the demand for female candidates in Myanmar.

Since patriarchal norms and attitudes occur across Myanmar society as a whole, we should expect to see them in all political parties. However, their effect on women's political representation may be accentuated in ethnic minority areas compared to other areas of the country. That is because the political and economic legacies of war and conflict have been found to produce gendered divisions of labour, along with physical, material, and emotional depletion among women (Hedström and Olivius 2020). Security concerns, especially those related to travelling and campaigning, might impact the supply of female candidates in ethnic minority regions more than of male candidates, potentially hindering women's ability and ambition to participate in politics (Schneider and Carroll 2019). On the demand side, in ethnic-minority areas, political parties—including ethnic parties—may be more hesitant to recruit female candidates due to these same concerns.

Given that ethnic parties primarily operate in the ethnic minority states where most of the conflict-affected areas in the country are concentrated, concerns related to gender norms and attitudes may impact the overall tally of candidates for ethnic parties more than for catch-all parties, which also operate in other areas of the country, where they might be less constrained in nominating women.[8] As such, if gender norms affect parties' praxis in Myanmar, we should expect ethnic parties to underperform in terms of women's representation compared to catch-all parties. To be clear, our claim is not that patriarchal attitudes are more pervasive in ethnic parties, but rather, that security concerns in the areas in which these parties are most likely to contest exacerbate such attitudes.

Party Institutionalization or Age

While limited, existing literature highlights institutionalization, specifically the regularity and transparency of candidate-recruitment and selection processes, as an important factor in facilitating women's representation (Wylie 2020). Parties with higher levels of institutionalization have been found to improve levels of women's representation (Caul 1999). That is because a more institutionalized candidate-recruitment process may make it easier for newcomers (including women) to understand and pursue the process, and may prevent the "arbitrary dismissal of candidates in favour of others" (Pitre 2003). Additionally, adaptability, or the ability of a party to survive environmental challenges and to last longer, indicates a higher level of organizational capacity, which is expected to improve a party's ability to support candidates and impact women's representation (GEN 2017).

It is generally thought that ethnic parties in Myanmar are weakly institutionalized (Stokke 2019). Indeed, many ethnic parties in Myanmar are young and under-developed. While catch-all parties such as the NLD and the USDP are likely more institutionalized than ethnic parties as a whole, generalizing about ethnic parties in this way masks significant variation among them. As discussed in a previous section, some ethnic parties have been mobilizing their communities since the late 1980s while others were founded just a few years prior to the 2015 election.

While party age is not equivalent to party institutionalization per se, there are reasons to expect that how long an ethnic party has been around serves as a good indicator for party institutionalization in Myanmar. That is because the longest surviving ethnic parties also tend to be those that have run successful campaigns, which means that they likely had, or have developed from that experience, some level of organizational acumen. In fact, all existing ethnic parties founded prior to the 1990 election had some level of success in their founding election in 1990. Furthermore, although the pre-1990 parties were disbanded, they were likely to have had some level of ongoing party-building opportunities, albeit underground.

It is important to note that party age in Myanmar may also be a proxy for a party's commitment to democratic values. The pre-1990 ethnic parties tend to be most closely associated with pro-democracy endeavours, having developed in opposition to the military junta. Ethnic minority voters are generally aware that many leaders of the pre-1990 ethnic parties were imprisoned, like the NLD's Aung San Suu Kyi. Additionally, these parties boycotted the 2010 election because many of their party leaders were still in prison, and they feared that the election would not be free and fair. In contrast, some of the newly formed ethnic parties that did compete in 2010 were co-opted by the military-backed party, the USDP, and were thought to be USDP proxy parties. Such variation in commitment to democratic values may affect the extent to which a party prioritizes women's representation.

In sum, compared to the ethnic parties founded in 2010 and later, the pre-1990 ethnic parties are not only more institutionalized, but may also be more committed to democracy and democratic values. These features are likely to impact how these ethnic parties facilitate women's political participation. We therefore expect the older ethnic parties to be the most proactive in selecting female candidates.

We investigate how closely evidence from Myanmar aligns with, or if it challenges, what these two theoretical approaches lead us to expect. In the next sections, we evaluate these strands in tandem to see which has the most support.

DO ETHNIC PARTIES PROMOTE WOMEN'S POLITICAL REPRESENTATION?

Recall that one strand in the literature suggests that ethnic parties may be *less* likely to nominate women, since these parties operate primarily in patriarchy-inspiring conflict zones (though gendered norms are endemic across all parties); and another finds that the age of parties in Myanmar may matter more than their constituency (ethnic or catch-all). So how *do* ethnic parties fare when it comes to increasing women's political representation in Myanmar?

To answer this question, we examine interview data from 50 in-depth interviews conducted from November 2018 to March 2019 with MPs and party gatekeepers from seven ethnic political parties in Myanmar, including: 1) Arakan National Party (ANP), 2) Kachin State Democracy Party (KSDP), 3) Lisu National Development Party (LNDP), 4) Mon National Party (MNP), 5) Pa-O National Organization (PNO), 6) Shan Nationalities League for Democracy (SNLD), and 7) Ta'ang National Party (TNP). (See Appendix One for party profiles.)

The selection of ethnic parties for this study was informed by both electoral success and party characteristics. We include the five ethnic parties that won the most seats across all parliaments in the 2015 election (ANP, SNLD, TNP, PNO and LNDP), as well as the most electorally successful Kachin and Mon ethnic parties (KSDP and MNP). These parties are also representative of ethnic parties of varying sizes, organizational structures, ages, and ideological platforms. In analysing these interviews, we focus here on cultural attitudes about women in politics and party rules and procedures, particularly as they relate to recruiting and supporting female candidates.

Cultural Attitudes as Barriers

Consistent with existing research on women's political engagement and representation in Myanmar, traditional cultural attitudes were a major theme among interviewee responses. Representatives from almost all ethnic parties mentioned cultural attitudes as a key challenge women face and as likely to contribute to the supply of and demand for female politicians in ethnic minority communities. As noted, though, we would expect similar attitudes in catch-all parties.[9]

Regarding the supply side, stereotypes and gendered expectations may disincentivize women from entering or remaining in politics across all political parties. Among interviewees from ethnic parties, we find many of them expressed concerns related to these stereotypes and expectations. A female TNP MP recounted her own experience this way: "Men don't respect women. When I talked in the campaign, they didn't respect me. Later, I heard that I am just a young girl in their eyes ... my words are a child's words".[10] In a similar vein, an SNLD party member explained how gendered stereotypes might detrimentally affect female political representatives: "If women rode motorcycles with male MPs or sit at the tea shop with men, people in the social environment will talk about her like she committed infidelity".[11] In another interview, a male MP from the MNP stated, "it is not appropriate to walk alone for a woman, they need a partner".[12] Similarly, MPs from the KSDP and ANP highlight how a woman must often get permission and support from her husband to participate in politics, with one KSDP MP claiming, "I think a woman's experience will be harder than man's because women need their husband's permission. And most of the husbands in my country do not want to prioritize their wives, so women will face more challenges than men".[13]

Even when women choose to enter politics, despite these cultural attitudes, their community may be less likely to support them compared to their male counterparts. Regarding the demand side, one woman MP from the SNLD claimed, "according to our culture, people are afraid of putting women as decision makers".[14] Similarly, a male MP from the ANP stated, "It depends on our culture and traditions ... some people still think that women should stay at home, cook and look after children. So, it is difficult to persuade women to participate in politics".[15] These demand-side issues are also likely to affect the supply side. Indeed, traditional attitudes about the role of women in society are likely to drive down women's political participation and representation.

It is important to reiterate that these attitudes are widespread across all segments of Myanmar society (Htun and Jensenius 2020). Thus, while cultural attitudes may explain why women's representation in Myanmar is much lower than it is in other countries or the global average, it is worthwhile to examine other factors that might explain the potential variation between catch-all and ethnic parties as well as among ethnic parties regarding women's candidate selection and representation.

Candidate Selection Procedures

Turning to institutional factors, ethnic party representatives expressed limited knowledge of formal procedures for candidate selection and recruitment of women. Many interview respondents recounted an informal selection process or a reliance on the Union Election Commission's broad guidelines.[16] For example, according to a member of LNDP, "We were not able to set proper rules and procedures at that time. We just checked the UEC's policies and tried to follow them ... the party did not give any guidelines".[17] In a similar vein, a member of the PNO stated, "The party's rules, criteria and procedures were nothing special. The party practiced the rules and policies prescribed by the government".[18]

One reason for an apparent lack of procedural guidelines may be the supply of candidates. For example, a member of the LNDP stated, "As a central committee, there was no control or monitoring needed in candidate selection because the candidates themselves came to the party and registered themselves".[19] This might indicate that there are not enough contenders to stand as potential candidates for ethnic parties, so a formal selection process is not necessary. Since both ethnic parties and catch-all parties recruit from ethnic minority communities, ethnic parties often must compete with catch-all parties for candidates, not just votes. Given this limited supply of candidates, a formal selection process might not be needed or might make it even more difficult for ethnic parties to find candidates.

Another reason for lacking procedural guidelines may be the relative newness of many ethnic parties; they may not have had the time to codify candidate selection process. Table 3.2 categorizes all political parties in Myanmar based on the year of the first election in which they contested. Of the ethnic parties included in our interview analysis, the ANP, MNP and SNLD first competed in 1990; the PNO and TNP, in 2010; and the KSDP and LNDP, in 2015. Based on our expectations that party institutionalization both increases with age and corresponds with women's access to candidacy, it is not surprising that representatives from the newer ethnic parties were most likely to describe their parties as lacking formal candidate selection procedures generally and for women specifically.

Two of the older ethnic parties interviewed, the MNP and ANP, were the most explicit in indicating a formal candidate selection procedure; in another interview, an SNLD representative insinuated that they had a formal procedure, too, though he did not describe it in detail. (Interviewees from the TNP, which first competed in 2010, also indicated a more formal process.) A member of the MNP described their procedure this way:

> We collect the candidates' lists from each township and there are about ten candidates in each list in every township. We have a selection team and the party's chairman and leaders are in that team. For example, if we have about ten candidates from each township, members of the TC [township committee] vote first before the CC [central committee]. Candidates who get the most votes go to the selection team. And the selection team selects them.[20]

A member of the ANP even indicated that potential candidates debated before the ultimate selection was made: "To compete in the internal election, we have to register in the township first. In front of the TEC [township executive committee], we have to debate with other competitors. At that time, the TEC and CEC [central executive committee] select candidates by voting. After the internal election, I competed in the general election".[21]

In other words, three of the four parties that indicated a formal candidate selection procedure (MNP, ANP, TNP, and SNLD) were the more "institutionalized" (i.e., older) ethnic parties (see Table 3.4). Moreover, the TNP is considered more institutionalized than other parties such as the LNDP and PNO, which described only limited candidate selection procedures. We discuss party institutionalization and its impact on women's representation in greater detail in a later section.

Interestingly, when asked, nearly all respondents claimed that their party had a specific policy in place to increase women's participation.[22] At the same time, many male respondents blamed women for their low level of participation. A member of the ANP stated, "We had a policy to increase the number of female candidates. We did not have any limit to participation for women in politics, but women lack desire. Women in urban areas dare to speak and have confidence, but not in the rural areas".[23] A member of the KSDP made a similar statement: "We have had a policy to encourage women and youth to become members of the party since the party was established, but Kachin women do not dare to get involved in politics. They still lack self-confidence".[24]

According to a PNO member, "In the 2015 election, the party had policies to put women up to 30 percent. The party just included the women, but they did not even attend the meeting. So, it is not effective".[25] Indeed, an SNLD member claimed that in their party, women and men have equal opportunities, but women thought leadership and politics are not their concerns.[26]

While many ethnic party representatives stated that they did not discriminate against female candidates and had policies in place to encourage more participation, there was limited evidence of specific efforts among ethnic parties to support and actively recruit female candidates. A response from a female member of the KSDP encapsulates the state of recruitment and selection of female candidates in ethnic parties: "No activity and no support. There was just talk about that kind of policy but no practice in reality".[27] While there seems to be a correlation between a party's age and the formality of general candidate selection procedures, there is no indication that this applies to policies associated with women's recruitment and selection more specifically among ethnic parties.

Our interview data indicate that traditional attitudes about women in politics permeate through ethnic minority communities (albeit, again, also through other communities) and ethnic parties generally had yet to institute more robust measures to recruit and support female candidates. Additionally, some ethnic parties appeared to have formal candidate selection procedures while others did not. All these factors contribute to rates of women's political participation and representation. At the same time, we recognize that we cannot draw inferences about how ethnic parties compare to catch-all parties based on the qualitative data we examined in this section alone. (For a deeper discussion of women's political participation among all parties in Myanmar, see Chapter Two.) Hence, we turn next to quantitative data that shed light on ethnic versus catch-all parties' performance in facilitating women's representation in Myanmar.

ARE ETHNIC PARTIES MORE EFFECTIVE THAN CATCH-ALL PARTIES IN ADVANCING WOMEN?

We know that gendered expectations are pervasive, that newer ethnic parties in particular may lack procedures sufficient to minimize bias—and that the seats for which ethnic parties contest are also more likely to be concentrated in conflict-affected areas, where women may be especially unlikely to seek, or to be selected to stand for, elected offices. But which of these factors matters most—especially since some of these factors are more subject to policy manipulation than others (e.g., parties can develop better policies), and some are also more likely to remain germane now, post-coup, for women's empowerment (e.g., even more women than previously, ethnic-minority and Bamar alike, are in conflict zones)?

We use data from the 2015 election and examine candidate selection and women's success rate in the election. Here, selection refers to whether women are fielded in elections and success refers to whether they win. Both facets are important: being selected to stand is the first gateway to women's representation, while success ultimately allows for their descriptive representation. This analysis includes data from all legislatures in Myanmar: Amyotha Hluttaw (the upper house of the national legislature), Pyithu Hluttaw (the lower house of the national legislature), and state and regional legislatures. Table 3.3 summarizes our main analysis. Our discussion focuses on the fourth column, which indicates the percentage of candidates who are women for the NLD, USDP, and all ethnic parties combined, as well as the final two columns, which indicate success rates for female and male candidates, respectively.

TABLE 3.3
2015 GE, Candidates and Winners by Gender and Party (all legislatures)

Party	Total Candidates	Total Female Candidates	Female Candidates (%)	Total Female MPs	Female Success Rate (%)	Male Success Rate (%)
All	5,884	777	13.2	151	19.4	19.6
Catch-all parties	4242	548	12.9	137	25.0	23.5
NLD	1,094	158	14.4	134	84.8	80.3
USDP	1,094	66	6.0	3	4.5	11.1
Ethnic parties	1,358	210	15.5	14	6.7	11.0

Source: Amyotha Hluttaw, Pyithu Hluttaw, and combined state and regional legislatures. "All" includes all candidates, including independents. "Catch-all parties" include all but ethnic parties and independent candidates. Authors' tabulation based on the election results released by the UEC.

Among several noteworthy patterns indicated in Table 3.3, one main takeaway is that we cannot draw a general conclusion about catch-all parties, among which the NLD and USDP are the main contenders. These parties differ vastly from one another in terms of commitment to democratic values, which likely has implications for their support for women's representation. Thus, it is not surprising that the NLD, the main pro-democracy party in the country, fielded more female candidates than the USDP, which is a military-backed party. In fact, the NLD (14.4 per cent) is more than twice as likely to field female candidates as the USDP (6 per cent).

Despite important variation among catch-all parties, Table 3.3 indicates that ethnic parties were more effective overall in fielding female candidates. Only 12.9 per cent of catch-all parties' candidates were female, versus 15.5 per cent for ethnic parties. Neither the USDP nor the NLD individually outperformed ethnic parties as a whole in recruiting female candidates, although the NLD came close.

That said, it is important to note that ethnic parties vary tremendously in the numbers of female candidates they nominated. For example, our estimates based on the UEC data indicate that for one of the seven ethnic parties on which we focused, the PNO, just 5 per cent of their candidates in the 2015 election were female, a level on par with the USDP's. In contrast, in ethnic parties like the SNLD and MNP, nearly 20 per cent of the candidates were female, which is significantly more than the NLD. As we describe above, this variation among ethnic parties likely correlates with the party's relative orientation towards democratic ideology. In fact, the PNO, the ethnic party with a similar record to the USDP's in nominating female candidates, was profiled as a USDP-affiliated party, locally referred to as a "proxy party" (Myanmar Times 2015). While there is no official list of proxy parties, the PNO is unlikely to be the only such party. We can assume that ethnic parties open to affiliation with the USDP are less committed to democratic values than others. Thus, it is possible that these ethnic parties' record of facilitating women's representation is very similar to that of the USDP.[28] These findings suggest that for both catch-all and ethnic parties, commitment to democratic values may be an especially important factor in whether they actively recruit and field women to compete in elections.

The recruitment of female candidates is an important initial step in facilitating women's representation, but it does not automatically lead to women's representation, because not all female candidates are successful. Thus, we also examine female candidates' success rate.

While ethnic parties fielded female candidates at a higher rate than other parties, including the NLD, there is no clear evidence that ethnic parties' female candidates performed better than those from catch-all parties. There is a clear cross-party difference in how female and male candidates performed. Remarkably, among NLD candidates, women performed better than their male counterparts; nearly 85 per cent of the NLD's female candidates won the election, compared with 80 per cent of male candidates. These figures stand in stark contrast to results for the USDP and ethnic parties. For the USDP, male candidates' 11.1 per cent success rate was more than double female candidates' 4.5 per cent. Ethnic parties as a whole did slightly better: 11 per cent of male candidates succeeded, versus 6.7 per cent of female candidates. The relative success rates of female and male candidates among the USDP and ethnic parties might reflect cultural factors related to gendered stereotypes among the electorate that are worth exploring in future research; for now, we limit our investigation to the party rather than voter level, based on available data and limitations.

Again, the pattern that emerged from examining female candidates' success rate indicates that ethnic parties are neither better nor worse as vehicles for women's election than catch-all parties. The catch-all party committed to democracy, the NLD, has a better track record than the ethnic parties as a whole, but the latter have a better track record than the catch-all party backed by the military, the USDP.

In sum, our analysis provides ambiguous findings regarding the factors behind women's nomination and election. There is no clear evidence that ethnic parties are more or less effective than catch-all parties in facilitating women's representation. While ethnic parties on the whole fielded a greater share of women than the catch-all parties did, the higher success rate of female NLD candidates compared to male NLD candidates suggests that the NLD was especially effective—and more so than ethnic parties—in supporting female candidates, once nominated.

WHAT EXPLAINS THE VARIATION AMONG ETHNIC PARTIES?

The NLD's exceptional success in getting female candidates elected may be attributable to its commitment to democratic values and its level of party institutionalization. It is possible that these same characteristics matter among ethnic parties. Thus, this section focuses on whether party age—which, among ethnic parties in Myanmar, is closely linked to party institutionalization—and commitment to democracy might account for the differing records of ethnic parties.

As previously discussed, ethnic parties in Myanmar are not all the same. Many ethnic parties share common demands related to the peace process and federalism, but they represent a diverse range of minority communities and geographic areas of the country. And perhaps most importantly for our analysis, they vary in terms of age. Based on 2015 electoral data for the lower and upper houses of the national legislature, or Pyidaungsu Hluttaw, this analysis aims to document the extent of variation in women's selection and success rates among ethnic parties and determine whether party age helps explain that variation.

Our analysis, summarized in Table 3.4, includes the ethnic parties and their candidates who competed in the states. Several ethnic parties fielded candidates in the regions as well, but these candidates are excluded from this analysis, because armed conflict primarily affects constituencies in the states. By excluding ethnic-party operation in the regions, we are able to better disentangle the effect of conflict—a factor we expect would reinforce traditional attitudes regarding gender— from the effect from party institutionalization. Parties in the first row, being oldest, are considered to be the most institutionalized ("high") among Myanmar's ethnic parties. The second group is considered to be moderately institutionalized ("medium"), and the third group, the least institutionalized ("low"). At the time of the 2015 election, parties with "high" institutionalization would have been around for about 25 years, those with "medium" institutionalization, for about five years, and those with "low" institutionalization, for less than a year.

In 2015, most ethnic parties competing were very new (see Table 3.2). In fact, more than 75 per cent had been around for five years or less. Thus, most ethnic parties in Myanmar are relatively young and therefore presumably less institutionalized. But does that matter for the extent to which ethnic parties facilitate women's representation?

Table 3.4 shows some evidence that institutionalization matters for women's representation, but the evidence is also inconsistent. Column 4 (the percentage of female candidates) shows that the ethnic parties that were more institutionalized ("medium" and "high") fielded more female candidates in 2015 than the least institutionalized parties. These findings are relatively consistent with our findings from interviews with ethnic party representatives. For example, a member of the LNDP party (considered to be one of the least institutionalized), indicated

TABLE 3.4
2015 Union Assembly, Candidates and Winners by Gender and Institutionalization (ethnic parties in the states only)

Level of Institutionalization	Number of Parties	Total Candidates	Female Candidates (%)	Total Female MPs	Female Success Rate (%)	Male Success Rate (%)	Ratio (%)
High	11	166	15.7	5	17.9	27.9	64.2
Medium	16	200	17.5	1	2.9	5.6	51.8
Low	22	136	11.8	0	0.0	4.2	0.0
All	49	502	15.3	6	6.6	12.5	52.8

Source: Authors' tabulation based on the election results released by the UEC.

that improving women's representation was not a feasible priority for the 2015 election: "it was in a rush, and since the party was just established, we could not do anything".[29] At the same time, there is no evidence that parties that are the most institutionalized fielded more female candidates than parties that were only moderately so.

Table 3.4 also shows that, regardless of the level of party institutionalization, male candidates in ethnic parties consistently outperformed female candidates. Among the most institutionalized ethnic parties, women's success rate was only 64.2 per cent that of men, and this ratio declined with party age—among the moderately institutionalized ethnic parties, women's success rate was only 51.8 per cent that of men. These findings regarding ethnic parties stand in stark contrast to the gender-differentiated success rate for NLD candidates (see Table 3.3): female NLD candidates performed slightly better than men. In sum, while institutionalization seems not to predict which parties *nominate* women, it does correlate with how well those female candidates *perform*, once given the opportunity to stand.

CONCLUDING REMARKS

Ethnic minorities and women both have a history of underrepresentation and discrimination in societies around the world. Yet, their shared marginalized status does not always translate into a shared focus on gender and ethnic equality among political institutions or organizations.

In fact, our analysis based on data from the democratic transition period in Myanmar (2010–20) presents rather mixed results. There is no clear evidence that ethnic parties prioritize recruiting women to become politicians. Our analysis of interviews with ethnic-party representatives demonstrates that traditional attitudes about women present cultural barriers to women's selection and political representation in these communities, just as in ethnic-majority communities. While there is no consistency among ethnic parties in their candidate selection procedures, many representatives expressed concerns related to implementing specific policies for the recruitment and selection of female candidates. At the same time, our analysis also indicates that ethnic parties fielded relatively more female candidates than did catch-all parties. However, ethnic parties were not effective in supporting these female candidates: male ethnic-party candidates outperformed their female counterparts to a significantly higher degree than for catch-all parties, compounding the latter's overall better odds of election.

An important takeaway from our study is that variation *within* categories of parties (i.e., different ethnic parties or different catch-all parties) are likely to be as great as those *across* categories (i.e., ethnic versus catch-all parties). Some catch-all parties, like Myanmar's USDP, have poor records of facilitating women's representation whereas others', like the NLD's, are much better. The same can be said about ethnic parties. Thus, our analysis of Myanmar suggests that being "ethnic" or "catch-all" hardly matters for whether a party selects and supports women. Further, we might also find this variation among ethnic organizations beyond political parties, operating in a context without formal elections.

Offering only partial support for extant theories, our case study of Myanmar provides some suggestive evidence that what matters most in terms of parties' relative proclivity to propel women into elected office is commitment to democratic values and party institutionalization. We suggest that, regardless of party label, democratic orientation and party institutionalization matter for women's representation in Myanmar and beyond. Parties committed to democratic values are more likely also to be committed to women's representation. Additionally, younger, less institutionalized parties may not have adequate capacity to recruit and support female politicians. Future studies, in a post-coup Myanmar or elsewhere, might more systematically investigate these hypotheses.

This study was conducted when democracy and most political parties in Myanmar were still in their infancy. Recall that more than 75 per cent of ethnic parties had been around for five years at most. Thus, they were often learning through trial and error and trying to build up their parties for future electoral success. Between the 2015 and 2020 elections, many ethnic parties merged in order to prevent vote-splitting within their communities; some mergers, like between the Mon Unity Party and Kayah State Democratic Party, had some success. Continuous party building might have enabled ethnic parties to deepen their commitment to democratic values and women's representation. However, this opportunity was cut short by the military coup on 1 February 2021.

POST-COUP CONSIDERATIONS

Following the 2021 military coup, Myanmar's new junta set up a State Administrative Council (SAC) to run the country and invited ethnic parties to join. While several ethnic parties accepted positions in the coup regime (including the ANP and the newly merged MUP), most declined. Some ethnic-party leaders issued clear statements that they would refuse any offers of positions from the military-led government (Nachemson 2021). Instead, many ethnic-party representatives, alongside ethnic armed organizations, joined forces with ousted NLD government representatives to form the National Unity Government (NUG). As a "shadow government", the NUG is striving to develop a unified multi-ethnic political and armed coalition to confront the military dictatorship. About one-third of the NUG's ministers come from ethnic-minority (non-Bamar) groups, and 9 of 37 (24.3 per cent) of current cabinet ministers are women (Wee and Paddock 2021); this is a significant increase in ethnic-minority and women's representation from the two previous NLD cabinets.[30]

These advances, we believe, are indicative of the NUG's deep commitment to democratic values. In a way, the NUG has shown stronger commitment towards democratic values than the NLD government, which at times had to accommodate the military. The NUG has indicated that it would repeal the 2008 constitution, which was drafted *by* and *for* the military. The NUG has also openly endorsed federalism, for which ethnic minorities have been advocating since

Myanmar gained independence. Indeed, although not without tension, NUG leaders are currently working with ethnic minorities and, in line with ethnic minority demands, recognizing the NLD's previous failures to maintain good relations with these groups. The renewed prospects for federalism in Myanmar could indicate an enhanced position for ethnic parties in the future.

Moreover, these post-coup experiences are also expected to enhance (some) ethnic parties' democratic orientations. As mentioned above, some newer ethnic parties were previously thought to be aligned with the military-backed USDP. In post-coup Myanmar, ethnic parties' alignment with the SAC or the NUG has elucidated which parties are pro-democracy and which are not. And these pro-democracy ethnic parties will no doubt further strengthen their democratic commitments.

The response to the coup by all segments of society has instilled some hope that political parties will improve their efforts to recruit and select female candidates in a post-coup Myanmar. According to reports by the Gender Equality Network, women make up approximately 60 per cent of frontline protest leaders and 70–80 per cent of leaders in broader civil society disobedience movements fighting against the military (Leigh 2021). Many of Myanmar's ethnic parties have a history of putting up female candidates with experience in social activism. For instance, one of the KSDP's successful candidates in the 2015 election is the founder of the Kachin Women's Union. In our interviews with party representatives, a female ANP MP from the 2015 election explained how her political ambition is rooted in her experience in the 2007 Saffron Revolution:

> In 2007, I actively participated in the Saffron Revolution. Actually, my ambition was just for better education, it was not about the politics. But I realised that we need to set up a good system, I got involved in politics because I believe that every citizen should have responsibilities. After 2007, I was a citizen who was involved in the transition process of our country.

Given the growing pool of female activists across communities in Myanmar, we expect a significant increase in the supply of female candidates in the future electoral landscape. Given the new fervour for democracy and democratic values, we also expect pro-democracy forces, in both catch-all and ethnic parties, to improve their recruitment and support of female politicians.

NOTES

1. According to a report by the Transnational Institute (TNI 2015), 45 ethnic parties competed in Myanmar elections in 1990, 24 in 2010, 55 in 2015, and 54 in 2020. The total number of political parties was 93 in 1990, 39 in 2010, 91 in 2015, and 91 in 2020.
2. In the 2015 Pyithu Hluttaw elections, the main catch-all parties competed in 315 of 325 townships across the country. This means that ethnic parties had to compete with both the NLD and USDP in most townships.
3. The winning party was the Anti-Fascist People's Freedom League, led by General Aung San.
4. What ignited the protests in 1988, leading to the eventual regime collapse, appeared to have been economic mismanagement and a demonetization crisis (Steinberg 2001; Taylor 2009). Persistent social unrest through 1988 forced the regime leader to promise a multi-party election, which propelled party formation. Taylor (2009, p. 403) describes the visible emergence of pro-democracy mobilization this way: "Following the army putsch and the renewal of the promise of a multi-party general election, politicians and activities withdrew from the streets in order to begin to organize their parties". Aung San Suu Kyi gave her first major public speech two weeks after the 8888 Uprising and the NLD was formally established on 27 September 1988. In short, by the time a visible pro-democracy movement emerged, the BSPP regime had already been replaced by a new group of military cadre.
5. While Table 3.2 is based on a briefing by the Transnational Institute, it also corresponds to existing studies on Myanmar's political parties, including Tan, Minoletti and Bjarnegård (2020).
6. See Chapter Six for a discussion of women's representation at subnational levels in Myanmar.
7. Other potential party-level factors affecting women's political representation in Myanmar include level of funding and infrastructure facilitating travel and campaigning on the ground. These factors are likely to vary among ethnic parties, as well as among newer parties specifically. However, we are unable to evaluate the effects of these factors due to lack of data.
8. Not all ethnic minority areas were similarly conflict-affected, and not all ethnic parties operated in conflict-affected areas. For example, generally speaking, the armed conflict was more active in Shan State than in Chin State. However, conflict level varies within each state as well. Thus, the extent to which conflict-related concerns impacted ethnic parties' candidate recruitment process likely varied. At the same time, conflict data at the locality level would be necessary to shed light on the variation among ethnic parties. Short of such data, our analysis is limited to examining ethnic parties as a unit.

9. See Chapter Two on candidate selection across all parties in Myanmar for more details.
10. Interview with HM-FMP14.
11. Interview with HM-MGK01.
12. Interview with SS-GKCECM02.
13. Interview with LR-MMP11.
14. Interview with HM-FMP11.
15. Interview with SS-GKCECM04.
16. The Union Electoral Commission provided a list of eligibility criteria for candidate nomination, including guidelines for age, residency, citizenship, criminal record, etc. For more details, see IDEA (2020).
17. Interview with LR-MMP07.
18. Interview with HM-MGK07.
19. Interview with LR-GKCECM05.
20. Interview with SS-MMP02.
21. Interview with SS-FMP02.
22. The phrase, "up to 30 per cent" often came up in these interviews.
23. Interview with SS-GKTECM04.
24. Interview with LR-GKCECM04.
25. Interview with HM-MGK04.
26. Interview with HM-FMP11.
27. Interview with LR-FMP07.
28. To draw a more precise inference than this speculation we offer would require identifying additional parties besides the PNO as proxy parties and comparing them to other ethnic parties. Future research should further examine the "proxy party" phenomenon among ethnic parties in Myanmar.
29. Interview with LR-GKCECM07.
30. There was just one female minister (Aung San Suu Kyi herself) in the first NLD cabinet (San Yamin Aung 2017).

REFERENCES

Bogaards, Matthijs. 2010. "Ethnic Party Bans and Institutional Engineering in Nigeria". *Democratization* 17, no. 4: 730–49. https://doi.org/10.1080/13510347.2010.491197.

Caul, Miki. 1999. "Women's Representation in Parliament: The Role of Political Parties". *Party Politics* 5, no. 1: 79–98. https://doi.org/10.1177/1354068899005001005.

Center for Peace and Conflict Studies (CPCS). 2011. "2010 Myanmar General Elections Learning and Sharing for Future". Observation Report. Siem Reap, Cambodia: CPCS. http://www.centrepeaceconflictstudies.org/wp-content/uploads/2010-Myanmar-Observer-report.pdf.

Chandra, Kanchan. 2005. "Ethnic Parties and Democratic Stability". *Perspectives on Politics* 3, no. 2: 235–52.

———. 2011. "What is an Ethnic Party?" *Party Politics* 17, no. 2: 151–69. https://doi.org/10.1177/1354068810391153.

Escobar-Lemmon, Maria, and Michelle M. Taylor-Robinson. 2009. "Getting to the Top: Career Paths of Women in Latin American Cabinets". *Political Research Quarterly* 62, no. 4: 685–99. https://doi.org/10.1177/1065912908322414.

Gender Equality Network (GEN). 2017. "Gender and Politics in Myanmar: Women and Men Candidates in the 2015 Elections". Yangon, Myanmar: GEN.

Goetz, Anne Marie. 1998. "Women in Politics & Gender Equity in Policy: South Africa & Uganda". *Review of African Political Economy* 25, no. 76: 241–62. https://doi.org/10.1080/03056249808704312.

Gunther, Richard, and Larry Diamond. 2003. "Species of Political Parties: A New Typology". *Party Politics* 9, no. 2: 167–99. https://doi.org/10.1177/13540688030092003.

Hedström, Jenny, and Elisabeth Olivius. 2020. "Insecurity, Dispossession, Depletion: Women's Experiences of Post-War Development in Myanmar". *The European Journal of Development Research* 32, no. 2: 379–403. https://doi.org/10.1057/s41287-020-00255-2.

Holmsten, Stephanie S., Robert G. Moser, and Mary C. Slosar. 2010. "Do Ethnic Parties Exclude Women?" *Comparative Political Studies* 43, no. 10: 1179–1201. https://doi.org/10.1177/0010414009347831.

Horowitz, Donald L. 1985. *Ethnic Groups in Conflict*. Berkeley, USA: University of California Press.

Htun, Mala, and Francesca R. Jensenius. 2020. "Political Change, Women's Rights, and Public Opinion on Gender Equality in Myanmar". *The European Journal of Development Research* 32, no. 2: 457–81. https://doi.org/10.1057/s41287-020-00266-z.

IDEA. 2020. "2020 General Election in Myanmar – Fact Sheet". Yangon, Myanmar: International IDEA Myanmar. https://www.idea.int/sites/default/files/news/news-pdfs/2020-General-Election-in-Myanmar-Fact-Sheet_14-July-2020.pdf.

International Crisis Group (ICG). 2015. "The Myanmar Elections: Results and Implications". *Crisis Group Asia Briefing* 147. Yangon, Myanmar: ICG. http://www.burmalibrary.org/docs21/ICG-2015-12-09-the-myanmar-elections-results-and-implications-en-red.pdf.

Jap, Jangai, and Adam Ziegfeld. 2020. "Ethnic Parties in New Democracies: The Case of Myanmar 2015". *Electoral Studies* 65 (June): 102131. https://doi.org/10.1016/j.electstud.2020.102131.

Kempel, Susanne, Chan Myawe Aung Sun, and Aung Tun. 2015. "Myanmar Political Parties at a Time of Transition: Political Party Dynamics at the National and Local Level". Yangon, Myanmar: Pyoe Pin Programme.

Kittilson, Miki Caul. 2006. *Challenging Parties, Changing Parliament: Women and Elected Office in Contemporary.* 1st ed. Columbus, USA: Ohio State University Press.

Leigh, Lottie. 2021. "The Sarong Revolution – Myanmar". 24 June 2021. Washington, D.C.: International Women's Initiative. https://www.theiwi.org/gpr-reports/the-sarong-revolution.

Lien, Pei-te, Dianne Pinderhughes, Carol Hardy-Fanta, and Christine Sierra. 2007. "The Voting Rights Act and the Election of Nonwhite Officials". *Carol Hardy-Fanta* 40 (July). https://doi.org/10.1017/S1049096507070746.

Lovenduski, Joni, and Pippa Norris. 1993. *Gender and Party Politics.* Thousand Oaks, Califorinia, USA: SAGE Publications.

Matland, Richard, and Michelle Taylor. 1997. "Electoral System Effects on Women's Representation: Theoretical Arguments and Evidence from Costa Rica". *Comparative Political Studies* 30, no. 2: 186–210. https://doi.org/10.1177/0010414097030002003.

McAllister, Ian, and Donley T. Studlar. 2002. "Electoral Systems and Women's Representation: A Long-term Perspective". *Representation* 39, no. 1: 3–14. https://doi.org/10.1080/00344890208523209.

Minoletti, Paul. 2014. "Women's Participation in the Subnational Governance of Myanmar". San Francisco, United States: The Asia Foundation. http://asiafoundation.org/publications/pdf/1374.

———. 2020. "Gender and Political Participation in Myanmar". Yangon, Myanmar: EMReF/IDRC.

Myanmar Times. 2015. "Election Parties". *The Myanmar Times*, 2 September 2015. https://www.mmtimes.com/national-news/16265-election-parties.html.

Nachemson, Andrew. 2021. "Will More Ethnic Minority Organizations Join Myanmar's Revolution?" *Foreign Policy* (blog). 7 January 2021. https://foreignpolicy.com/2021/07/01/myanmar-ethnic-minority-organizations-coup-revolution-federal-army/.

Okin, Susan Moller. 1999. *Is Multiculturalism Bad for Women?* Princeton: Princeton University Press. https://press.princeton.edu/books/paperback/9780691004327/is-multiculturalism-bad-for-women.

Peace Support Fund. 2016. "The Women are Ready: An Opportunity to Transform Peace in Myanmar". Yangon, Myanmar: The Peace Support Fund. https://reliefweb.int/sites/reliefweb.int/files/resources/the_women_are_ready_english__1.pdf.

Pedersen, Morten B. 2008. "Burma's Ethnic Minorities". *Critical Asian Studies* 40, no. 1: 45–66. https://doi.org/10.1080/14672710801959133.

Pitre, Sonia. 2003. "Women's Struggle for Legislative Power: The Role of Political Parties". *Atlantis: Critical Studies in Gender, Culture & Social Justice* 27, no. 2: 102–9.

Rabushka, Alvin, and Kenneth A. Shepsle. 1972. *Politics in Plural Societies: A Theory of Democratic Instability*. Columbus, Ohio, USA: Charles Merrill. https://doi.org/10.1177/000271627240400123.

Schneider, Paige, and David Carroll. 2019. "Conceptualizing More Inclusive Elections: Violence Against Women in Elections and Gendered Electoral Violence". *Policy Studies* 41 (November): 1–18. https://doi.org/10.1080/01442872.2019.1694651.

Steinberg, David L. 2001. *Burma: The State of Myanmar*. Washington, D.C.: Georgetown University Press.

Stokke, Kristian. 2019. "Political Representation by Ethnic Parties? Electoral Performance and Party-Building Processes among Ethnic Parties in Myanmar". *Journal of Current Southeast Asian Affairs* 38, no. 3: 307–36. https://doi.org/10.1177/1868103419893530.

Tan, Netina, Paul Minoletti, Elin Bjarnegard, and Aye Lei Tun. 2020. "Party Building and Candidate Selection: Intraparty Politics and Promoting Gender Equality in Myanmar". Yangon, Myanmar: IDRC, EMReF.

Taylor, Robert H. 2009. *The State in Myanmar*. Singapore: NUS Press.

Thawnghmung, Ardeth Maung. 2011. "Beyond Armed Resistance: Ethnonational Politics in Burma (Myanmar)". Honolulu, USA: East-West Center. https://www.eastwestcenter.org/publications/beyond-armed-resistance-ethnonational-politics-burma-myanmar.

Transnational Institute (TNI). 2015. "Ethnic Politics and the 2015 Elections in Myanmar". *Myanmar Policy Briefing* 16. Amsterdam, Netherlands: TNI. https://www.tni.org/files/publication-downloads/bpb16_web_16092015.pdf.

Wängnerud, Lena. 2009. "Women in Parliaments: Descriptive and Substantive Representation". *Annual Review of Political Science* 12: 51–69. https://doi.org/10.1146/annurev.polisci.11.053106.123839.

Wee, Sui-Lee, and Richard C. Paddock. 2021. "Aung San Suu Kyi Falls, but Myanmar's Democratic Hopes Move On". *The New York Times*, 6 December 2021. https://www.nytimes.com/2021/12/06/world/asia/myanmar-aung-san-suu-kyi.html.

Wylie, Kristin N. 2020. *Party Institutionalization and Women's Representation in Democratic Brazil*. Cambridge MA, USA: Cambridge University Press.

4

ATTITUDES TOWARDS WOMEN AND POLITICAL LEADERSHIP

Anor Mu, Paul Minoletti, Guillem Riambau, and Michelle Dion

As explained in the introduction to this volume, political parties play an important role in shaping the demand for women's representation and participation in politics, while gendered cultural values and norms often influence whether women opt to participate in politics. In this chapter, we explore the ways that attitudes and experiences correlate with men and women's sense of political efficacy and their attitudes towards women's participation in politics in Myanmar as of 2019—i.e., before the 2021 coup. Though the 2015 election resulted in a higher proportion of female members of parliament (MPs) being elected (10 per cent) than at any other previous time in the country's history, women's parliamentary representation remained very low compared to other countries in the region and globally (Gender Equality Network 2017, pp. 10–11). To better understand the sources of women's political underrepresentation in Myanmar, we examine the experiences and attitudes that affect political participation through a nationwide survey conducted between September and December 2019. As detailed in

Chapter One, our survey asked a total of 2,889 respondents in four states/ regions that cover a range of Myanmar's geographic and demographic characteristics (Mon, Mandalay, Ayeyarwady, and southern Shan) to reflect on their experiences and attitudes about politics and women's participation in politics.

We begin by analysing men and women's attitudes towards gender equality and gender roles. We find that men and women did not differ much in their overall opinions about gender roles in society. However, when we examine potential reasons *why* men and women held certain opinions about gender equality, we find that age, political knowledge, satisfaction with democracy, and early life experiences, such as witnessing violence against their mother, have different associations with expressions of support for gender equality among men compared to women.

Then, we turn to three attitudes related to women's participation in politics. First, we examine internal political efficacy, which refers to whether someone feels they are able to participate in politics, which is an important determinant of whether they engage in political behaviour, such as voting, contacting a government official, or running for political office (Finkel 1985). If women feel less politically capable of participating in politics than men, they also will be less likely to engage in politics. We find that men in Myanmar were more likely to express political self-efficacy than women, in general. At the same time, some personal characteristics, such as political knowledge and satisfaction with democracy, were equally associated with political efficacy for men and women. Two notable exceptions were education and age. Among men, having completed high school was associated with greater political efficacy, whereas this trait did not significantly explain political efficacy for women.[1] The relationship between age and political efficacy also varied by gender.

Next, we examine whether women and men think women *should* be involved in politics, noting that support for women in politics tends to coincide with democratic values (Inglehart, Norris, and Welzel 2003). Specifically, we consider whether men and women believe women in Myanmar should participate in politics and whether they would support a daughter participating in politics. The latter question focuses on a specific, potentially hypothetical instance of women's participation that is likely to bring into relief real tensions or concerns related to women's participation in politics, such as social status or violence.[2] This inquiry also captures a future-oriented perspective on how people in Myanmar believe women *should* engage politically in the future, albeit measured at the distinct historical moment when our survey was conducted. Interestingly, overall, women were more likely to believe women should participate as much as men, but less likely to support a daughter's participation in politics. When we examine the reasons *why* men and women held these views, we find that attitudes and early life experiences associated with support for women's involvement in politics varied by gender.

We begin with an overview of the extant literature on these attitudes in Myanmar, highlighting common factors that correlate with men and women's attitudes towards equality in family and social roles, political efficacy, and political participation, which are our primary outcomes of interest. Then, we describe our survey, including average differences between women and men on various political attitudes and experiences, before turning to multivariate regression models that explain variation in attitudes towards gender equality, political efficacy, and attitudes towards women's participation in politics in Myanmar. We conclude with a discussion of the implications of all this for the future in Myanmar, bearing in mind that, at the time of writing this chapter, the dictatorship that originated from the 2021 coup still prevails.

GENDER, LIFE EXPERIENCES, POLITICAL EFFICACY AND WOMEN'S PARTICIPATION IN POLITICS

In this section, we situate our analysis in the existing literature on attitudes towards gender equality, political efficacy among men and women, and how such attitudes and experiences may relate to stances on the extent to which women *should* participate in politics. Because few studies have examined these questions in Myanmar, we necessarily draw on insights from elsewhere in the region or beyond, with the aim of understanding whether and when existing explanations may apply in our case. The small but growing literature on gender relations, attitudes, and women's participation in politics in Myanmar yields a range of common observations, many of which are consistent with our data and analysis.

Attitudes about Gender Equality and Gendered Social Roles

As noted in Chapter One, particular religious, cultural, or social attitudes are widely recognized to be associated with less support for gender equality in general and for women's participation in politics in particular (Inglehart and Norris 2003; Inglehart, Norris, and Welzel 2003; Paxton, Kunovich, and Hughes 2007; Paxton, Hughes, and Barnes 2020). In Myanmar, the pervasiveness of gender inequality and attitudes that reinforce that inequality throughout society is a common thread in existing research. For example, Htun and Jensenius's (2020) analysis of two national surveys conducted in 2014 highlights a preference for male children and more education for sons than daughters, and the belief that men are better in business than women. In many of their analyses, only education explains variation in these attitudes, with women and men often expressing similar support for gender inequality. They note that traditionalism, which they define as "familism, deference, conflict-avoidance, and an aversion to self assertation" (Htun and Jensenius 2020, pp. 468–69), is also pervasive in Myanmar, and that such values and beliefs transcend age, gender, and employment status. Buddhism and religiosity, they note, are likewise strongly associated with traditional values and gender roles; they point specifically to various legal movements based in Buddhist nationalism or ethnic and religious rights that have been used recently to reinforce gender inequality or stop efforts to promote greater gender equality (see also Barrow 2015). For these reasons, our empirical analysis below begins first with describing differences in attitudes towards gender equality between men and women and exploring potential explanations for why men and women expressed different views about gender equality and roles in society generally.

Sources of Internal Political Efficacy

When women are accorded a diminished role in the family and public sphere, as in Myanmar, it is not surprising that women are then less likely to have a sense of internal political efficacy, which is our second outcome of interest in this chapter. Internal political efficacy refers to the belief that one is capable of understanding, communicating about, and participating in politics (Wolak 2018, pp. 765–66). Internal political efficacy is important in part because it is associated with political participation (Finkel 1985) and regime maintenance in democracies

(Easton and Dennis 1967). Recent work elsewhere in East and Southeast Asia suggests that internal political efficacy is positively associated with various types of political participation (Liu 2020, p. 7; Wen, Hao, and George 2013).

Most research on internal political efficacy focuses on education (Rasmussen and Nørgaard 2018), or other individual-level characteristics. For example, Fraile and de Miguel Moyer (2021) suggest that men's greater willingness to take risks compared to women provides a partial explanation for the gender gap in internal political efficacy in Europe. Other work on internal political efficacy emphasizes earlier childhood or adolescent experiences (e.g., Easton and Dennis 1967; Rodgers 1974). In Myanmar, intrafamily violence, particularly against women—which may feature among these formative experiences—is fairly prevalent (Larsen, Aye, and Bjertness 2021; Kabir et al. 2019; Gender Equality Network 2015). Beliefs about the use of violence within the family are also gendered in Myanmar; the Myanmar Demographic and Health Survey from 2015–17 found that women are more likely than men to justify husbands' beating their wives (Ministry of Health and Sports 2017). We know of no studies that examine the relationship between childhood experiences of family violence and future internal political efficacy, specifically. However, research elsewhere suggests that being the target or recipient of household violence as a child is associated with significantly lower levels of self-efficacy in general, while evidence from Israel finds witnessing violence against a parent to be only weakly negatively associated with lower self-efficacy (Haj-Yahia et al. 2021; also see Chapter Five).

These studies have not explicitly considered the ways in which experiencing intrafamilial violence is both gendered and may differ in its impact across genders. However, given the gendered nature of domestic violence and the high levels of social inequality between genders in Myanmar, we expect that being the target of intrafamilial violence will produce a stronger negative association with political efficacy for women than men, and witnessing intrafamilial violence against one's mother, which would reinforce unequal gender roles, would be associated with less support for gender equality or women's participation in politics, particularly among men.

Though most studies of internal political efficacy focus on individual characteristics or experiences, some recent work suggests that political context may also explain relative levels. Wolak (2018) argues that people will feel more efficacious when they believe their government is more responsive to them, which may be the case when it is run by co-partisans or those who share similar ideological positions, gender, or racial or ethnic background. Along these lines, she finds that women in US states with more female state legislators express higher levels of internal efficacy (ibid., p. 774). In light of her findings, we would expect those who approve of the Myanmar government or are satisfied with democracy in Myanmar to also express greater internal political efficacy, and, to the extent that women remain underrepresented in elected office in Myanmar, we would expect the gender gap in political efficacy and, by extension, political participation to remain large.

Attitudes About Women's Participation in Politics

Given the pervasive attitudes that reinforce gender inequality in Myanmar, including deference to men within families and resistance to roles for women in the public sphere, it is unsurprising that many people in Myanmar would be reluctant to believe women should be more involved in politics. In her interviews with female activists, Loring (2018, p. 75) highlights Buddhist traditions that reinforce gendered roles and the idea that women should not be involved in politics. Similarly, Ma Agatha, Poe Ei Phyu, and Knapman (2018, p. 462) highlight the role of cultural norms in Myanmar, including deference to elders and men, as barriers to women's participation in politics. They also note that families worry about their female family members' being imprisoned for their political work and are concerned about the stigma associated with women's travelling or being perceived as not sufficiently committed to their families (ibid., pp. 470–71). In Chapter Five, Bjarnegård further documents the ways in which harassment and violence have been normalized as part of electoral politics in Myanmar.

Consistent with this qualitative evidence, the only survey analysis of attitudes towards women's participation in politics in Myanmar using national data from 2014 confirms that a large plurality of men (34 per cent) and women (43 per cent) somewhat or strongly agree that women should not be involved in politics so much as men (Htun and Jensenius 2020, p. 465). Htun and Jensenius (2020, pp. 473–74) also find that resistance to women's involvement in politics is most associated with traditional values and religiosity, which is broadly consistent with claims that economic and political progress tend to go hand in hand with support for gender equality and women's involvement in politics (Inglehart, Norris, and Welzel 2003; Inglehart and Norris 2003). We build and extend upon these insights here by not only examining whether men and women share similar attitudes about women's participation in politics, but by also asking whether our respondents would support a daughter's participation in politics. In this way, we attempt not only to replicate the findings of the earlier study, but also to extend the analysis to consider normative attitudes towards women's future political participation.

METHODS AND DATA

As detailed in Chapter One, our survey was carried out between September and December 2019 by a team of 13 enumerators under the Enlightened Myanmar Research Foundation (EMReF). Our team decided to conduct our surveys in four states/regions: Mon, southern Shan,[3] Mandalay, and Ayeyarwady. We excluded Kachin State, Rakhine State, and northern Shan State, as these were sites of active conflict, which presented safety risks and would have made it extremely difficult to secure permission from the relevant authorities to conduct surveys with broad geographical coverage. Our selection of Mon, southern Shan, Mandalay, and Ayeyarwady as survey sites, moreover, reflected the wide variety of geographical, economic, and cultural features in Myanmar. To illustrate the differences among these states and regions vary, Table 4.1 presents descriptive statistics of key demographic characteristics in our sample. Specifically, we chose Ayeyarwady and Mandalay as relatively more economically developed regions that were also fully controlled by the Myanmar government and had a majoritarian Bamar ethnic population. Next, we selected Mon State for its large ethnic Mon population and economy that relied on migration to Thailand. While Mon has armed ethnic organizations, it remained predominantly controlled by the Myanmar government. Lastly, we focused on southern Shan, a predominantly hilly and agricultural region that is largely populated by Shan and Pa'O ethnic groups, as an area of mixed governing authority, with some parts wholly or partially controlled by local ethnic armed groups and militias, and their associated political organizations.

At the time of our survey, our survey locations largely excluded areas that had experienced the most intense conflict in Myanmar over the preceding two decades, such as Karen State and Karenni State in the 2000s, and Kachin State, northern Shan State and Rakhine State in the 2010s. Given the relationship between conflict and (typically male-dominated) militarization of society, it is possible that our results may indicate a lower gender gap on measures such as political efficacy than may be found in areas that have more recently experienced conflict. However, we are not able to test for this.

TABLE 4.1
Descriptive Statistics by Region/State, 2018

	Shan	Mon	Mandalay	Ayeyarwady
Percent female	54.4	64.1	55.5	56.2
Mean age	43.9	47.8	46.2	47.3
Percent middle school or above[1]	35.4	32.2	33.3	34.6
Percent urban	50	49.9	50.1	50.1
Percent employed[2]	81	62.8	74.8	61.7
Mean phones in household	2.3	1.9	1.9	1.7
Percent where privacy limited[3]	19.8	15.9	4.7	10.1
Observations	720	724	721	724

(1) Completed middle school. Includes complete vocational qualification (N=19), religious education (N=5), and ethnic post-10 education (N=3). (2) At least once during the previous 12 months. (3) Enumerators' subjective assessment to the question: "Was it easy to get private answers?". Percentage reported is the share of "NO" (i.e., privacy at stake).

Aside from the deliberate selection of four regions or states as our key survey sites, we selected townships, ward/village tracts, and villages randomly based on weights, in order to get a representative sample of the population within each region/state.[4] In each state or region, we randomly selected three townships, then interviewed around 240 people in each. Within each township, we again randomly selected eight to ten villages (or wards in urban areas).[5] If residents who opened the door agreed to participate, we asked them to list all adults living in the household. From that list, the enumerator picked one of the adults at random using a random number generator app on their mobile device. If the person was not in the house at that moment, another enumerator would return later. If the person refused, the enumerator would move to the next house. We collected a total of 2,889 survey responses in this manner, approximately 25 per cent from each of the states or regions, and within each of these, one third from each township.[6]

Our survey included a range of questions about respondents' sociodemographic background, life experiences, and attitudes. We asked respondents their age and binary gender identity,[7] and coded whether they lived in an urban or rural area, following government designations. We also asked enumerators to indicate whether the interview was conducted in private, which we include as a control variable in the regressions below. In addition, our enumerators differentiated between instances when respondents declined to answer a question and when they volunteered that they could not choose or did not know how to answer. Like for other surveys in Myanmar, we observed a relatively large number of "don't know" responses. We have included these responses in the denominator in all analyses that follow, following Htun and Jensenius (2020, p. 462).

Attitudes about gender equality, life experiences, and political participation by gender

Before moving to our multivariate analysis, we begin by presenting descriptive statistics of key concepts or indicators disaggregated by gender. Figure 4.1 illustrates the proportion of men and women who agree or strongly agree with attitudes that are consistent with equal gender roles within families and society in general. When the original statement expressed a sentiment contrary to support for gender equality, we present the proportion who disagreed or strongly disagreed with the statement. Some of these questions are included in an additive index of overall support for gender equality that we include in our multivariate analyses in the next section. Overall, Figure 4.1 suggests that men and women in Myanmar shared similar views about the roles that women and men should play in families and society in general, and that these views were, on average, somewhat biased towards traditional gender roles.

FIGURE 4.1
Support for Gender Equality Among Men and Women in Myanmar, 2018

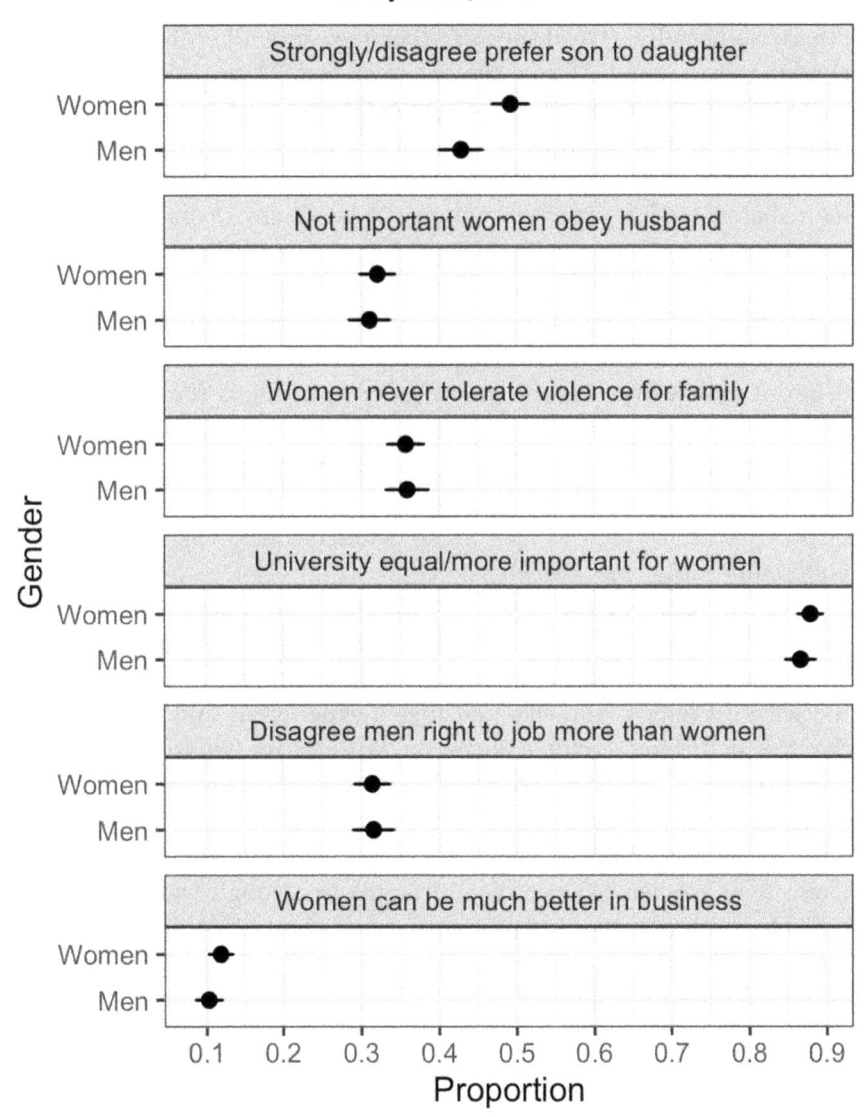

Note: Proportions with 95 per cent confidence intervals.

In total, 49 per cent of women and 43 per cent of men strongly disagreed or disagreed that they would prefer a son to a daughter; this difference is statistically significant. However, women and men otherwise broadly agreed on our other measures of attitudes towards gender roles. About 31 per cent of men and 32 per cent of women agreed that it is not important for women always to obey their husbands, and 36 per cent of both men and women agreed that women should never tolerate violence to keep a family together. Similarly, women and men shared similar views on whether it is equally or more important for women to get university education than men (87 per cent of men, 89 per cent of women), and 31 per cent for both genders disagreed that men have more of a right to a job than women. Finally, similarly small proportions of men (10 per cent) and women (12 per cent) believed that women can be much better in business than men. These findings are consistent with a 2014 nationwide survey in Myanmar that also found that there was very little difference by gender in attitudes towards the importance for women and men of attending university, or on whether women or men make better business leaders (The Asia Foundation 2014, pp. 78–79).

Next, we examine the extent to which these attitudes about women's roles were also reflected in the lived experiences and views about politics among men and women in Myanmar. Figure 4.2 highlights the ways in which women's and men's experiences and beliefs about the world differed, with a focus on self-efficacy regarding political participation, experiences with intrafamilial violence before adulthood, perceived safety travelling at night, trust in outsiders, and satisfaction with democracy. Notably, men (54 per cent) were significantly more likely than women (43 per cent) to agree or strongly agree that they are able to participate in politics, our measure of political efficacy. We return to this finding below, in our multivariate models of internal political efficacy by gender.

The other indicators included in Figure 4.2 capture key life experiences and attitudes that we expect to be associated with internal political efficacy or attitudes about women's participation in politics. In light of the pervasiveness of interpersonal and gendered violence in Myanmar and its potential impact on political efficacy and related attitudes, we asked respondents about their experiences with such

FIGURE 4.2
Political Efficacy, Life Experiences, and Perceptions of Trust, Safety, and Democracy Among Men and Women in Myanmar, 2018

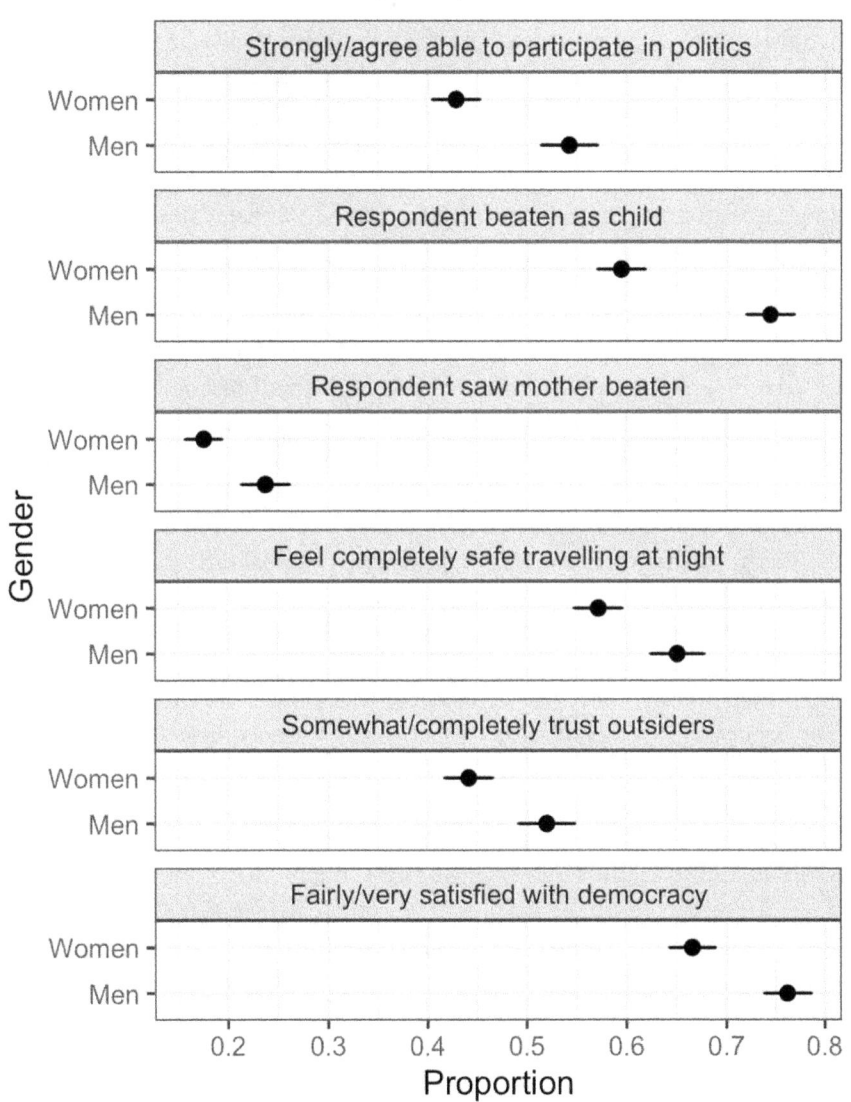

Note: Proportions with 95 per cent confidence intervals.

violence. We found significant differences in the proportions of men and women who experienced interpersonal violence in their households before adulthood, felt safe travelling at night, or trusted outsiders. Women were significantly less likely to report that they were beaten when children (59 per cent) or that their mother was beaten when they were underage (18 per cent), compared to men (74 per cent and 24 per cent, respectively). Women were also significantly less likely to somewhat or completely trust outsiders (44 per cent) or to feel completely safe travelling in their township at night (57 per cent)—the corresponding figures for men were 52 per cent and 65 per cent, respectively. Participation in politics at all levels can require travelling at night, including for parliamentary candidates or elected members, ward/village tract administrators, and citizens who wish to participate in meetings. Further, violence and harassment have been normalized as part of politics in Myanmar (Bjarnegård, this volume). That women in our sample felt less safe and are less likely to trust outsiders than men reflects the ways in which violence can be a barrier to women's political participation, which is further reinforced in the qualitative evidence Bjarnegård presents in Chapter 5.

Because existing research suggests that political efficacy and support for women's political participation can depend on people's beliefs about the political system, we also asked respondents whether they were satisfied with democracy. Again, women were significantly less likely than men to say they are fairly or very satisfied with democracy (67 per cent vs. 76 per cent). We expect this difference in satisfaction with democracy will be correlated with internal political efficacy because people who feel their government is less responsive often feel that their participation does not matter. Similarly, if women are less satisfied with democracy, they may also be less likely to believe that women should engage more in politics. We return to these questions in our multivariate analyses. In many ways, these differences between women and men's experiences reinforce the gender inequality and attitudes about women's roles that Figure 4.1 highlights.

Finally, in Figure 4.3, we present the proportion of men and women who express certain attitudes, particularly about women's role in politics. We asked whether women should participate as much as men in politics, and whether they would support their daughter's participation in politics. These are the final outcomes we consider in

FIGURE 4.3
Support for Women's Participation in Politics and Political interest and Knowledge Among Men and Women in Myanmar, 2018

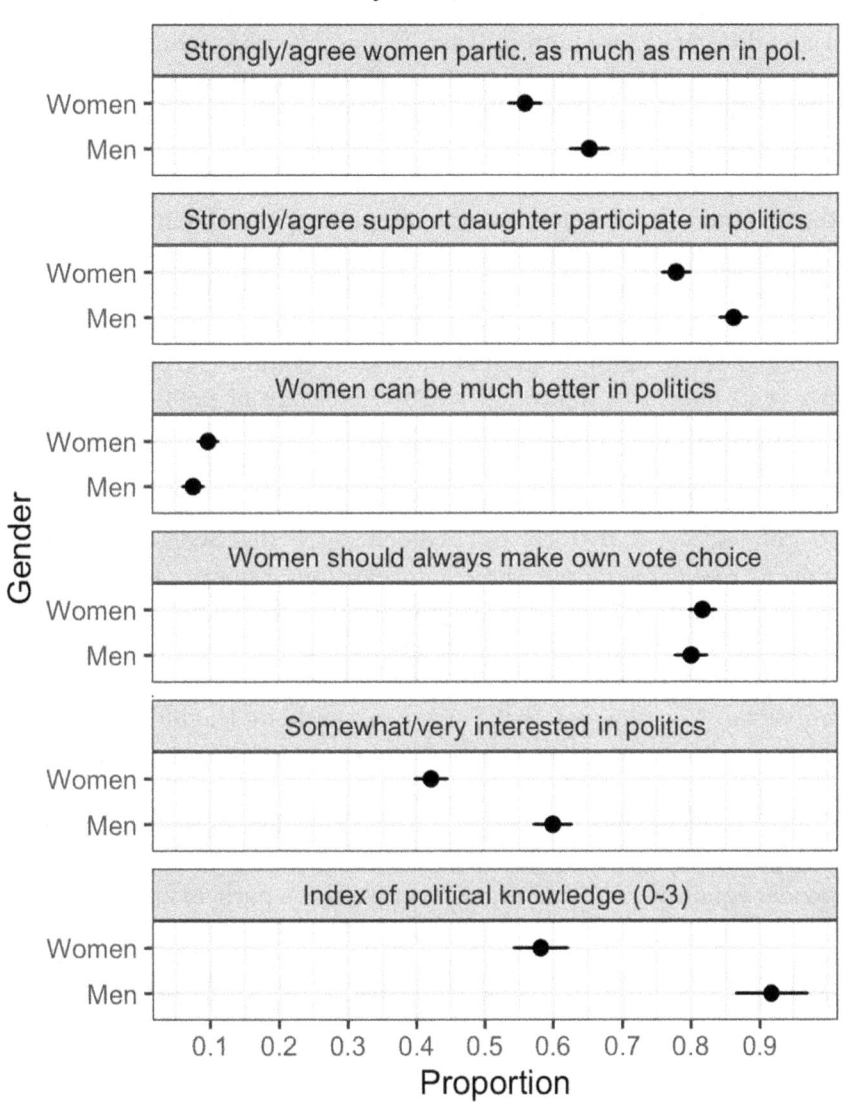

Note: Proportions with 95 per cent confidence intervals.

our multivariate analysis below. We found that women are less likely than men to express support for women's participation in politics (56 per cent of women, 65 per cent of men), or for their daughter to participate in politics (78 per cent of women, 86 per cent of men). These differences are both statistically significant. A nationwide survey conducted in Myanmar in 2019 similarly found that women were more likely than men to think that women should be less involved in politics than men (Welsh et al. 2020, p. 27). Therefore, it is not surprising that few men (8 per cent) or women (10 per cent) believe that women can be much better at politics than men. In contrast, overwhelming majorities of men (80 per cent) and women (82 per cent) agreed that women should always make their own choices when voting in elections. Consistent with previous findings, women also expressed significantly less interest in politics (42 per cent vs. 60 per cent) and have significantly less knowledge of politics than men.[8]

Together, these descriptive statistics describe a context in which women are less interested in and less informed about politics, and women tend to be less supportive than men of women's participation in politics, yet both men and women agree that women should be able to make their own choices in elections. These patterns would be consistent with a society where both men and women have reservations about women's participation in politics, but nonetheless believe that the right to choose candidates without interference is universal. We suggest that future research in fragile democracies further explore the ways in which political attitudes and support for women's participation vary.

In the following section, we seek to understand the individual characteristics most associated with men's and women's support for gender equality, political efficacy, and women's participation in politics.

EXPLAINING GENDERED VALUES AND ATTITUDES

In this section, we present several multivariate regression analyses to better understand men's and women's attitudes about gender roles, political efficacy, and women's participation in politics in Myanmar. In particular, we are interested in understanding what individual characteristics are most associated with different attitudes towards gender equality, internal political efficacy, and women's participation in politics, across genders. Therefore, we estimate separate regressions for men and women, and interpret those results separately. In addition to some of the measures already discussed, we also include other demographic characteristics, such as age, education, income, marital status, occupation, location, and various measures of trust in different institutions, as well as attitudes towards individualism and the family.[9]

Attitudes Towards Gender Equality

We start by examining attitudes towards gender equality. To do so, we construct an additive index that measures individual attitudes towards gender equality, using the following four questions:

1. How important is it that a wife obeys her husband even when she does not agree?
2. In general, who do you think make better business leaders? [men or women]
3. When jobs are scarce, men should have more right to jobs than women. [agree/disagree]
4. Is university education more important for men or for women?

For each of these questions, we code the answer as +1 if it relatively favours gender equality, –1 if it goes against gender equality, and 0 if the answer is neutral or respondents do not know what to answer.[10] For instance, for the first one, we code +1 if the answer is slightly important or not important at all, and –1 if the answer is somewhat or very important. As a result, our index ranges from –4 (those against gender equality on all four fronts) to +4 (those in favour of gender equality on all four fronts). The mean for men is –1.1, with a standard deviation of 1.72; those figures are –1.1 and 1.73 for women. Figure 4.4 plots the linear regression coefficients and 95 per cent confidence intervals for demographic characteristics and attitudes we expect help explain variation in support for gender equality.

Throughout this section, rather than discuss each result in detail, we focus on results that are statistically significant and differentiated by gender. For women, only education, political knowledge, and collective values are significantly associated with attitudes favouring gender equality. For men, age, education, satisfaction with democracy, interest in politics, and reporting not having witnessed violence against

FIGURE 4.4
Factors Associated with Gender Equality in Myanmar, 2018

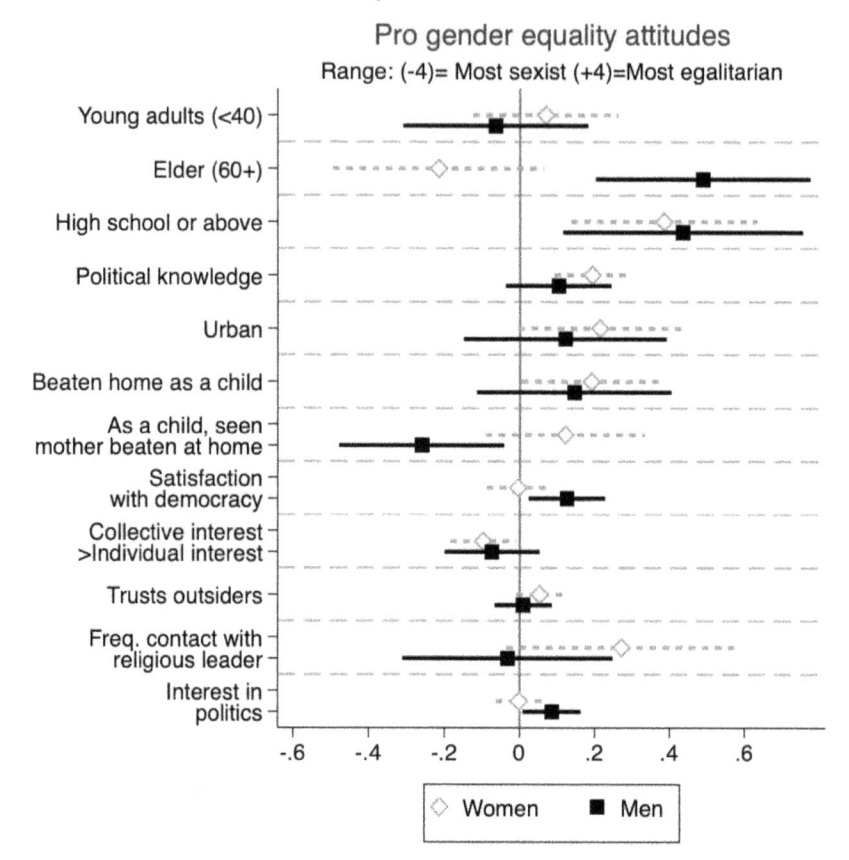

Pro gender equality attitudes
Range: (-4)= Most sexist (+4)=Most egalitarian

Young adults (<40)
Elder (60+)
High school or above
Political knowledge
Urban
Beaten home as a child
As a child, seen mother beaten at home
Satisfaction with democracy
Collective interest >Individual interest
Trusts outsiders
Freq. contact with religious leader
Interest in politics

◇ Women   ■ Men

Note: Linear regression coefficients with 95 per cent confidence intervals. Models also include controls for marital status, number of cell phones in the household (as a proxy for income), language of the interview, occupation, trust in parliament, trust in the military, willingness to obey mother-in-law even when she is deemed to be wrong, trust towards outsiders, privacy of the interview, location, and state/region, which are not included in the figures above. All standard errors are clustered at the village/ward level. R^2 for female regression: 0.13. R^2 for male regression: 0.13.

their mother in childhood are good predictors of pro-equality attitudes. For both men and women, inclinations towards gender equality were relatively similar for those under 40 and between 40 and 60. However, men over 60 expressed significantly higher support for gender equality than men under 60; conversely, women over 60 expressed significantly less support for gender equality than their peers under 60. Put differently, older women expressed more conservative attitudes than younger women, while older men expressed more progressive attitudes than their younger peers. This contrast suggests both that older generations differ in their attitudes about gender equality and that the association between age and views on gender equality differs by gender. In contrast, men and women who had completed high school or higher education expressed stronger support for gender equality, both statistically and substantively.

Turning to experiences and attitudes, we note that notwithstanding some differences across genders, all the statistically significant associations we find between experiences and attitudes are generally consistent with theoretical expectations. Women with more political knowledge expressed significantly greater support for gender equality and women with more collectivist values expressed significantly less. Meanwhile, neither political knowledge nor collectivist values could be significantly associated with support for gender equality among men. Instead, satisfaction with democracy and interest in politics were positively and significantly associated with pro-gender equality attitudes. Together, these findings are consistent with arguments associating collectivist interests or satisfaction with democracy with post-materialist values, such as gender equality. More research is needed to understand the reasons for these differences between men and women.

Finally, we explore the effect of early experiences with intrafamilial violence on attitudes towards gender equality. As noted above, domestic violence is pervasive in Myanmar (Larsen, Aye, and Bjertness 2021; Kabir et al. 2019; Gender Equality Network 2015), and women are more likely to believe domestic violence against women is justified (Ministry of Health and Sports 2017). Research in other contexts suggests that early life experiences help shape internal efficacy in general in adulthood (Easton and Dennis 1967; Rodgers 1974), and that experiences with domestic violence specifically can have a negative impact on general personal efficacy in adulthood (Haj-Yahia et al. 2021). We find a positive association, albeit statistically insignificant, between being the target of domestic violence as a child and support for gender equality. More discouraging, however, is the statistically significant association for men between reporting witnessing domestic abuse of one's mother before adulthood and lower reported support for gender equality, which is consistent with our expectations. This association implies that men who witnessed violence against their mother carry into adulthood less support for gender equality. In contrast, women who report seeing domestic violence against their mothers tended to express slightly (though not statistically significant) more support for gender equality. The asymmetry between men and women highlights the ways in which gendered violence can have differential long-term consequences for social values, a topic that begs further exploration in future research.

Gendered Explanations of Internal Political Efficacy

We next examine the predictors of internal political efficacy (see Figure 4.5). The main takeaway here is that interest in politics has the largest positive association with internal political efficacy for both men and women. This is not surprising because the two concepts are hypothesized to be closely related (for example, see Kenski and Stroud 2006). We also observe that the following are positively associated with a higher internal political efficacy (even if not always at conventional significance levels) for both women and men: trust in outsiders, age (being younger than 60), interest in politics, satisfaction with democracy, and political knowledge. Frequency of contact with a religious leader (measured as a dummy variable: 1 means the respondent had such contact at least once during the past year[11]) also correlates positively with efficacy. We note, though, that this variable may capture social status and connections as much as religiosity; we therefore need to be cautious when interpreting it.

However, there are some differences across genders: Higher levels of formal education are associated with higher perceptions of efficacy for men, but the effect is nowhere to be seen for women. This is surprising as qualitative studies have found that female MPs are more likely than male counterparts to report having a high level of education as an important factor that gave them confidence to enter politics and/or that lent them credibility with their party or voters. A female hundred-household leader confirms:

> I do not want to be a member of parliament because I do not have high education background. I regret now for the fact that I did not

FIGURE 4.5
Factors Associated with Internal Political Efficacy by Gender in Myanmar, 2018

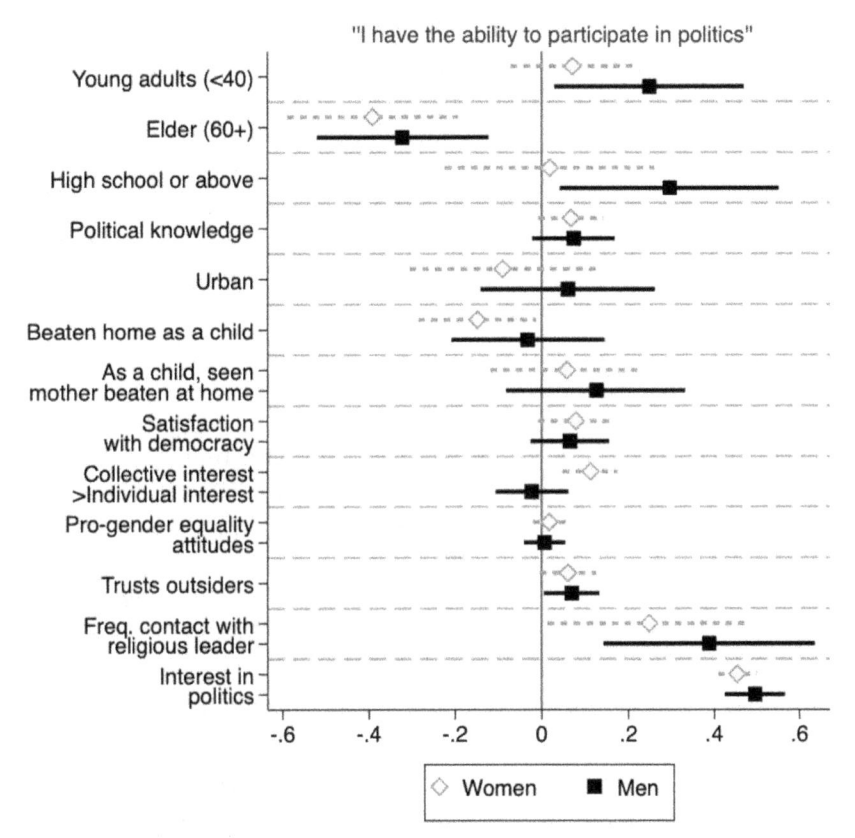

"I have the ability to participate in politics"

[Forest plot showing linear regression coefficients for Women (◇) and Men (■) across the following factors: Young adults (<40), Elder (60+), High school or above, Political knowledge, Urban, Beaten home as a child, As a child, seen mother beaten at home, Satisfaction with democracy, Collective interest >Individual interest, Pro-gender equality attitudes, Trusts outsiders, Freq. contact with religious leader, Interest in politics. X-axis ranges from -.6 to .6.]

Note: Linear regression coefficients with 95 per cent confidence intervals. Models also include controls for marital status, number of cell phones in the household (as a proxy for income), language of the interview, occupation, trust in parliament, trust in the military, willingness to obey mother-in-law even when she is deemed to be wrong, trust towards outsiders, privacy of the interview, location, and state/region, which are not included in the figures above. All standard errors are clustered at the village/ward level. R^2 for female regression: 0.25. R^2 for male regression: 0.32.

continue the school till graduate. If I am educated, I will try to be a member of parliament.

A possible reason for this difference may be that our study contrasts those with at least high school education with those who have not completed high school education, whereas most female MPs have completed undergraduate or postgraduate university education (Gender Equality Network 2017, p. 25).[12]

We also note that women who report experiencing intrafamilial violence before adulthood express lower levels of political efficacy, while similar experiences among men have no association with their internal political efficacy. This suggests that when men experience childhood violence, they are able to overcome or rebound from such experiences and express similar levels of internal political efficacy as men who shared no similar experience. In contrast, such experiences appear to have lingering effects among women, reducing their sense of political efficacy compared to other women. Interestingly, witnessing violence against their mother before adulthood has no significant association with internal political efficacy for either men or women in our sample.

Last, marital status is another characteristic that has radically different effects for men and women: while women who were never married are, on average, five percentage points more likely to state that they disagree or strongly disagree that they have the ability to participate in politics, there is no such effect for men (results not included in the figure).

Gendered attitudes and support for women in politics

Next, we examine the predictors of support for women's participation in politics in Myanmar. The shared characteristics associated with higher support are formal education, political knowledge, trust in outsiders, favouring gender equality, interest in politics, and the belief that individuals should sacrifice their individual interests to benefit the collective (although the latter two qualities fail to reach conventional significant levels). See Figure 4.6 for regression coefficient estimates with confidence intervals. None of these results are particularly surprising in light of the studies from Myanmar or elsewhere discussed earlier. Education, political knowledge, interest in politics, and being pro-gender equality are all generally expected to have a positive association with support for women's participation in politics.

However, experience of intrafamilial violence again produces a key difference across genders. Men who observed their mothers being beaten at home before adulthood tend to express less support for

FIGURE 4.6
Factors Associated with Support for Women's Participation in Politics by Gender

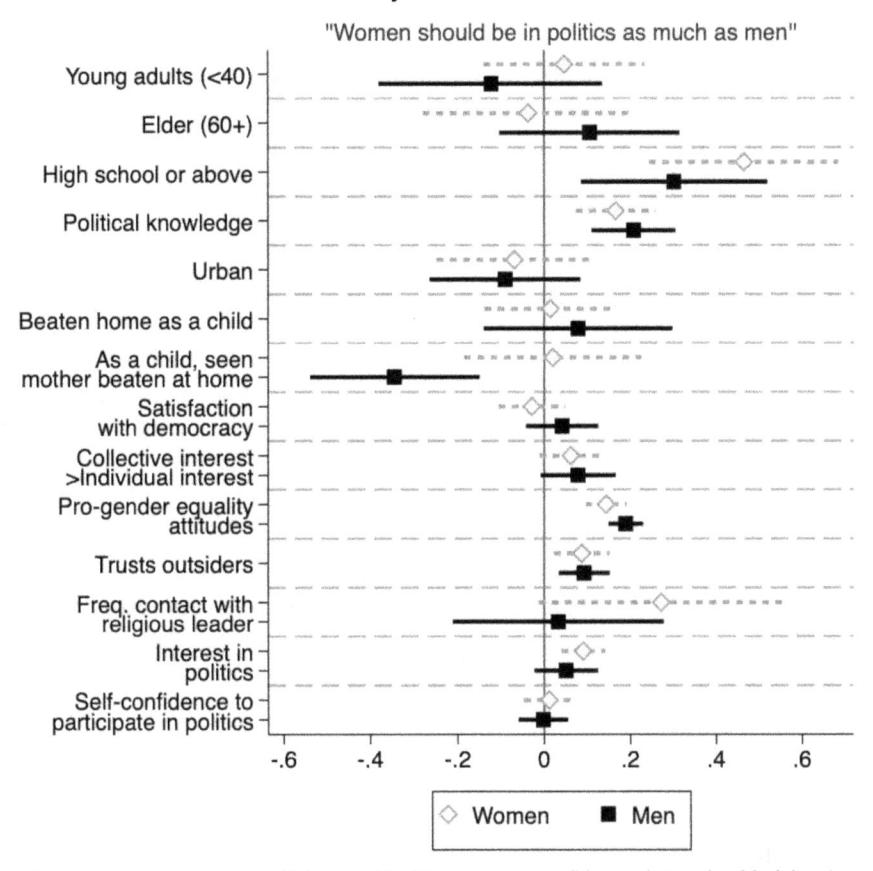

"Women should be in politics as much as men"

[Forest plot showing linear regression coefficients for Women (◇) and Men (■) across the following variables: Young adults (<40), Elder (60+), High school or above, Political knowledge, Urban, Beaten home as a child, As a child, seen mother beaten at home, Satisfaction with democracy, Collective interest >Individual interest, Pro-gender equality attitudes, Trusts outsiders, Freq. contact with religious leader, Interest in politics, Self-confidence to participate in politics. X-axis ranges from -.6 to .6.]

Note: Linear egression coefficients with 95 per cent confidence intervals. Models also include controls for marital status, number of cell phones in the household (as a proxy for income), language of the interview, occupation, trust in parliament, trust in the military, willingness to obey mother-in-law even when she is deemed to be wrong, trust towards outsiders, privacy of the interview, location, and state/region, which are not included in the figures above. All standard errors are clustered at the village/ward level. R^2 for female regression: 0.15. R^2 for male regression: 0.20.

women's participation in politics than men who did not have such an experience. This is consistent with our earlier results (see Figure 4.4); men who witnessed gendered intrafamily violence in childhood (an indicator for a gendered household upbringing) tended to express less support for gender equality. Our findings suggest that men who grow up in a context of intrafamilial violence are likely to internalize less gender-equal and more patriarchal attitudes and behaviours. In other words, our results suggest that observing intramarital violence as kids does not enhance a feeling of empathy towards females (which could be another feasible long-run response): instead, men seem to internalize the values and attitudes of their abusive fathers.

Last, perceptions of safety ("Do you feel safe to travel through your township during the nighttime [the daytime]?") seem to have an effect for women, but not for men (results not included in the figure): women who feel safer in their townships (either at night or during the day) are more willing to support women's participation in politics. This finding also highlights the ways in which gendered experiences of context, in this instance, the perception of personal safety, can produce heterogenous effects across genders. This is consistent with other research in which women cite safety concerns as barriers to participation in politics (Ma Agatha, Poe Ei Phyu, and Knapman 2018, pp. 470–71; Bjarnegård, this volume).

Attitudes Towards Future Generations of Women Participating in Politics

Lastly, we examine what may explain willingness to support younger women's participation in politics—with the reminder that we carried out the survey before the 2021 coup. To make the question salient to respondents, we asked them to agree/disagree with the following statement: "I would support my daughter to join parties and participate in politics if she so wished". Figure 4.7 presents the model coefficients with 95 per cent confidence intervals.

As in the above cases, we find that when a given characteristic predicts support among respondents of one gender, it also does for the other: interest in politics, satisfaction with how democracy works, internal political efficacy, trust in outsiders, beliefs that individuals should sacrifice their individual interests to benefit the collective, and living in rural areas are positively associated with support for daughters' engaging in politics (although in some cases only at a 10 per cent significance level).

In this case, only one observable characteristic predicts support, for one gender: political knowledge, and only for men. Men with higher

FIGURE 4.7
Factors Associated with Support for Daughter's Participation in Politics by Gender

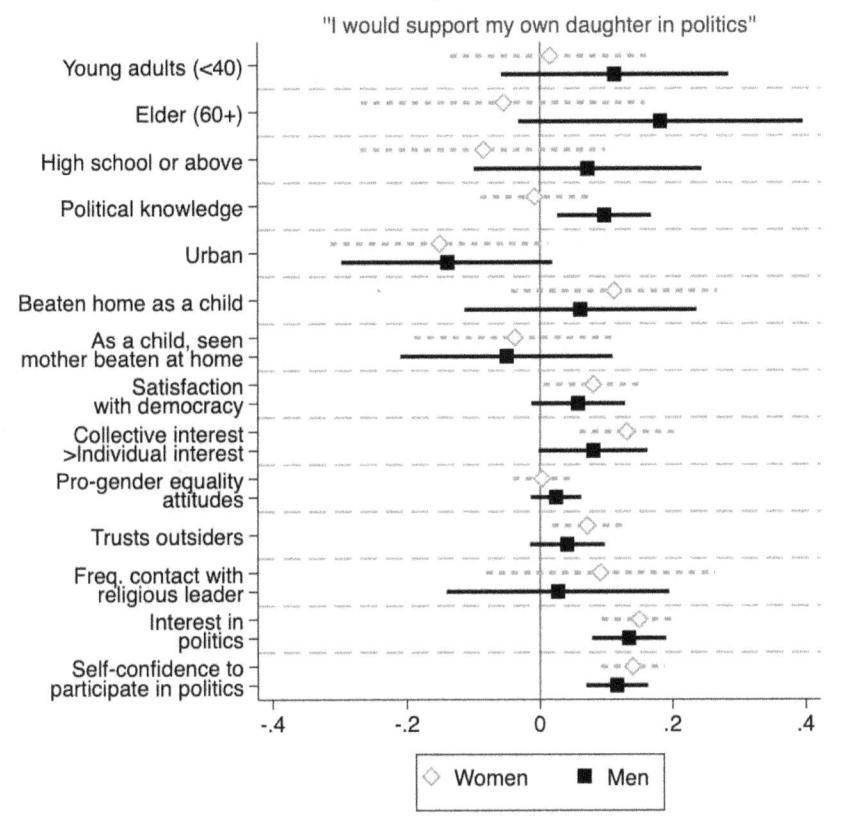

"I would support my own daughter in politics"

[Forest plot showing linear regression coefficients with 95% confidence intervals for Women (open diamonds) and Men (filled squares) across the following variables: Young adults (<40), Elder (60+), High school or above, Political knowledge, Urban, Beaten home as a child, As a child, seen mother beaten at home, Satisfaction with democracy, Collective interest >Individual interest, Pro-gender equality attitudes, Trusts outsiders, Freq. contact with religious leader, Interest in politics, Self-confidence to participate in politics. X-axis ranges from -.4 to .4.]

Note: Linear egression coefficients with 95 per cent confidence intervals. Models also include controls for marital status, number of cell phones in the household (as a proxy for income), language of the interview, occupation, trust in parliament, trust in the military, willingness to obey mother-in-law even when she is deemed to be wrong, trust towards outsiders, privacy of the interview, location, and state/region, which are not included in the figures above. All standard errors are clustered at the village/ward level. R^2 for female regression: 0.14. R^2 for male regression: 0.13.

political knowledge seem more likely to be willing to support their daughters in politics; this quality seems to play no role for women. We would like to highlight that perceptions of safety do not seem to be associated with willingness to support their daughters' participation in politics. Neither measure of perception of safety seems to add any explanatory power. Similarly, overall positions in favour of a more egalitarian society in terms of gender do not seem to predict support for one's own daughter's participation in politics. We suggest future research should further examine how political knowledge relates to normative beliefs about gender equality in fragile democracies, for both men and women.

DISCUSSION AND CONCLUSION

The results presented above show that some sociodemographic factors and life experiences affect women and men differently with regards to their approach to politics, and to gender and participation in particular. Our descriptive statistics show that men and women in Myanmar tended to express similarly low levels of support for gender equality in family and society (see Figure 4.1), but the factors that explain these levels differed between men and women (see Figure 4.4). Support for women's participation in politics followed a similar pattern, in general, except that men tended to support women's participation at significantly higher rates than did women (see Figure 4.3). Nonetheless, the factors that explained support for women's participation in politics were similar across men and women, just like general pro-equality gender equality attitudes (see Figures 4.6 and 4.7).

At the same time, men and women differed in one important way in both our models of general gender equality (see Figure 4.4) and gender equality in political participation (see Figures 4.6 and 4.7): childhood experiences with intrafamilial violence and, in the latter case, perceptions of personal safety. That is, men who reported seeing their mothers beaten in childhood also were significantly more likely than otherwise to express lower levels of support for both gender equality in society and women's participation in politics. We found no such difference among women. This suggests that gendered domestic violence reinforces and perpetuates patriarchal values and attitudes among men. While some research has examined adolescent experiences of violence and of political violence in adulthood (e.g., Bjarnegård, Brounéus, and Melander 2017), none that we know of has examined how experiences of gendered domestic violence in childhood affect adults' support for gender equality or women's participation in politics. We believe this should be an important area for future research in fragile democracies with highly patriarchal social systems, like Myanmar in 2018.

In addition, we find that being the target of intrafamilial violence in childhood also has gendered effects on internal political efficacy. Among women, experiencing domestic violence as a child is associated with lower confidence as adults to take part in politics, compared to women who did not experience such violence. In contrast, we find no significant difference in internal political efficacy between men who were and were not beaten as children (see Figure 4.5). This is even though men in general were more likely to report having been beaten as children than women in our sample (see Figure 4.2). Nonetheless, we also see that being the target of domestic violence or witnessing violence against one's mother does not have significant or gendered associations with willingness to support one's daughter's participation in politics.

Together, these various findings suggest that past experiences with intrafamilial violence may have long-lasting psychological effects on internal political efficacy and attitudes towards gender equality and women's participation in politics. For men, seeing violence against their mother can reinforce patriarchal values, and for women, while being the target can negatively affect their political efficacy, it does not dissuade them from thinking their daughters should be involved in politics.

Furthermore, we would like to highlight a finding that will require further inquiry: while more educated men tend to have higher political self-confidence, we observe no such effect among women. It is important to note that this difference does not likely reflect lack of power—women tend to be better educated than men in our sample, reflecting the general pattern in Myanmar society (Gender Equality Network 2017, p. 25).[13]

Finally, though we do not have the space to present and discuss these results in detail, we would like to note that our findings do not hold equally in all states we visited. In Southern Shan, women are much less favourable to female participation in politics than are women in the other three states. We also find women in Shan much less supportive of their daughters' taking part in politics than their female counterparts in Mon, Mandalay, and Ayeyarwady. We find no such patterns among men. These differences could perhaps be influenced by the historically higher level of militarization of society and politics in southern Shan State than in our other study areas. However, it could also be due to attitudes towards gender among some or all of the ethnic communities residing in southern Shan State, versus those of the predominant ethnic groups in other states/regions surveyed. We believe regional differences within Myanmar should be an area for future researchers interested in questions of gender and political participation.

We also check for major rural–urban differences. Women in urban areas exhibited attitudes more in favour of gender equality in general than their rural counterparts (see Figure 4.4). We found differences between urban and rural respondents in attitudes towards participation, too (see Figures 4.5–4.7). Urban women were no more feminist than rural women, nor were urban men more feminist than rural men, on any of our measures. Similarly, a 2014 survey found that rural dwellers were only slightly more likely than urban dwellers (72 per cent vs. 69 per cent) to agree with the statement that men make better political leaders than women (The Asia Foundation 2014, pp. 78–79). Female MPs in the national lower house were also roughly equally likely to represent more rural as urban constituencies (Gender Equality Network 2017, p. 41). Therefore, although general attitudes may be more conservative or anti-feminist in rural areas, there does not seem to be a big urban/rural divide with regard to political participation.

The findings presented above have some clear policy-relevant takeaways. Life experience matters; self-confidence matters; safety matters. All of these aspects matter as much as or even more than education. They matter not only for women's own participation, but also for their willingness to encourage their daughters to take part in politics. These and other patterns are worth exploring further, such as the reason behind observed regional/state-level effects, and, in particular, why these are gender-biased.

How can this all help us understand political participation currently in Myanmar, after the 2021 coup and under a non-democratic regime? The military have not been shy to use repression: they have killed more than five thousand people in relation to the coup (Institute for Strategy and Policy – Myanmar 2022a), while more than twenty thousand homes and buildings have been torched since the coup (Institute for Strategy and Policy – Myanmar 2022b). At the time of our writing, it is very hard to predict if, and when and how, democracy will return to Myanmar. The public is participating strongly in Myanmar's spring revolution in different ways, and the revolution has pushed the public into the centre. At present, a popular phrase is "the public has only the public", i.e., the people have become aware that they will have to pave their own way during the revolution. Therefore, even if democracy returns, it will be hard to assume that the factors explaining political participation will be largely unchanged. The revolution is having a large impact on how and why people participate in politics. It is too soon to conjecture how this might impact attitudes and levels of participation in a possible post-revolutionary system.

NOTES

1. Note that high school education is still rare in Myanmar: the 2014 census showed that among those aged 25 and above, only 16.1 per cent had completed high school (Government of Myanmar 2017, p. 51).
2. See Appendix Four for our survey questions.
3. For logistical reasons only the following townships were included in our sampling frame for southern Shan State: Taunggyi Township, Hsi Hseng Township, Hopong Township, Nyaung Shwe Township, Kalaw Township, Pinlaung Township, Pekon Township, Pindaya Township, Ywa Ngan Township.
4. Weighting corrected for different township sizes, so that each individual in the state had an equal chance of being randomly selected for an interview.
5. Once villages or wards had been chosen, enumerators visited them for two to three days, conducting surveys all day. Once in the village or ward, enumerators would start at a house at random and walk around the village, knocking at every N^{th} door (N varying depending on the size of the village/ward).
6. The randomly selected townships were Taungyi Nyaung Shwe and Hsihseng (Shan); Thabeikkyin, Tada U, and Singu (Mon); Nyaung Done, Kyaunggon, and Nga Pu Daw (Mandalay); Bilin, Kyaikmaraw, and Kyaik Htoe (Ayeyarwady).
7. Thirty-seven respondents did not identify as either male or female. That small subsample does not allow enough statistical power to analyse patterns that may explain their behaviour and attitudes; we exclude them from the analysis.
8. To measure political knowledge, we asked three questions (all open-ended) about the current political situation in Myanmar, including: "Who elects

the president?"; "Do you know the name of an MP of this township in the state/region hluttaw?"; and "Do you know the name of an MP of this township in the Pyithu/Amyothar Hluttaw [lower or upper house of the federal parliament]?" Our index of political knowledge sums the number of correct answers each respondent provided. The average correct responses were 0.58 for women and 0.92 for men.
9. All our regressions include state/region fixed effects and cluster standard errors at the village/ward level. Figure footnotes include lists of additional covariates included in the models.
10. When respondents refused to answer a question, the response is excluded from analysis.
11. 12.5 per cent of respondents state having met a religious leader (from once to very frequently) during the past 12 months (8 per cent of women and 18 per cent of men).
12. We note that this is a well-identified null result for women: the sample size for all educational categories is large enough for us to be confident that this finding is robust (14 per cent of men and 17 per cent of women have at least higher education in our sample).
13. The 2015 Labour Force Survey (LFS) report describes, "Women are slightly less likely than men to have ever attended school, and they are more likely to be illiterate. However, women are slightly more likely than men to have completed high school (13.5% vs 13.1%) and almost 50% more likely than men to hold an undergraduate degree or above (6.8% vs 4.6%)". Our survey was conducted after the LFS, by which time educational differences had tilted further in favour of women.

REFERENCES

Barrow, Amy. 2015. "Contested Spaces during Transition: Regime Change in Myanmar and Its Implications for Women". *Cardozo Journal of Law & Gender* 22, no. 1: 75–108.

Bjarnegård, Elin, Karen Brounéus, and Erik Melander. 2017. "Honor and Political Violence: Micro-Level Findings from a Survey in Thailand". *Journal of Peace Research* 54, no. 6: 748–61. https://doi.org/10.1177/0022343317711241.

Easton, David, and Jack Dennis. 1967. "The Child's Acquisition of Regime Norms: Political Efficacy". *The American Political Science Review* 61, no. 1: 25–38. https://doi.org/10.2307/1953873.

Finkel, Steven E. 1985. "Reciprocal Effects of Participation and Political Efficacy: A Panel Analysis". *American Journal of Political Science* 29, no. 4: 891–913. https://doi.org/10.2307/2111186.

Fraile, Marta, and Carolina de Miguel Moyer. 2021. "Risk and the Gender Gap in Internal Political Efficacy in Europe". *West European Politics* 45, no. 7: 1–19. https://doi.org/10.1080/01402382.2021.1969146.

Gender Equality Network (GEN). 2015. "Raising the Curtain: Cultural Norms, Social Practices and Gender Equality in Myanmar". Yangon, Myanmar: GEN.

Government of Myanmar. 2017. *Myanmar 2014 Census: Thematic Report on Education*.

Haj-Yahia, Muhammad M., Niveen Hassan-Abbas, Menny Malka, and Shireen Sokar. 2021. "Exposure to Family Violence in Childhood, Self-Efficacy, and Posttraumatic Stress Symptoms in Young Adulthood". *Journal of Interpersonal Violence* 36, nos. 17–18: NP9548–75. https://doi.org/10.1177/0886260519860080.

Htun, Mala, and Francesca R. Jensenius. 2020. "Political Change, Women's Rights, and Public Opinion on Gender Equality in Myanmar". *The European Journal of Development Research* 32, no. 2: 457–81. https://doi.org/10.1057/s41287-020-00266-z.

Inglehart, Ronald, and Pippa Norris. 2003. *Rising Tide: Gender Equality and Cultural Change Around the World*. Illustrated edition. Cambridge, UK; New York: Cambridge University Press.

Inglehart, Ronald, Pippa Norris, and Christian Welzel. 2003. "Gender Equality and Democracy". In *Human Values and Social Change*, edited by Ronald Inglehart, pp. 91–115. Leiden, The Netherlands: Brill.

Institute for Strategy and Policy – Myanmar (ISP – Myanmar). 2022a. "Over 5,600 Civilians Killed Within a Year of the Coup". 14 May 2022. https://www.ispmyanmar.com/over-5600-civilians-killed-within-a-year-of-the-coup/ (accessed 11 September 2022).

———. 2022b. "More Than 22,000 Homes and Buildings Torched After the Coup". 4 June 2022. https://www.ispmyanmar.com/more-than-22000-homes-and-buildings-torched-after-the-coup/ (accessed 11 September 2022).

Kabir, Russell, Mainul Haque, Masoud Mohammadnezhad, Nandeeta Samad, Shabnam Mostari, Shiny Jabin, Md Anwarul Azim Majumder, and Md Golam Rabbani. 2019. "Domestic Violence and Decision-Making Power of Married Women in Myanmar: Analysis of a Nationally Representative Sample". *Annals of Saudi Medicine* 39, no. 6: 395–402. https://doi.org/10.5144/0256-4947.2019.395.

Kenski, Kate, and Natalie Jomini Stroud. 2006. "Connections Between Internet Use and Political Efficacy, Knowledge, and Participation". *Journal of Broadcasting & Electronic Media* 50, no. 2: 173–92. https://doi.org/10.1207/s15506878jobem5002_1.

Larsen, Lise Wessel, Win Thuzar Aye, and Espen Bjertness. 2021. "Prevalence of Intimate Partner Violence and Association with Wealth in Myanmar". *Journal of Family Violence* 36, no. 4: 417–28. https://doi.org/10.1007/s10896-020-00190-0.

Liu, Shan-Jan Sarah. 2020. "Gender Gaps in Political Participation in Asia". *International Political Science Review* (August). https://doi.org/10.1177/0192512120935517.

Paxton, Pamela, Melanie M. Hughes, and Tiffany Barnes. 2020. *Women, Politics, and Power: A Global Perspective*. Lanham, Maryland: Rowman & Littlefield.

Paxton, Pamela, Sheri Kunovich, and Melanie M. Hughes. 2007. "Gender in Politics". *Annual Review of Sociology* 33, no. 1: 263–84. https://doi.org/10.1146/annurev.soc.33.040406.131651.

Rasmussen, Stig Hebbelstrup Rye, and Asbjørn Sonne Nørgaard. 2018. "When and Why Does Education Matter? Motivation and Resource Effects in Political Efficacy". *European Journal of Political Research* 57, no. 1: 24–46. https://doi.org/10.1111/1475-6765.12213.

Rodgers, Harrell R. 1974. "Toward Explanation of the Political Efficacy and Political Cynicism of Black Adolescents: An Exploratory Study". *American Journal of Political Science* 18, no. 2: 257–82. https://doi.org/10.2307/2110702.

Welsh, Bridget, Myat Thu, Chong Hua Kueh, and Arkar Soe. 2020. "Myanmar: Grappling with Transition: 2019 Asian Barometer Survey Report". Selangor: Strategic Information and Research Development Centre.

Wen, Nainan, Hao Xiaoming, and Cherian George. 2013. "Gender and Political Participation: News Consumption, Political Efficacy and Interpersonal Communication". *Asian Journal of Women's Studies* 19, no. 4: 124–49. https://doi.org/10.1080/12259276.2013.11666168.

Wolak, Jennifer. 2018. "Feelings of Political Efficacy in the Fifty States". *Political Behavior* 40, no. 3: 763–84. https://doi.org/10.1007/s11109-017-9421-9.

5

VIOLENCE, GENDER, AND POLITICS

Elin Bjarnegård (with important contributions from an anonymous co-author)[1]

Violence is a constant factor influencing Myanmar politics. The return to repressive, military rule in 2021 demonstrates how relevant violence is—and probably always was—for understanding political participation in Myanmar. This chapter investigates the political and gendered roles that violence plays, and the interlinkages between violence taking place in the public and private spheres. Whether violence is carried out by the Tatmadaw (Myanmar military) during an armed conflict or by an intimate partner against another, it follows gendered patterns and contributes to a gendered culture of violence. The relevance of the feminist slogan "the personal is political" is striking in the many examples of how this culture of violence affects the formal political process in gendered ways. This chapter brings together findings from previous parts of the book to shed light on how party politics and political candidates are affected by and experience gendered public attitudes and how a persistent culture of violence—public manifestations of militarization as well as tolerance of domestic violence—shapes gendered politics, even in a period of relative liberalization.

The chapter will demonstrate why and how the culture of violence in general, and domestic violence in particular, is crucial in shedding light on the opportunities and hurdles for "putting women up" in pre-coup Myanmar. It draws on the findings about violence that emerged from the various data collection efforts of the project as well as on sources external to the project. In doing so, it recognizes that violence is complex and continuous. It operates along a continuum that stretches from armed conflict to legacies that remain in peacetime (Cockburn 2004). The chapter also shows how violence that takes psychological forms, such as harassment and intimidation, and that takes place in the private sphere, such as domestic abuse, also has political and gendered repercussions (Bjarnegård 2018). The more democratic and peaceful period that Myanmar experienced around the elections of 2015 is here seen and analysed in light of the fact that it was both preceded and succeeded by more violent and repressive forms of governance. For a while, the introduction of democratic elections in Myanmar seemed to constitute an important step towards the peaceful resolution of conflict in the violence-ridden country, but political actors nevertheless operated with political violence in fresh memory and the period was not itself free of political violence. In a conflict-affected political environment such as Myanmar, even the widely praised elections of 2015 come with increased risk of violence and violations of electoral and personal integrity. As we know, in 2021, not long after the next round of elections, the military took power in a coup d'état, reinforcing a culture of political violence. Against the background of this repressive turn, this chapter investigates the interconnections among personal experiences of violence, attitudes to political participation, and the experience of violence of those politicians who participated in the seemingly peaceful general elections of 2015.

Recent research suggests that political violence can be gendered in different ways, including in motive, form, and impact (Bardall, Bjarnegård, and Piscopo 2020). Research has also demonstrated that experiences of violence in one's childhood household have gender-differentiated and long-lasting effects (Whitfield et al. 2003). We use these findings as a point of departure for analysing the role that violence played in determining the gendered conditions for political participation in Myanmar. We investigate whether the extent of violent experiences differed between politically active men and women in

Myanmar, and if they faced different forms of violence. We map and describe the gendered experiences of male and female candidates at the national level, drawing on extensive interviews and focus-group discussions, as described below. Furthermore, we explore the gendered impact of violence in the population at large by revisiting the survey data presented in Chapter 4. We take a closer look at how childhood experiences of violence have shaped attitudes to the political participation of women in the broader population.

Taken together, the different types of data used here demonstrate that violence is normalized in Myanmar, and that attacks and abuse are seen as part of politics, just as they are expected in many other areas of life. Although most political candidates interviewed saw improvements compared to previous political experiences, a majority nevertheless reported some form of intimidation also during their 2015 election campaign. Verbal or online harassment reports included ethnic or religious aspects. While it was difficult to discern any gendered differences in the *extent* of harassment and verbal abuse, there were discernible differences in the *form* of harassment that men and women face. Women were more often the victims of personal accusations, including degrading talk directed against family members as well as rumours about their person. A large part of this harassment took place online. In the general population, we can also see that experiencing different types of violence in childhood has a gendered impact on attitudes to gender equality. This emphasizes the continuum of violence whereby even childhood experiences of violence can have long-lasting political effects.

SPIRALS OF VIOLENCE AND GENDER INEQUALITY

Political participation of different kinds has been associated with violence and intimidation throughout Myanmar's modern history. During the decades of military rule preceding the brief liberalization phase in focus here, demonstrating against the regime or participating in the few elections that were held could lead to violent repression or imprisonment. People who decided to become politically active knew they were risking their lives (Croissant and Kamerling 2013). Members of the opposition, including the high-profile leader of the National League for Democracy (NLD), Aung San Sui Kyi, were imprisoned for years. In addition, there have been persistent ethnic conflicts and civil war in different areas of the ethnically diverse country. Ethnic armed forces have battled the Tatmadaw in order not to give up what they consider their lands (Nilsen 2013; Kipgen 2015; Cheesman and Farrelly 2016). State-sponsored violence carried out by the Tatmadaw against ethnic minority groups has included widespread sexual violence against women. It is still unclear exactly how widespread, but reports suggest that the over 100 documented cases only constitute a small fraction of actual cases and a report by the Women's League of Burma described gang rape by the Tatmadaw as an institutionalized counter-insurgency strategy (WLB 2014).

Against this background, it is understandable that the political liberalization that the military set into motion in the early 2000s was initially met with scepticism. As the military proceeded with their roadmap and drafted a constitution, installed a civilian government through the 2010 elections, and finally conceded power to the NLD in the elections of 2015, scepticism was increasingly replaced with cautious hope that the country's conflicts might finally be peacefully resolved in elections and by a civilian government (Bünte 2016; Stokke and Aung 2020).

In the aftermath of turnover, the elections of 2015 were widely lauded as relatively free and fair, and for their low levels of violence. Expectations for the new government ran high, both domestically and internationally. Many failed to see that the military still had a firm grip on power, and that the constitution legitimized a persistent masculinization of politics. For instance, the Tatmadaw could appoint 25 per cent of the legislature, and a military background was required for certain military positions. Male dominance within the military institution perpetuated militarized masculinity as a feature of Myanmar politics. This ideal was also manifest in the low number of female representatives from the military-backed Union Solidarity and Development Party (USDP) (Bardall and Bjarnegård 2021; Khin Khin Mra 2021; Khin Khin Mra and Livingstone 2023). In this context, the new NLD government failed to meet the high expectations of the international community. The Rohingya crisis in 2017 changed many international observers' view of the NLD and Aung San Suu Kyi (Bjarnegård 2020; Décobert and Wells 2020), but the government still had considerable domestic support. The NLD won another landslide victory in 2020, but any hopes of democratic progress were dashed as the military took over in a coup d'état in 2021.

At the time, international observers as well as domestic activists saw the general elections in 2015 as a political turning point for Myanmar. Ahead of the elections, there was a great degree of apprehension. Observers feared that all dimensions of electoral integrity would be violated and that violence would be rampant (Nilsen and Tonnesson 2013). Afterwards, most election-observation reports instead expressed relief and even surprise. The reports were largely positive, claiming not only that the military-affiliated USDP accepted their loss but that the election process itself had also been relatively smooth and free from electoral malpractice and violence (e.g. The Carter Center 2016; ANFREL 2015; GEOM 2015). The coup that came a few months after the 2020 general elections has raised questions about how much of a breaking point with the past the elections of 2015 actually constituted (Bardall and Bjarnegård 2021). How misguided, and possibly naïve, were the positive assessments of 2015 election? One clear indication that assessments were overblown was the extent of ongoing militarization, which soon breached its constraints.

The assessment of political violence is generally based on media reports, or, in the case of elections, on the official reports of election-observation missions. These types of reports are more likely to observe physical forms of violence that take place in the public sphere than less visible forms of violence (Bjarnegård 2018). When elections are introduced in countries with a recent experience of repressive authoritarianism, such as Myanmar, democratic institutions are new and often weak, and candidates as well as voters are unaccustomed to the electoral game and its rules. It is not uncommon that undemocratic forms of sticks and carrots, such as harassment and intimidation, but also the use of state resources and co-optation of civil society, are used to affect the outcome of an election (Collier 2010; Norris 2013). To capture such experiences, however, we need to directly ask the targets of violence about their personal experiences. Threats or slander delivered directly to an individual will only become publicly known if that individual chooses to report it. In a context scarred by coercion and violence, there may not be a clear distinction between criticism as a natural part of a democratic election campaign and forms of personal intimidation (Krook 2020).

Intimidation and harassment during an election campaign imply that someone has tried to have an impact on the election by illegitimate means and in a manner that simultaneously violates electoral integrity and personal integrity. One way of doing this is to use physical violence, but threats and degrading talk can achieve similar results (Bjarnegård 2018). Such psychological forms of election violence have also gained in importance as social media have increasingly become an important platform for campaign and political debate—as well as for hate speech and intimidation (Bardall 2017). In a country like Myanmar, where political actors have experienced violent repression and have come to see fear for their life as a likely consequence of political engagement, a harsh political climate may be expected, and slander may not be seen as worth reporting. It is thus possible that violations of electoral integrity remain out of view for the majority of people assessing the quality of elections.

This chapter revisits this period of political liberalization, focusing on the 2015 election as a landmark event of the period. To assess whether the elections really were the peaceful break with the violent past that they were sometimes described as being, we need to move beyond external observers' assessments and physical and public acts of violence. We base our analysis on first-hand experiences of individuals who were politically active at different levels of Myanmar politics and we take a range of intimidating experiences and actions into account, as these exist on a continuum of violence (Bjarnegård 2023). In particular, this chapter investigates the extent to which politically active individuals experienced violence, intimidation, and harassment related to the election, and if there were gendered dimensions to these experiences. Violence can be gendered in different ways, and a broader take on violations of electoral integrity is more likely to unveil incidents targeting women (e.g. Bardall 2011; Bjarnegård 2023). In our analysis, we revisit the question of prevalence of violence in the 2015 election, as well as the extent to which male and female politicians experience different forms (Bardall, Bjarnegård, and Piscopo 2020).

Taking a step back, we also consider the broader societal context in which politicians in Myanmar operated at the time. As raised in Chapter One, gender differentiated experiences of political violence come from somewhere and are shaped by existing attitudes and values among citizens, pertaining both to the use of violence and to gender.

A body of research has connected sexist attitudes to a propensity for violence, both at the societal level (Caprioli 2000; Caprioli and Boyer 2001; Hudson et al. 2009; Melander 2005a, 2005b) and the personal level (Tessler and Warriner 1997; Tessler, Nachtwey, and Grant 1999; Bjarnegård, Brounéus, and Melander 2019; Bjarnegård and Melander 2017). A study of attitudes in countries around the Pacific Ocean demonstrated that individuals with more gender-equal attitudes also exhibited higher levels of tolerance for other nationalities and religious groups. This was true for both men and women (Bjarnegård and Melander 2017). Studies carried out in nearby Thailand have also demonstrated that male political activists who took to arms in otherwise peaceful demonstrations were more likely to subscribe to patriarchal values (Bjarnegård, Brounéus, and Melander 2017) and to have experienced violence in childhood (Bjarnegård, Brounéus, and Melander 2019). Another study from the conflict-ridden deep south of Thailand shows that young men with more patriarchal values are more likely to volunteer for paramilitary groups than are men with a more egalitarian outlook (Bjarnegård et al. 2022).

Taken together, these findings suggest a vicious circle of gender inequality and violence, with intergenerational effects. Childhood experiences of family violence—corporal punishment or violence against women in the household—increase the risk of participating in violence as an adult. Moreover, childhood experiences of violence, particularly seeing one's mother being beaten, also seem to instil gender-unequal values that remain into adulthood (Whitfield et al. 2003).

Public opinion surveys carried out in Myanmar in 2014 and 2015, during the more liberal period between phases of military rule, revealed attitudes to gender roles that were largely conservative and traditional. Most people across all age groups believed that men were more capable leaders in business as well as in politics and that it is more important for boys than girls to receive a university education, and most respondents expressed a preference for sons (Htun and Jensenius 2020). As Chapter Four reports, our survey a few years later, in 2019, largely replicated these findings. Earlier and coincident studies have also concluded that family violence is pervasive in Myanmar (Kyu and Kanai 2005; Larsen, Win Thuzar Aye, and Bjertness 2021). A survey from 2015 demonstrated that intimate partner violence is not just common, but also that many respondents, including women themselves, see it as justified (Larsen, Win Thuzar Aye, and Bjertness 2021). Other studies have found that the prevalence of corporal punishment of children is high, both as a family practice and in the education system (Pa Pa Thwin, May Than Nwe, and Mon Mon Aye 2021; Nyan Linn, Kallawicha, and Chuemchit 2022). Khin Khin Mra and Livingstone (2023) provide a feminist institutionalist analysis of how informal gendered norms influenced the implementation of new, seemingly more equal, formal democratic institutions, perpetuating unequal power dynamics and societal acceptance of domestic violence. Even during the ten-year long transition period, women's groups met strong resistance as they advocated for a Prevention of Violence Against Women (PoVAW) law (Aye Thiri Kyaw 2023)

As we know, our survey mirrors many of these findings. For instance, a majority of our survey respondents in Myanmar also reported being beaten as children (see Figure 4.2). However, our survey makes it possible to go a step further and to bring experiences of violence and attitudes to women in politics together in the same analysis. In order to better understand patterns of gendered violence in politics in Myanmar, we need to situate political violence in a broader context of patriarchal values and violent norms in the population at large. In this chapter we will take a closer look at items in our survey pertaining to experiences of violence to investigate how they may have affected the political climate in which male and female politicians operated.

The analysis below thus reassesses the degree of violations of electoral integrity in the 2015 election, using more gender-sensitive measurements than election-observation missions were able to do: asking political actors directly, and including a broader definition of violence. The analysis also seeks to discern potential gender differences in the forms of violence that men and women experience. Some research has suggested that men experience more physical violence and women, more psychological violence (Bardall 2011). Research in different contexts has demonstrated that the violence women experience, particularly online, is more likely to have sexual connotations than the rumours and threats that men receive (Bjarnegård 2023; Bjarnegård, Håkansson, and Zetterberg 2020). Regardless of the frequency and form of violence, however, it may have gendered impacts. Men and women may interpret the violence they encounter differently, whether they have experienced it directly or as a member of the community

(Bardall, Bjarnegård, and Piscopo 2020). Finally, we return to the survey data to investigate how the experience of violence in childhood may affect political attitudes in adulthood, contributing to a spiralling legacy of violence linking war and peace, as well as the private and political spheres.

DESIGN AND METHODS

The analyses in this chapter build on the research carried out in the collaborative project funded by the International Development Research Center (IDRC), and in close collaboration with Enlightened Myanmar Research Foundation (EMReF). The analysis, as well as some of the initial writing of a first draft, were carried out jointly by a local researcher in Myanmar and me. The current circumstances made it impossible for my co-author to complete the work on the chapter, and I am unable to properly acknowledge the contributions they made. I wish to make it clear that this chapter builds on data collection and an understanding of that data that would never have been possible without close collaboration with local researchers. In the event that the situation in Myanmar changes, I hope there will be a way for me to revise the authorship of this chapter and make the contributions and name of my coauthor public.

The focus of this chapter is gendered violence in different shapes and forms. This was not an initial focus of the data-collection efforts of the project at large, but it was an aspect that came up in interviews and on which we touched in the survey. The present situation in Myanmar further confirms the need to understand the culture of political violence in the country. We have taken the data that we have from various facets of the research effort to shed light on the phenomenon of violence from a number of different aspects. This means that this chapter combines data from different groups of respondents: 72 interviews with gatekeepers and national candidates from nine political parties, 99 focus group discussions (FGDs) and 98 semi-structured interviews with local-level politicians, and a survey with 2,889 citizens.[2]

Our analysis of the interviews with both national- and local-level politicians relies heavily on what was question number 12 in both instances: *"Did you face any intimidation or harassment during your campaign?"* The focus-group guide had no specific questions about violence, but in some cases the issue arose, anyway. In the survey data, we focus on linking questions about experiences of violence to political attitudes. This means a focus on question 601, which asked respondents to assess how often they were beaten at home or saw their mother being beaten before the age of 18.

POLITICIANS' OWN EXPERIENCES OF ELECTION VIOLENCE

We start by assessing the first-hand experiences of national and local candidates as they competed in the 2015 election. The majority of our national candidate interviewees reported experiencing some form of intimidation during their election campaign. They also said that verbal or online harassment quite frequently included ethnic or religious aspects. The situation seemed calmer at the local level, where only around one quarter of the elected local leaders interviewed for this study reported experiencing intimidation, harassment, or election fraud as part of their election process. Further, none of our local interviewees reported violent threats or physical violence. Therefore, it seems that local elected leaders were less likely than parliamentary candidates to face harassment or intimidation as part of their election campaign, and when this did occur it was less likely to be in the form of threats of or actual physical violence.

We did not discern any clear gender differences in the *extent* of harassment and verbal abuse at the national level. The gender differences at the local level, however, were more visible. Here, around 30 per cent of the female interviewees said that they had faced harassment or intimidation during their campaign, compared to around 20 per cent of the male interviewees. This is despite the fact that our sample of interviewees under-represented women in the most powerful and prestigious positions, such as among ward or village tract administrators. Thus, there are clearer gender differences in the extent of violence at the local level than at the national level, though the overall incidence of harassment is lower among local-level candidates.

One possible interpretation is that women at the national level enter a set game of politics, where electoral integrity is frequently violated. These violations take place regardless of the gender of the candidate. At the local community level, however, women are more likely to be targeted as women. Traditional gender norms still permeate local communities and although they are less violent, they are also less accepting of women.

NORMALIZATION OF VIOLENCE

The legacy of violence is evident when politicians talk about their experiences. Politicians in contemporary Myanmar have lived in a conflict-prone political environment for a long time. They have become accustomed to expecting conflict, hardship or even torture and imprisonment when they engage politically. Political activity has put not only themselves, but also their family members, at risk. The majority of candidates, with the potential exception of the very young, thus have a very violent point of reference when they evaluate their experiences in the 2015 election. One male Ta'ang National Party (TNP) national candidate recounts his experience of campaigning in areas the Kachin Independence Army (KIA) controlled before the elections in 2010. At this time, KIA members pointed their guns at him, but he was able to persuade them to allow him to campaign in their area. Elsewhere, in what he referred to as "USDP-controlled areas", it was instead the local militia that pointed their guns at him and refused to allow him to campaign in their area. However, he did not face such issues in 2015.[3]

A male Shan Nationalities League for Democracy (SNLD) candidate at the national level said that he is used to having inspectors watching and tracing every step, always passing by his house, but that this was more common earlier than in the 2015 election.[4] Many candidates, particularly from NLD, simply, and perhaps understandably, focused on the improvement they have seen in their ability to participate in politics and recounted a mainly positive and violence-free story.[5] While these narratives may capture a real diminution in physical forms of political violence, they also demonstrate that Myanmar politicians have normalized attacks and abuse, and that it is difficult to compare these narratives with those from politicians in other contexts. However, analyses carried out in other conflict-affected contexts, such as post-conflict Sri Lanka, have shown similar patterns of normalization of violence as a way of politics (Bjarnegård, Håkansson, and Zetterberg 2020).

Even though the election of 2015 showed improvement compared to 2010, there were still incidents of physical violence and threats of physical violence. One Lisu National Development Party (LNDP) gatekeeper received a death threat after having organized events that criticized KIA and after having suggested that a Lisu Social Service Society be established.[6] A female NLD candidate recounted how the Association for the Protection of Race and Religion, better known as *Ma Ba Tha*, came to her rallies armed with knives. Some people were wounded, and in other places she had to cancel public meetings. Some of her campaign workers were also threatened because they were working for her, and the *Ma Ba Tha* were against her campaign.[7]

Certain threats are more subtle. One male village tract administrator was told, "You can play or do what you want now, but be careful. Who knows what will happen to you when you are no longer in that position".[8] While such threats are not as direct, they nevertheless instil a sense of fear into the electoral game.

GENDERED FORMS OF VIOLENCE

There seem to be differences in the *type* of harassment that men and women face. Women are more often the victims of personal accusations, including degrading talk directed against family members as well as rumours about their person. In Kachin State Democracy Party (KSDP), for instance, male candidates reported that it was their party that was being criticized, while their only female candidate was personally attacked and accused of land-grabbing by other Kachin parties.[9] One 29-year-old female TNP candidate experienced belittling talk, hearing rumours saying that she was no more than a child and that one cannot trust a child.[10] Another female member of parliament (MP) experienced degrading talk related to her daughter's marriage to a man from a different ethnic group. She said:

> Some people attack me because my daughter has married a Burmese. They ask me why I did not stop my daughter's marriage. When someone is not satisfied with my actions in parliament, they post these things on social media. So, I never post pictures of my children and grandchildren on social media.[11]

Among local community leaders, harassment of female candidates was not just more common than harassment of men, it was also more directly and outspokenly motivated by their gender. For example, a female village tract administrator said, "I was insulted by some people because they prefer to have a male ward administrator. Therefore, there were big problems during the election".[12] Another female village tract administrator did not seem to take the gossip very seriously, but nevertheless recognized its gendered forms, as she said, "I did not really face any harassment except from some gossip making fun of me, such as, 'a little woman is going to be our village tract administrator, why not a man?'"[13]

This type of harassment does not only come from men. Traditional gender norms are shared by men and women alike, and women also attack the personal qualifications of other women. One of the local women said, "Sometimes I faced some gossip, especially from some woman. The gossip was about my education level and what I can do for the community. But I did not care much and I neglected whatever they said".[14] Even if such gendered slander is expected and not taken seriously, it may have gendered consequences (see discussion on gendered impacts in Bardall, Bjarnegård, and Piscopo 2020). For instance, a female local politician said that she had no intention of trying to become a parliamentarian because "if I become an MP, I would be insulted as a 'fucking woman' by the community".[15]

Around 50 per cent of women compared to 35 per cent of men said that their participation in community life had resulted in difficulties or challenges in their home life. Some interviewees specifically described facing opposition from or arguing with family members over this issue. The nature of opposition by family members seems to be shaped by the gendered roles that men and women are expected to perform in the family. The criticism a few men described was from their wives, who claimed that their community leadership activities came at the expense of their business or other income-generating activities.[16] The women who had experienced criticism from their families were instead criticized because political activities took time from housework and childcare.[17] No female interviewees mentioned family members' objecting to their neglecting business/income-generating activities, and no male interviewees mentioned being criticized by family members for neglecting housework or childcare. In this case, a gendered analysis of what is *not* mentioned as opposition to political activity is as revealing as what is mentioned. These findings are in themselves not indications of violence, but they indicate an increased risk of intimate-partner violence for women as a result of their political activity. Five women and only one man stated the importance of receiving support from family members for being able to take on their role.[18]

Notably, quite a few candidates also said they did not experience any harassment. To be well-known and respected helped in certain cases. Two candidates who were long-time teachers said that with so many former and current students in the area, and with the respect they had gained, they were protected from violence, intimidation or harassment.[19]

ONLINE HARASSMENT

It is, by now, an almost universal experience that rumours spread more quickly than they used to. There are few places in which the change has been as rapid as in Myanmar, and much of the change happened between the elections of 2010 and 2015. As Table 5.1 illustrates, as late as 2011, less than 1 per cent of Myanmar's population were using the internet; by 2015, this level had risen to more than 20 per cent (WDI 2021).

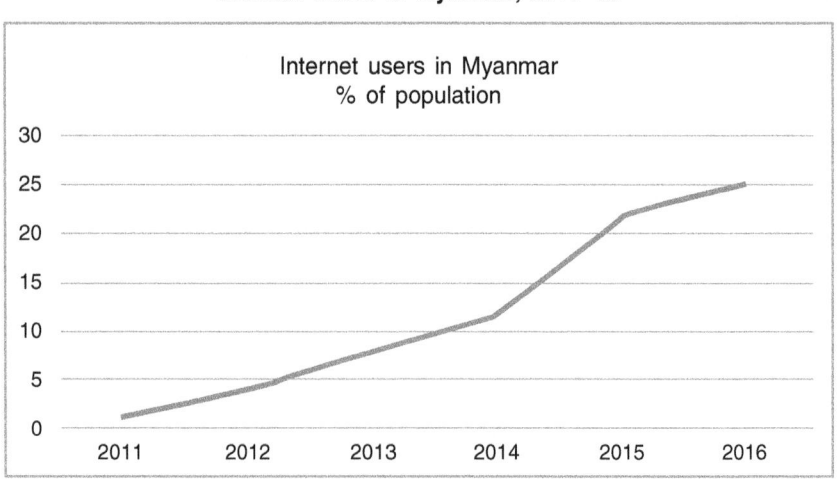

TABLE 5.1
Internet Users in Myanmar, 2011–16

Source: World Development Indicators, the World Bank.

A lot of harassment seems to have moved online in the 2015 elections, particularly at the national level. This could potentially be part of the reason for why we find a difference in harassment between national and local levels—a substantial share of local interviewees was presumably in areas with more limited internet access. Online harassment included spreading fake photos as well as accusations and attacks on Facebook. Mobile phones and texting services were also used to spread rumours.[20] One female candidate from NLD said she was harassed on Facebook and someone produced a fake news article defaming her in order to convince people to vote for someone else.[21] A male candidate for SNLD was accused online of meddling with foreigners, due to his background working with NGOs.[22] One MP explained that people said that he is a drinker and had been a prisoner. As he described,

> [T]here are more attacks after 2015 when social media has become popular. Before that, there were fewer attacks on social media. Some people who use fake accounts on Facebook attack whatever I do.[23]

Sometimes, however, online violence does not stay online. One NLD female candidate recounts that people used social media to tell the community that she was arrogant and not liked by anyone in her neighbourhood.[24] Those social media attacks were followed by physical attacks on her property: the steel gate to her house was destroyed and a glass wall in her office was smashed.[25]

Ethnic intolerance was clearly present online as well. One SNLD gatekeeper was called a "Shan Racist" on Facebook.[26] A (Buddhist) USDP male candidate said that rumours were spread on Facebook about his having a Muslim name.[27] He interpreted it as an attempt to make people misunderstand his ethnicity. Both men and women experienced online threats, but it seems somewhat more common that women reported online intimidation. It is important to remember that the internet is not a cause of intimidation, but a vehicle for transporting and spreading rumours and insults. Areas without internet are of course not free of slander, although it cannot take place online. As one respondent noted, "I didn't face harassment on social media at that time because we do not have access much to social media in my constituency, but I was insulted by another party after I had been elected. USDP was not happy with my being elected, they objected to me".[28]

EXPERIENCES OF FAMILY VIOLENCE

The survey allows us to study the broader society in which the experiences of individual politicians were embedded. Although the survey is not nationwide, it gives us a much better view of how normalized violence is in the family and how this might impact the environment in which politicians were campaigning. It also allows us to address broader manifestations of political violence, including against voters. The survey was carried out among representative samples of the population in the following states and regions: Mon, southern Shan, Mandalay, and Ayeyarwady. This mix gives us reasonable variation in geography, economic development, and culture.[29]

When it comes to experiences of political violence, only about 5 per cent of our respondents thought that voters had been threatened with violence at the polls in the 2015 election. The relationships we are looking for when it comes to the impact of violence are thus slightly more complex and indirect. We turn to look at the experience of family violence and how this is connected to politics. Looking at attitudes to and experiences of violence in the family, we see a picture in which violence is, in many ways, an everyday experience. A majority of both men and women were beaten at home as children. Around a fifth of our respondents also saw their mother being beaten when they were themselves children. The experience of growing up with violence contributes to a normalization of violence as a way of solving conflicts.

How do these experiences of violence affect individuals as political beings? Can we discern any linkages between experiences of violence in the private sphere and the political role of these citizens? And how are those linkages gendered?

POLITICAL AND GENDERED EFFECTS OF FAMILY VIOLENCE

In Myanmar, more boys than girls seem to be the victims of family violence, indicating that violence is, in itself, a gendered phenomenon. Men are more likely to have been beaten as children, indicating that corporal punishment was used for chastising boys even more than girls. A full 74 per cent of men were beaten at home before the age of 18; this number was significantly lower for female respondents (59 per cent) (see Figure 4.2). This means that although both men and women are likely to have grown up in households where violence took place, boys were more likely to be its targets. Boys were also more likely to be beaten at school and to participate in fights with other young children.

Experiences of physical violence as children are not just gendered in themselves, they also have differential gendered impact in adulthood. Boys and girls internalize violent experiences in different ways. Our survey demonstrates that this is also true in Myanmar. Women who were beaten as children are less likely to see themselves being able to participate in politics as adults. The experience of being beaten as a child seems to lower the political self-confidence of women, more so than for men (see Figure 4.5). The fact that violence against boys and men is more common than for women, both in homes and in public spheres such as schools, contributes to a visible linking of being a boy and being subject to violence. Whereas the experience of violence in the home does not suppress boys' political ambition, it does so for women—a visible and long-lasting psychological effect of physical violence. However, the experience of violence in childhood rather seems to increase women's expressed support for their own daughters' engaging in politics (see Figure 4.7). These results are not conclusive, but they suggest that the lived injustice of being a victim of violence can also be turned to empowerment.

Violence is a societal problem with both direct and indirect effects. Seeing one's mother being beaten is an indirect childhood experience of violence that affects men well into their adulthood. Our survey data demonstrate that men who saw their mothers being beaten are less likely to support gender equality as adults (see Figure 4.4), and they tend to express lower support for women's participation in politics (see Figure 4.6). This is perhaps not strange, given that the violence they are exposed to is clearly gender-based and likely to send strong signals about the lower value of women as well as about the power relations between the sexes. This experience has a marked effect on men, but no similar effect on women's views of gender equality (see Figure 4.4) or women's political participation (see Figure 4.6). This may be because the process of "othering" that is inherent in the act of causing physical harm to another person is emphasized more strongly when a signal is sent to young boys about the "otherness" of women. Young girls are more likely to identify with, rather than distance themselves from, the woman being beaten. Rather, they are likely to internalize the sense of lower value that acts of violence signal, doubting their own value and capabilities. This is line with findings in the research field on intergenerational violence. Whereas boys who are exposed to violence in their families are more likely to grow up to become perpetrators of violence themselves, girls who are exposed to violence in childhood are overrepresented among victims of violence as adults (Whitfield et al. 2003).

The personal is political, in Myanmar as elsewhere. Experiences of violence in childhood shape the values and behaviour of future citizens and voters. While democratic institutions can be put in place rather quickly, it takes a long time to nurture the values that underpin and protect those institutions. Where violence is taught as a means to resolve conflict in the family, it will ultimately weaken political procedures and undermine the peaceful resolution of conflict that is democracy. Because legacies of violence are gender-differentiated, men who were exposed to violence in their childhood family are both less likely to support women's political participation and more likely to become perpetrators of violence themselves. This relationship may also exist at a more aggregate level. Hudson et al. (2009) argue that the manner in which women are treated and protected in a state is a strong predictor for violent conflict and disregard of international treaties. While the elections of 2015 in Myanmar demonstrated that short-term institutional changes could lead to less electoral violence, they also suggested that the threat of violence was never far from the minds of candidates.

CONCLUDING DISCUSSION

The costs of political participation in Myanmar are potentially extremely high, and the military takeover in early 2021 raised the stakes even further. Being politically active is closely associated with personal risk, and candidates going into politics expected harassment, even during the period of relative political liberalization. In 2015, systematic repression of opposition politicians was no longer so common as it had been in the previous election, but some degree of harassment of candidates was largely normalized and costs of political participation were still seen as high for the individual, their community, and society at large. The violent legacy of politics in Myanmar meant that a new norm for peaceful campaigning had not been institutionalized. Given the low expectations of politicians, violent incidents were likely to be underreported and it is thus difficult to compare Myanmar with other contexts. It is important to remember that part of the reason why the 2015 election was lauded was precisely because everyone's expectations were so low, and apprehension, so high.

The expansion of internet usage has changed the way that public figures, including politicians, can be reached—and harassed. This is true in Myanmar as elsewhere, but in Myanmar, the internet and elections appeared at about the same time, and both were fairly new phenomena in 2015. Online harassment that takes place on social media platforms also has the implication of being visible to a large number of people. Whereas other forms of violence may primarily involve the perpetrator and the victim, harassment on social media distorts publicly available political information and causes wide-reaching harm due to its velocity and spread.

Online platforms are vehicles for the spread of the views and values of citizens, just like political institutions are likely to mirror the attitudes and priorities of the majority of the population. As Htun and Jensenius (2020, p. 478) said of Myanmar in an article published just before the military coup, "As long as public opinion on women and gender remains conservative, traditional, and authoritarian, there is likely to be support for nationalism and skepticism of moves toward gender equality."

Public opinion, in turn, relies on the values of the population, many of which are established already in childhood. While there is a need for continued support for the reintroduction of democracy and elections, there is a simultaneous need to support long-term value change, starting with addressing a culture of violence in families, schools, and communities. Taken together, this chapter and other research in the field point in the same direction: prevention of political violence does not only happen in the political sphere, but also in the private sphere. Reducing family violence and socializing girls and boys into awareness of gender equality are good ways of preventing political violence in the long run.

The military coup implies a reinforcement of the vicious circle of violence as intrinsic to politics in Myanmar. A better understanding of how persistent violent legacies were in the last transition offers a useful warning for the next transition (hopefully) to come. While levels of physical violence may diminish quite quickly, it will likely be hard to shake expectations of risk among potential candidates, or to achieve a norm of peaceful campaign engagement.

NOTES

1. As explained below, this chapter reflects contributions from a local researcher in Myanmar who cannot be named under present circumstances.
2. For more information about data collection, see Chapter One. For specific information on data-collection strategies pertaining to the survey, see Chapter Four.
3. Interview with HM-MMP05.
4. Interview with HM-MGK01.
5. For example, interview with SS-GKTECM02.
6. Interview with LR-GKCECM05.
7. Interview with LR-FMP02.
8. Interview with LR14.
9. Interviews with LR-FMP07, LR-MMP10, and LR-MMP11.
10. Interview with HM-FMP14.
11. Interview with SS-FMP01.
12. Interview with SS29.
13. Interview with LR29.
14. Interview with LR09.
15. Interview with HM14. N.b. "fucking" here is used as a general expletive, rather than implying any particular sexual promiscuity/behaviour.
16. Interviews with HM04, HM10, LR03, and SS12.
17. Interviews with SS31 and SS32.
18. Interviews with HM02, HM12, LR09, LR10, LR21, and LR29.
19. Interviews with LR-MMP01, and LR-MMP04.
20. Interviews with HM-MMP04, HM-MMP10, HM-FMP15, LR-FMP01, LR-FMP02, LR-FMP03, HM-FMP11, LR-GKCECM05, SS-GKCECM04, SS-MMP04, and SS-MMP08.
21. Interview with LR-FMP03.
22. Interview with HM-MMP04.
23. Interview with SS-MMP04.
24. Interview with LR-FMP02.
25. Interview with LR-FMP02.

26. Interview with HM-MGK05.
27. Interview with SS-MMP08.
28. Interview with LR-MMP06.
29. For more information, see Chapter Four.

REFERENCES

Asian Network for Free Elections (ANFREL). 2015. "Myanmar 2015 General Election: Assessment Mission Analysis". 1–12 September 2015. https://anfrel.org/wp-content/uploads/2016/06/ANFREL-Assessment-Mission-Report-Myanmar.pdf.

Aye Thiri Kyaw. 2023. "Women's Mobilization, Activism and Policy-Making in Myanmar's Transition". In *Waves of Upheaval in Myanmar: Gendered Transformations and Political Transitions*, edited by Jenny Hedström and Elisabeth Olivius. Copenhagen, Denmark: NIAS Press.

Bardall, Gabrielle. 2011. "Breaking the Mold: Understanding Gender and Electoral Violence". Washington, D.C.: International Foundation for Electoral Systems (IFES).

———. 2017. "The Role of Information and Communication Technologies in Facilitating and Resisting Gendered Forms of Political Violence". In *Gender, Technology and Violence*, edited by Marie Segrave and Laura Vitis, pp. 100–17. Routledge. https://doi.org/10.4324/9781315441160-7.

Bardall, Gabrielle, and Elin Bjarnegård. 2021. "The Exclusion of Women in Myanmar Politics Helped Fuel the Military Coup". *The Conversation*, 21 February 2021. http://theconversation.com/the-exclusion-of-women-in-myanmar-politics-helped-fuel-the-military-coup-154701.

Bardall, Gabrielle, Elin Bjarnegård, and Jennifer M. Piscopo. 2020. "How is Political Violence Gendered? Disentangling Motives, Forms, and Impacts". *Political Studies* 68, no. 4: 916–35. https://doi.org/10.1177/0032321719881812.

Bjarnegård, Elin. 2018. "Making Gender Visible in Election Violence: Strategies for Data Collection". *Politics & Gender* 14, no. 4: 690–95. https://doi.org/10.1017/S1743923X18000624.

———. 2020. "Introduction: Development Challenges in Myanmar: Political Development and Politics of Development Intertwined". *The European Journal of Development Research* 32, no. 2: 255–73. https://doi.org/10.1057/s41287-020-00263-2.

———. 2023. "The Continuum of Election Violence: Gendered Candidate Experiences in the Maldives". *International Political Science Review* 44, no. 1: 107–21.

Bjarnegård, Elin, Karen Brounéus, and Erik Melander. 2017. "Honor and Political Violence: Micro-Level Findings from a Survey in Thailand". *Journal of Peace Research* 54, no. 6: 748–61. https://doi.org/10.1177/0022343317711241.

———. 2019. "Violent Boyhoods, Masculine Honor Ideology, and Political Violence: Survey Findings From Thailand". *Journal of Interpersonal Violence* (March). https://doi.org/10.1177/0886260519832926.

Bjarnegård, Elin, Anders Engvall, Srisompob Jitpiromsri, and Erik Melander. 2022. "Armed Violence and Patriarchal Values: A Survey of Young Men in Thailand and Their Military Experiences". *American Political Science Review* (August). https://doi.org/10.1017/S0003055422000594.

Bjarnegård, Elin, Sandra Håkansson, and Pär Zetterberg. 2020. "Gender and Violence against Political Candidates: Lessons from Sri Lanka". *Politics & Gender*. https://doi.org/10.1017/S1743923X20000471.

Bjarnegård, Elin, and Erik Melander. 2017. "Pacific Men: How the Feminist Gap Explains Hostility". *The Pacific Review* 30, no. 4: 478–93. https://doi.org/10.1080/09512748.2016.1264456.

Bünte, Marco. 2016. "Myanmar's Protracted Transition". *Asian Survey* 56, no. 2: 369–91. https://doi.org/10.1525/as.2016.56.2.369.

Caprioli, Mary. 2000. "Gendered Conflict". *Journal of Peace Research* 37, no. 1: 51–68. https://doi.org/10.1177/0022343300037001003.

Caprioli, Mary, and Mark A. Boyer. 2001. "Gender, Violence, and International Crisis". *Journal of Conflict Resolution* 45, no. 4: 503–18. https://doi.org/10.1177/0022002701045004005.

Carter Center, The. 2016. "Observing Myanmar's 2015 General Elections: Final Report". Atlanta, Georgia, US: The Carter Center. https://www.cartercenter.org/resources/pdfs/news/peace_publications/election_reports/myanmar-2015-final.pdf.

Cheesman, Nick, and Nicholas Farrelly. 2016. *Conflict in Myanmar: War, Politics, Religion*. Singapore: ISEAS – Yusof Ishak Institute.

Cockburn, Cynthia. 2004. "The Continuum of Violence: A Gender Perspective on War and Peace". June 2004. https://doi.org/10.1525/california/9780520230729.003.0002.

Collier, Paul. 2010. *Wars, Guns and Votes: Democracy in Dangerous Places*. New York: Harper Collins.

Croissant, Aurel, and Jil Kamerling. 2013. "Why Do Military Regimes Institutionalize? Constitution-Making and Elections as Political Survival Strategy in Myanmar". *Asian Journal of Political Science* 21, no. 2: 105–25. https://doi.org/10.1080/02185377.2013.823797.

Décobert, Anne, and Tamas Wells. 2020. "Interpretive Complexity and Crisis: The History of International Aid to Myanmar". *The European Journal of Development Research* 32, no. 2: 294–315. https://doi.org/10.1057/s41287-019-00238-y.

Gender Election Observation Missions (GEOM). 2015. "The Myanmar Elections 2015: A Historic Opportunity for Women Voters to Build Momentum for

Inclusive Governance". http://www.genderconcerns.org/pdfs/GEOM%20MM%20English.pdf.
Htun, Mala, and Francesca R. Jensenius. 2020. "Political Change, Women's Rights, and Public Opinion on Gender Equality in Myanmar". *The European Journal of Development Research* 32, no. 2: 457–81. https://doi.org/10.1057/s41287-020-00266-z.
Hudson, Valerie M., Mary Caprioli, Bonnie Ballif-Spanvill, Rose McDermott, and Chad F. Emmett. 2009. "The Heart of the Matter: The Security of Women and the Security of States". *International Security* 33, no. 3: 7–45. https://doi.org/10.1162/isec.2009.33.3.7.
Khin Khin Mra. 2021. "Women Fight the Dual Evils of Dictatorship and Patriarchal Norms in Myanmar". *New Mandala* (blog). https://www.newmandala.org/women-in-the-fight-against-the-dual-evils-of-dictatorship-and-patriarchal-norms-in-myanmar/.
Khin Khin Mra, and Deborah Livingstone. 2023. "When Heads of the Household Become Heads of the Village: Gender and Institutional Change in Local Governance Settings in Myanmar". In *Waves of Upheaval in Myanmar: Gendered Transformations and Political Transitions*, edited by Jenny Hedström and Elisabeth Olivius. Copenhagen, Denmark: NIAS Press.
Kipgen, Nehginpao. 2015. "Ethnic Nationalities and the Peace Process in Myanmar". *Social Research* 82, no. 2: 28.
Krook, Mona Lena. 2020. *Violence Against Women in Politics*. 1st ed. New York: Oxford University Press.
Kyu, Nilar, and Atsuko Kanai. 2005. "Prevalence, Antecedent Causes and Consequences of Domestic Violence in Myanmar". *Asian Journal of Social Psychology* 8, no. 3: 244–71. https://doi.org/10.1111/j.1467-839X.2005.00170.x.
Larsen, Lise Wessel, Win Thuzar Aye, and Espen Bjertness. 2021. "Prevalence of Intimate Partner Violence and Association with Wealth in Myanmar". *Journal of Family Violence* 36, no. 4: 417–28. https://doi.org/10.1007/s10896-020-00190-0.
Melander, Erik. 2005a. "Political Gender Equality and State Human Rights Abuse". *Journal of Peace Research* 42, no. 2: 149–66. https://doi.org/10.1177/0022343305050688.
———. 2005b. "Gender Equality and Intrastate Armed Conflict". *International Studies Quarterly* 49, no. 4: 695–714. https://doi.org/10.1111/j.1468-2478.2005.00384.x.
Nilsen, Marte. 2013. "Will Democracy Bring Peace to Myanmar?" *International Area Studies Review* 16, no. 2: 115–41. https://doi.org/10.1177/2233865913492961.
Nilsen, Marte, and Stein Tonnesson. 2013. "Political Parties and Peacebuilding in Myanmar". *PRIO Policy Brief* 5. Oslo, Norway: Peace Research Institute Oslo (PRIO). https://www.prio.org/Publications/Publication/?x=5853.

Norris, Pippa. 2013. "The New Research Agenda Studying Electoral Integrity". *Electoral Studies*, Special Symposium: The New Research Agenda on Electoral Integrity 32, no. 4: 563–75. https://doi.org/10.1016/j.electstud.2013.07.015.

Nyan Linn, Kraiwuth Kallawicha, and Montakarn Chuemchit. 2022. "The Use of Corporal Punishment against Children in Myanmar: An Analysis of Data from the 2015-2016 Myanmar Demographic and Health Survey". *Child Abuse & Neglect* 131 (September). https://doi.org/10.1016/j.chiabu.2022.105692.

Pa Pa Thwin, May Than Nwe, and Mon Mon Aye. 2021. "Violence Against Children: The Practice of Corporal Punishment in Primary Schools of Myanmar". *Journal of Human Rights and Peace Studies* 7. https://so03.tci-thaijo.org/index.php/HRPS/article/view/254113.

Stokke, Kristian, and Soe Myint Aung. 2020. "Transition to Democracy or Hybrid Regime? The Dynamics and Outcomes of Democratization in Myanmar". *The European Journal of Development Research* 32, no. 2. https://doi.org/10.1057/s41287-019-00247-x.

Tessler, Mark, Jodi Nachtwey, and Audra Grant. 1999. "Further Tests of the Women and Peace Hypothesis: Evidence from Cross-National Survey Research in the Middle East". *International Studies Quarterly* 43, no. 3: 519–31. https://doi.org/10.1111/0020-8833.00133.

Tessler, Mark, and Ina Warriner. 1997. "Gender, Feminism, and Attitudes toward International Conflict: Exploring Relationships with Survey Data from the Middle East". *World Politics* 49, no. 2: 250–81. https://doi.org/10.1353/wp.1997.0005.

Whitfield, Charles L., Robert F. Anda, Shanta R. Dube, and Vincent J. Felitti. 2003. "Violent Childhood Experiences and the Risk of Intimate Partner Violence in Adults: Assessment in a Large Health Maintenance Organization". *Journal of Interpersonal Violence* 18, no. 2: 166–85. https://doi.org/10.1177/0886260502238733.

Women's League of Burma (WLB). 2014. "'If They Had Hope, They Would Speak': The Ongoing Use of State-Sponsored Sexual Violence in Burma's Ethnic Communities". Chiang Mai, Thailand: WLB.

6

NAVIGATING LOCAL POLITICS AND GENDER

Cassandra Preece, La Ring Pausa and Paul Minoletti

Conventional assumptions about women's representation posit that higher proportions of women will be found at local levels of government where barriers to entry are minimal than at higher levels (Mariani 2008; Eder, Fortin-Rittberger, and Kroeber 2016). Indeed, studies on established democracies have found that the number of women in politics decreases when one moves from local to national governments (Vengroff, Nyiri, and Fugiero 2003; Kjaer 2010). This literature has shown that lower-level offices tend to be more open and accessible to women (Brodie 1985; Lovenduski and Norris 1993; Vengroff, Nyiri, and Fugiero 2003). However, evidence of this trend is inconclusive in less established or newer democracies, where limited formal institutions and lack of political party activity might prevent women from entering local politics (Kyed, Harrisson, and McCarthy 2016; Aydogan, Marschall, and Shalaby 2016).

Existing literature on Myanmar highlights structural, cultural, and institutional barriers to women's political participation at all levels of government (Löfving 2011; Latt et al. 2017). Yet, the discrepancy between the percentage of women represented at the local level and at the national and state/region level in Myanmar in the late 2010s challenges the "pyramid" model of women's representation: that women will be better represented closer to the ground. Following the 2015 general election (GE), women made up approximately 13.7 per cent of all elected members of parliament (MPs) in the Union (national) parliament and approximately 12.7 per cent of all MPs in the state/region parliaments across the country (excluding military seats). Meanwhile, women represented less than 1 per cent of elected ward/village tract administrators at the local level across the country. Why was women's representation so low at the local level in Myanmar? Drawing on extensive qualitative evidence from local interviews and focus-group discussions (see Chapter One for details), along with secondary data on local elections and politics, we investigate how women participated in local politics and why so few female local leaders were elected in Myanmar prior to the February 2021 military coup.

Following the coup, the military suspended national and state/region parliaments. The military has tried to maintain existing local governance arrangements, as stipulated in the 2008 Constitution. However, the democratic opposition rejects that constitution. In most of the country, the junta-controlled local administration has either completely broken down or is severely weak.

The Myanmar people's revolution against the military resulted not only major political change, but also considerable economic, social, and cultural change. We draw data from pre-coup Myanmar in the late 2010s, but anticipate that the underlying social conditions we investigate remain germane to issues of community leadership, even absent elections, and will remain so assuming elections are ultimately restored.

This chapter focuses on the institutional and structural barriers that impact the supply of women who are willing to participate in local politics, and the demand of women by local leaders and community members in the electoral process. We present qualitative data related to women's attendance and participation in local politics through public meetings, and women's election to and representation in local leadership positions, including as ward/village tract administrators (W/VTAs), 100-household heads (100 HHs) and 10-household heads

(10 HHs). In brief, W/VTAs are elected by their local community. They are responsible for carrying out instructions at the local level from the township administration and are intended to represent local communities to township level authorities. 100 HHs and 10 HHs are below the W/VTAs in the local administrative structure and are both elected as well. While the duties are not clearly defined, all HHs are expected to assist the W/VTA in both safety and administrative matters.[1]

We find that while women were more likely than men to attend local public meetings in many villages, they were less likely to participate actively in group settings. Furthermore, women were significantly less likely to hold leadership positions at the local level in Myanmar. While the data on 100 HHs and 10 HHs are limited, evidence suggests that women were severely underrepresented across all local leadership positions.

This chapter briefly reviews the literature on local politics and women's representation in government. It then outlines the research method and data sources we used to explore gender and local politics in Myanmar. This is followed by a discussion of our qualitative findings related to women's participation and representation in local politics, identifying how they are consistent with existing explanations of women's representation at all levels of government in Myanmar. We present two key findings focusing on institutional barriers associated with local elections and structural barriers related to time and resource constraints, and safety concerns associated with the responsibilities of local leaders. Finally, we outline key implications of our focus-group discussions and interview findings for women's participation and post-coup local politics in Myanmar.

LOCAL POLITICS AND WOMEN'S REPRESENTATION

Local politics, broadly speaking, remains a critical arena for policy development and implementation. Despite growing trends of globalization and centralization within states, the most significant issues facing citizens are often everyday concerns that are the responsibility of local officials (Baldersheim and Wollmann 2006). Further, the prospects for democracy at the national level are often contingent on the presence and strength of democracy at the local level (Gabriel, Hoffmann-Martinot, and Savitch 2000). Local authorities are often responsible for the implementation of state/national policy programmes but can also be an important source of policy ideas and creative solutions (Schreurs 2008). Finally, local authorities are believed to be in a strong position to address issues of inequality, since they are closest to citizens (Celis and Erzeel 2017).

The political participation of women at all levels of government matters and helps address women's diverse priorities (Dovi 2002; Mansbridge 1999). At the local level, women's participation can ensure that decisions and budgets are responsive to the conditions and needs of both men and women and equitable in the provision of public services and goods (Khosla and Barth 2008). Even where welfare spending is comparatively high, many local governments fail to adequately cover the costs of childcare and dependent care that are of greater concern and consequence for women compared to men. If women are part of the local decision-making process, these policy concerns are more likely to be appropriately addressed and funded (Celis and Erzeel 2017).

Studies conducted in South Asia and Myanmar have found that increasing gender parity in local governance bodies can result in increased efficiency and effectiveness (Agarwal 2001, 2009; Minoletti 2014). In Myanmar, a largely male-led budgetary process means that budgetary allocations targeting women's practical and strategic needs have been low (Burnley, Ei Phyu, and Hilton 2016). Unfortunately, gender equality at the local level has remained a significant issue in Myanmar.

Formal legal, policymaking and budgetary powers in Myanmar are historically highly centralized. However, decision-making at ward, village tract, and village levels is central to citizens' lives, especially related to local development, basic administration, security and dispute resolution, and social/religious activities. Many of the main elected leaders at the local level in Myanmar have acted as important interlocutors between ordinary people and higher levels of the state (Kempel and Tun 2016). Public service provision is organized and funded either entirely at local levels by local community organizations that act independently from the state or in conjunction with the state village/village tract/ward or township levels. While the majority of the government's budget is centrally controlled, much revenue collection and service delivery are decided at local levels (McCarthy 2016). In addition, wards and villages are the central location for many social and religious activities that directly impact citizens' lives.

Studies on Myanmar often highlight the role of political parties, demographic characteristics such as education and political experience, and gendered stereotypes that favour men in politics and hinder women's ability and confidence to participate (Peace Support Fund 2016; Asian Development Bank 2016; Gender Equality Network 2017). Recent work on women and local politics in Myanmar has found a variety of cultural and structural factors that obstruct women's participation. Cultural norms assign greater status to men than women, and often act as barriers to women's participation in public life (Löfving 2011; Gender Equality Network 2017). Traditional attitudes and gender norms view men as natural leaders and authority figures, diminishing women's roles to household and family work (Minoletti 2016). The expectations for women to perform all household tasks result in significant time constraints for women interested in participating in local politics. Findings from prior studies suggest that women in Myanmar who engage in paid work typically remain responsible for a larger share of unpaid domestic work and childcare (Williscroft 2020), making local leadership less appealing and more challenging for women. It is hardly surprising, then, that women who take on the role of W/VTAs are disproportionately likely to be unmarried, meaning they likely have fewer domestic responsibilities (Röell 2015).

Other structural barriers studies of local politics in Myanmar included educational and political experience requirements for candidates. Although women and men are attaining similar levels of education (Ahmed et al. 2020), female politicians are expected to have more education than their male counterparts at the national level (Latt et al. 2017). This finding is consistent with ours among local leaders. While women's formal educational attainment might not present a significant barrier for all women, these expectations might disproportionately affect older and less educated women who are interested in becoming political leaders (Gender Equality Network 2017). Women's lack of political experience in public decision-making roles also negatively affects their participation at local levels (Minoletti 2014). Wealth disparities between women and men pose an additional constraint. That W/VTAs need to have sufficient funds for their livelihoods hinders women's involvement in local politics (Kyed, Harrisson, and McCarthy 2016). Additionally, issues associated with travel and security have been found to impact women's ability to hold local leadership positions (Minoletti 2014; Kyed, Harrisson, and McCarthy 2016). We explore these structural barriers in greater depth below.

Less discussed in existing studies are institutional factors associated with the process of local politics in Myanmar. The process of elections for local W/VTAs, as implemented by the *Ward and Village Tract Administration Law 2012*, has been criticized as undemocratic and for often excluding women and young people from voting. Limited transparency and public knowledge about local elections means that people are often unaware that women are eligible to participate and run as candidates for local politics (Kyed, Harrisson, and McCarthy 2016). Further, candidate recruitment or selection at the local level is often driven by male elders of the community (Röell 2015) and is structured by existing gender dynamics and historical legacies (Khin Khin Mra and Livingstone 2022).[2] To address this gap in existing research, we investigate the institutional barriers associated with women's participation in local politics.

METHOD AND DATA

This chapter draws upon data collected from focus group discussions (FGDs) and semi-structured interviews conducted in wards and villages from September to November 2019 in Ayeyarwady Region, Mandalay Region, Mon State, and southern Shan State.[3] We chose these states and regions to reflect a variety of geographical, economic, and cultural features and based on accessibility for qualitative research.[4] In each, we then chose townships (three in each region/state), wards/village tracts, and villages through random selection. The study sites were all located in parts of Myanmar governed in line with the 2008 Constitution. Even prior to the 2021 coup, some ethnic-minority territories in Myanmar had different governance arrangements in place. Since 2021, such alternative arrangements have expanded rapidly, while the junta's local administration systems have broken down in many areas, most acutely in rural areas.

As detailed in Chapter One, a total of 99 FGDs were conducted across all selected wards and villages, for men and women, either aged 18–34 or 35 and older. Each FGD had 3–15 participants, although

75 per cent included 5–7 participants. Participants in each FGD were encouraged to discuss topics related to decision-making as well as opportunities for and hurdles to participation in local politics. We systematically analysed the data we collected in these FGDs to identify differences among states and regions, between rural and urban dwellers, and between young and old participants.

In addition to FGDs, we also carried out semi-structured interviews in each of our wards/villages. Our final sample consisted of twenty-three W/VTAs, thirty-seven 100 HHs, fourteen 10 HHs, nine elders and fifteen other community leaders. Only 28 per cent of respondents were women, spread unevenly across categories (9 per cent of W/VTAs we interviewed, 16 per cent of 100 HHs, 57 per cent of 10 HHs, 22 per cent of elders, and 60 per cent of other community leaders).[5] Similar to the FGDs, interview questions covered topics related to local decision-making processes, along with the interviewees' experience in local governance, including their background, motivation, and opportunities to become leaders, and challenges they faced. We supplement our FGD and interview data with reports from international organizations.

WOMEN AND LOCAL POLITICS

Myanmar's 2008 Constitution established a subnational administrative structure comprised of 14 states/regions, 74 districts, 330 townships, and 16,753 wards (urban) and village tracts (rural). There were also five self-administered zones (SAZs) and one self-administered division between the state/region and district level, mostly located in Shan State. Most village tracts included more than one village, with a total of 63,938 villages.[6] Wards/village tracts were led by W/VTAs who were elected by their local community rather than civil servants. W/VTAs were assisted by a clerk: a civil servant from the General Administrative Department (GAD) who reported to the unelected GAD at the township level. Below W/VTAs in the official administrative structure were 100 HHs and then 10 HHs, who were also elected. Most villages had only one 100 HH (usually the village leader). Additionally, there was often a significant role in local decision-making for local community elders, religious leaders, and leaders of local community-based organizations.[7]

Most official responsibilities assigned to W/VTAs were related to security, although other responsibilities included giving permission for public ceremonies and festivals, registration of births and deaths, public health activities, fire prevention, land administration and tax collection, emergency response, maintenance of local infrastructure, monitoring development projects, and coordinating with the township GAD and other government departments as required (Batcheler 2018). Myanmar law did not clearly outline official responsibilities for 100 HHs and 10 HHs, but they were expected to assist the W/VTA in their public safety and administrative duties (Government of Myanmar 2012). When we asked FGD participants what their W/VTA does for their community, the most common responses were carrying out basic administration (55 per cent), providing general leadership for the community (29 per cent), solving problems and disputes within the community (21 per cent), providing security (17 per cent), and promoting local development and improving service delivery (17 per cent).

Existing research on Myanmar suggests that some W/VTAs have felt they have little to no influence on township planning and budgeting and many residents in local wards/villages have deemed government planning and budgeting to be top-down (Minoletti 2019). However, there were several avenues for local-level involvement and influence. First, in many townships, W/VTAs were able to submit a list of community needs to township-level authorities to be included in the township annual budgeting process. W/VTAs were also able to submit proposals for how the township should allocate funds through the Constituency Development Fund and Poverty Reduction Fund.[8] There has been limited direction or policy specifying how this consultation process should have occurred, however, and it was not present in all townships.

Second, village-level committees engaged local residents to support large-scale projects related to development planning, including the Enhancing Rural Livelihoods and Incomes Project, the National Community Driven Development Programme and the Village Development Planning Project. Third, Township Development Affairs Committees (TDACs) were set up as elected bodies that worked with Development Affairs Organizations on annual planning of and budgeting for municipal service provision. Unfortunately, there is limited information regarding how, when, or under what circumstances decision-makers consulted and included TDAC members (Batcheler 2019). Yet, TDACs did provide the opportunity for village-level committees comprised of local residents to have some direct input into how the government allocated funds.

In all of the villages/wards covered in this study, at least some of the FGD participants described public meetings of some kind occurring. Among interviewees, approximately 40 per cent of W/VTAs and 55 per cent of 100 HHs mentioned holding public meetings and many local leaders expressed that they did not see these meetings as being key bodies for decision-making. Our data therefore indicate considerable variation in the importance that local leaders have given to public meetings, and how frequently they have held them. Some interviewees described community meetings only being held for religious and special occasions, while others claim that meetings have been held to discuss local development and service delivery issues. Prior to the coup, our data indicate that public meetings were held more frequently and were more common in rural areas than urban areas, and in wards that were geographically concentrated than village tracts typically covering multiple villages and a larger geographical area.

Women's Participation in Local Politics

Women represented less than 1 per cent of W/VTAs across the country, despite an increase since the first local elections in 2012 (Peace Support Fund 2016; Asian Development Bank 2016; Gender Equality Network 2017). While data on the exact numbers of female and male 100 HHs and 10 HHs are limited, evidence from our FGDs and interviews suggests that a large majority of both were men. However, women were more frequently 10 HHs than W/VTAs or 100 HHs. Local-level committees were also dominated by men, except for committees created by the National Community Driven Development Project (NCDDP)[9] which included a 50 per cent gender quota (Minoletti 2019). The NCDDP was designed to allow village-tract and village-level committees to influence decisions on budget spending. While female leaders in the NCDDP appreciated this scope for influence, most planning and budgeting was still controlled at the national level, where men dominated decision-making.

Our qualitative interview and FGD data found women more likely to attend local meetings than men. Participants in 85 per cent of the

26 FGDs that addressed public meeting attendance claimed that more women than men attended. Of the 46 interviewees who specified the approximate gender balance among meeting attendees in their ward/village, 63 per cent said that more women than men attended, 20 per cent said more men than women, and 17 per cent said either that equal numbers of men and women attended or that rates varied.

Unfortunately, higher female attendance did not translate to higher rates of active participation at meetings. In fact, women in our FGDs were more likely than men to describe having a lack of agency in meetings. One female FGD participant stated, "Men can discuss during meetings, women just stay silent and listen to the leaders. I think it is because they are less educated than men". None of the interviews or FGD participants said that women consistently talked more than men in meetings, although two interviewees said that women might speak more than men on certain topics, such as those regarding social and religious ceremonies. Similarly, one FGD participant and one interviewee noted that whether more women or men attend meetings depends on what is being discussed. While security and land issues often attracted more men, discussions related to health issues attracted more female participants. Women's status and/or family connections also played a role in their participation. One FGD participant described, "During meetings, some people participate in discussions, but some just stay silent and most of the active ones are the wives of 100 HHs".

Respondents attributed lower male attendance to their work habits and circumstances, with a consensus among participants in several FGDs that men are too busy with work or have migrated abroad for work and cannot attend public meetings. One female FGD participant claimed:

> My husband is a 10 HH leader but I do most of his work as a 10 HH leader. I inform the 10 households if there is a meeting. Because most of the time my husband is away from home. He needs to work to earn so most of the time I do his work on his behalf.

While our interview and FGD data suggest that the impact of time constraints on women's and men's ability to participate in local meetings has favoured women, much as this respondent described, we still found overall that the gendered dimensions of paid and domestic work resulted in fewer women becoming local leaders in their own right. As stated, much of our qualitative data mimic established explanations for women's low levels of representation at all levels of government in Myanmar. In particular, our interview and FGD participants addressed structural explanations related to education. Approximately 15 per cent of women and less than 2 per cent of men mentioned education as an important skill or ability in their becoming a local leader. Women's being less educated than men was also among the top answers FGD participants offered when prompted to explain why they think women had less ability to become leaders. A group of female participants, for example, claimed, "We are satisfied that there are no female leaders in the village because we don't have education, we can't read and write or speak like the men". Lower levels of political participation among women at the local level can be partially explained by expectations that female leaders be highly educated, and the gender gap for specific segments of the population in educational attainment rates. In Myanmar, older women tend to have less schooling than men and are more likely to be illiterate, although this pattern is reversed in younger segments.

Both FGD and interview participants also discussed culture and traditional gender norms. Several FGD participants discussed cultural traditions of male leadership that largely exclude women, while others simply mentioned a preference to have men as local leaders. One FGD participant stated, "In our [Muslim] society, women mostly do the housework and stay at home". Similarly, a female FGD participant expressed, "I think it is only traditional norms that deter women from being village leaders. People usually say that men are more suitable to be the leaders".

In fact, some male FGD participants explicitly expressed strong opposition to women's leadership. One male FGD participant asserted, "I do not like to see women in leadership positions because I am not used to it." Gender preferences for leadership arose less often in interviews, although 10 per cent of women and 5 per cent of men interviewed specifically mentioned that the community preferred male to female leaders. For FGDs, only 22 per cent agreed that women are as able as men to become W/VTA leaders, with female FGD participants twice as likely as males to think this. In comparison, almost 60 per cent of both men and women in our FGDs agreed that women and men did *not* have the same ability to become W/VTAs. When asked to explain why women have less ability to become leaders, FGD participants highlighted perceived issues including that men are better at public speaking, more active, more able to travel, and physically stronger; that women are too talkative, less educated than men, insufficiently decisive, and more likely to face gossip and criticism; it is not suitable for women to go out at night; and that women should stay at home and attend to family matters.

While some of these are practical and realistic concerns for women (i.e. that it is unsafe to travel at night), many of these issues demonstrate clear cultural norms and gender stereotypes that have hindered women's participation in local politics. These cultural norms not only contribute to societal perceptions of women as unable to hold leadership positions, but also impact women's confidence in their own ability to participate in public life. The following sections highlight key institutional and structural barriers our qualitative data uncovered to explain patterns of women's representation and participation in Myanmar's local politics.

INSTITUTIONAL BARRIERS TO PARTICIPATION IN LOCAL POLITICS

Elections for local leadership positions in Myanmar have not been direct or open to everyone. Under the 2008 Constitution, all elections were overseen by an Advisory Board, which is made up of five designated village elders who were appointed by the township administrator and under the supervision of the township administration office. Each household voted to select their household head in a grouping of ten households (their 10 HH). After all such communities had submitted the names of their 10 HHs to the Advisory Board, each household then voted through a secret ballot for their preferred 100 HH out of the 10 HHs. Depending on the population and geographic size of the village tract/ward, each village/ward had one or more 100 HH. If the village tract/ward had only one 100 HH, then that person was automatically the W/VTA, as well. If a village tract/ward had multiple 100 HHs, then each household voted for their preferred W/VTA from among the 100 HHs. The W/VTA was a single position at the apex of the local governance structure, and we believe was viewed as the head of local government.[10]

Local elections in Myanmar have been problematic for women, often disproportionately favouring men. The voting process significantly limited women's participation in the electoral process because most household votes were conducted by the man of the house, especially given gendered cultural norms (Khin Khin Mra and Livingstone 2022). This lower level of participation in the local electoral process is likely to have contributed to a general marginalization of women from local politics as it reinforces the "maleness" of this sphere of action. It may (or may not) also be the case that men were more likely to vote for men, and women to vote for women, in local elections in Myanmar. The local voting process is comparable to that of single-member-district electoral systems, which have been found to be less favourable for women and minorities than proportional ones (Rule 1987; Norris 2006). The voting system was reported negatively to affect women and to magnify rather than mitigate sociocultural hierarchies associated with gender.[11]

While political parties at the national level have often commented on local elections in Myanmar (BBC 2015), they have not historically been involved in the selection of 10 HHs, 100 HHs, or W/VTAs. Existing studies on parties in Myanmar indicate that engagement between parties and local constituencies was low, with many parties lacking key strategies to ensure local priorities are reflected in either national or state/region party politics (Kempel, Sun, and Tun 2015). Further, election reports have also found parties rarely to be involved in local elections and unsupportive of candidates for the W/VTA or other local positions (Kyed, Harrisson, and McCarthy 2016). Despite some candidates in the 2016 local elections who claimed to align with NLD objectives, there is no evidence of parties' participating in candidate recruitment or selection at the local level. It is therefore unsurprising that the levels of women's nomination and election at the local level differed from those at the national and state/region level, since parties do not serve a gatekeeping role.

Further, 81 per cent of all interviewees who held local leadership positions stated that they were not interested in joining a political party. Many interviewees cited their age (too old) as a key factor in their lack of interest in pursuing politics at a higher level. Other reasons for not joining a political party include their lack of experience and their commitment to helping their own communities. A 35-year-old

VTA stated, "Politics is very big to me, and I have to learn so many more things", while a 46-year-old local leader explained,

> I believe that if I join a particular political party, I would only be working for that party and must obey the rules and regulations of that party. There is no guarantee that I would still be able to work for my community's development.

While some of the reasons interviewees provided for not joining political parties can be attributed to personal ambition, confidence, and values, it is possible that the lack of party involvement at the local level has inadvertently undermined the links among the local, state/region, and national levels. Without efforts by the party or national leaders to implement gender quotas, gendered stereotypes are more likely to go unchecked, excluding women in local political positions. While gender quotas and involvement of local party politics would not guarantee more female participation, they would help to offer more opportunities for women to pursue public office and mitigate the barriers for women to come forward.

STRUCTURAL BARRIERS TO PARTICIPATION IN LOCAL POLITICS

Key structural barriers that have impacted women's participation in local politics specifically include time and resource constraints, and safety concerns associated with the responsibilities of local leadership positions. The compensation for W/VTAs and other local leadership positions has impacted the participation of both men and women. According to recent reports, W/VTAs received only monthly stipends (K70,000 and K50,000 or US$40 and US$30) to cover office expenses (Mon 2021). While W/VTAs were assisted by a salaried administrator from the GAD, their resources were not sufficient for the range of duties and responsibilities they often take on.

Both men and women we interviewed noted that they have often used their own money to cover costs associated with the position. A male VTA explained, "Of course. I have to attend to meetings that are held in town. So, I have to use my own money for travelling and food. I get the salary of K70,000, which is not enough". Similarly, a female 100 HH clarified, "I spend money from my own pocket for some tea and coffee whenever we have ward administrative meetings with other 100 HHs, 10 HHs and W/VTAs". Other times, W/VTAs used their own money to assist other local leaders. One male VTA explained, "I used my own finances but not for my own position, just to help the 100 HH. When they go to a township meeting instead of me, I paid some money for their travel and meal". Others stated that they used their own money to support community members and activities. A female 100 HH, for example, claimed that, "If there is a funeral, I sponsor the family for digging the grave to bury the body as well as for some snacks for them". Low salaries for local leadership positions have negatively impacted both the leaders and their families. One female elder explained that:

> We faced some difficulties such as food deficiency due to the limited funds for the household. We did not have money for sufficient food at that time because the salary is low. But the villagers gave us some food like vegetables which helped us a lot.

Many interviewees (both men and women) claimed to have other occupations outside of their local leadership positions. While several female interviewees noted that they were retired and/or supported by family members, many of them identified at least one other occupation. One female 10 HH stated, "I sell tofu and noodles in the morning where I earn some money for my family. And I rent the shop to one of my friends who sells barbeque in the evening".

Although both male and female local leaders have been affected by the minimal compensation and many of them had additional jobs and income streams, we believe these resource constraints negatively impact women's likelihood of participating in local politics more than men's. Male interviewees were more likely to mention experiencing financial issues or an impact on their business/income. However, the gender wage gap in Myanmar has remained significant across both urban and rural settings, with women making considerably less than men (Hansen, Rand, and Win 2020). If local leaders were required to use their own financial resources to fulfil their responsibilities, men were more likely than women to have additional resources to use.

Female interviewees were more likely to mention issues of having less time for family/social life and having to work inconvenient hours. Female interviewees across all local positions were also more likely to refer to difficulties or challenges in their home life due to their participation in public life. A female 10 HH expressed, "As I have to do community work, my family faces some difficulties. Since I have to make time for the community, someone has to compensate and double up on household work". Similarly, a female VTA explained,

> After being elected as VTA, I could not give as much of my time to my family, such as for taking care of my kids, and I was absent a lot from the role of a housewife, but my husband understands ... my parents are also very supportive.

Gendered stereotypes in Myanmar have contributed to placing a higher care burden on women compared to men. The time and resource constraints associated with local leadership positions have made it more difficult for women to carry out their household and care-related responsibilities. This strain has not only presented challenges for female leaders but might have also hindered women from getting involved in local politics at all.

Male dominance of public life in Myanmar has also contributed to gender stereotypes that associate men with public safety and security. Dispute resolution, crime-fighting, and security are established responsibilities of local political leaders. Further, high levels of distrust of the police and court system have contributed to a context in which local leaders—especially the W/VTA—have played key roles in maintaining security, dispute resolution, and justice (My Justice 2018). Interview findings support this gendered stereotype, with many interviewees identifying the ability to deal with security issues as a significant challenge for female leaders. Almost 20 per cent of interviewees who said women and men faced different challenges claimed that women find it more difficult to deal with crime-fighting. One female 10 HH stated, "Women would face more difficulties in solving some problems like fights among men ... to arrest a sexual offender is dangerous for a woman". Similarly, a young female FGD participant claimed, "Men can go everywhere, but some issues like robbery are not appropriate for women to handle".

Women faced additional difficulties in tackling security-related issues since many of these instances occur at night. More than 30 per cent of interviewees who said that men and women faced different challenges claimed that it was not possible for women to go out at night due to real or perceived security concerns. A male 100 HH stated, for example:

> There is one thing that in the middle of the night, women cannot go out alone and solve the problem, such as a fight over drugs. Even Daw Aung San Suu Kyi went out with her bodyguard whenever she went out.

Issues of travelling alone, safety and security have been found to impact women at all levels of government in Myanmar. Yet, the unique leadership responsibilities at the local level contribute more to women being perceived as unqualified or unable to take on local leadership positions. A male FGD participant, for example, stated, "We want men as leaders because they can go out easily at any time and everywhere".

CONCLUSION

Findings from both interviews and FGD data about local politics in Myanmar indicate that while women were more likely to attend public and committee meetings than men, they were less likely to hold local leadership positions and participate in meetings. Their willingness to attend public meetings leaves women's lower local representation, pre-coup, than in state/region and union-level governments puzzling.

Our FGD findings confirm that structural, institutional, and cultural barriers deter women at the local level. Institutional barriers include the local voting process and lack of party participation in local politics, while structural barriers relate to resource and time constraints. Cultural biases such as the perception of women being unable to hold leadership positions also affect women's confidence in their ability to participate in public life. Women are more likely than men to find lack of time for family or social life a key constraint. That women take on a disproportionate amount of the home and care burdens in Myanmar makes the time commitments and minimal compensation for local leadership positions especially discouraging for them. Other factors include education levels and political experience as potential barriers to participating in local politics. Finally, the responsibilities associated with local leadership positions related to security and crime are also viewed as inappropriate for women to handle. Practical safety concerns and cultural expectations that women perform domestic tasks and stay indoors after dark have limited women's participation in local politics.

The coup in February 2021 led to the military's suspension of the Union and state/region parliaments. However, the democratic opposition has established an executive—the National Unity Government, (NUG)—that is overseen by two legislative bodies, the Committee Representing the Pyidaungsu Hluttaw (CRPH) and the National Unity Consultative Council (NUCC). The NUG, NUCC, and CRPH have higher levels of youth and female representation than was the case for Myanmar's previous executives and national parliaments. At local levels, the junta-controlled administration has broken down in many areas and severely weakened elsewhere. Communities have set up various alternative local governance arrangements, and the NUG has also created a new framework for township, village tract, and ward level governance that is being followed in some areas. Also, certain long-established ethnic revolutionary organizations have expanded their territorial authority and are spreading and consolidating their existing local governance arrangements.

We do not yet have clear insight into how these new socio-political developments might affect women's engagement in local politics, but emerging studies suggest greater youth participation and increased female participation at the local level in newly conflict-affected areas in Myanmar's dry zone (McCarthy and Yin Nyein, forthcoming).[12] While long-established gendered stereotypes are not likely to disappear quickly, future studies should pay attention to how these changes impact women's likelihood to participate in local politics and how they are viewed as local leaders. More democratic election processes and greater compensation for local leaders can help attract more women to come forward. Future research should explore ways to recruit young women and create incentives to mobilize them for local politics.

NOTES

1. For more details on the roles, responsibilities, and elections of local officials, see Kempel and Aung Tun (2016); or Minoletti, Pausa, and Bjarnegård (2020).
2. It should also be noted that gender-based discrimination persists in Myanmar due to prolonged conflict and the militarization of culture and politics for most of Myanmar's history. For more on the intersection of conflict and

women's political participation, see Khin Mar Mar Kyi (2018), as well as Bjarnegåd, this volume.
3. We draw on these same data in Minoletti, Pausa, and Bjarnegård (2020).
4. For these reasons, we did not consider Kachin State, Rakhine State, and northern Shan State as study areas.
5. The research design originally aimed for gender parity among interviewees, but the extent of male dominance among these positions made that difficult to achieve.
6. For a detailed review of Myanmar's subnational structure, see Batcheler (2018).
7. In some areas of Myanmar, ethnic armed organizations (EAOs) also play a significant role in public-service delivery and goods provision (Batcheler 2019).
8. Part of the Union Budget, these funds provide resources to each township for the construction and maintenance of small-scale infrastructure projects (such as water supply, buildings, or road and bridge repairs). The funds are managed by the Township Development Implementation Committee and provide MPs with an opportunity to review projects (Robertson, Joelene, and Dunn 2015).
9. The NCDDP is funded by the World Bank and implemented through the Department of Rural Development (DRD) for rural development in Myanmar.
10. It is worth noting here then that the supply and demand of women leaders was likely to differ among these positions, and attitudes towards a female W/VTA might have been more negative than toward women holding 10 HH or 100 HH positions.
11. While data are limited, there is evidence of township administrators' rejecting female candidates that households had selected in the 2012 W/VTA elections (BBC 2015).
12. Existing studies suggest that more women are involved in local politics in conflict-affected areas due to the absence of men (who are either involved in fighting or have been killed). For further research on the intersection between armed conflict and women's participation in local governance, see KWO (2010); Kempel and Aung Tun (2016); Khin Khin Mra and Deborah Livingstone (2022).

REFERENCES

Agarwal, Bina. 2001. "Participatory Exclusions, Community Forestry, and Gender: An Analysis for South Asia and a Conceptual Framework". *World Development* 29, no. 10: 1623–48. https://doi.org/10.1016/S0305-750X(01)00066-3.

———. 2009. "Gender and Forest Conservation: The Impact of Women's Participation in Community Forest Governance". *Ecological Economics* 68, no. 11: 2785–99. https://doi.org/10.1016/j.ecolecon.2009.04.025.

Ahmed, Syeda Kashfee, Toby Carslake, Anna Dabrowski, and Petra Lietz. 2020. "Gender and Ethnicity in Myanmar Education. Baseline Study Report for the Convention on the Elimination of All Forms of Discrimination against Women (CEDAW) Committee". Camberwell, Australia: Australian Council for Educational Research. https://research.acer.edu.au/boys_edu/4.

Asian Development Bank. 2016. "Gender Equality and Women's Rights in Myanmar a Situation Analysis". Manila, Philippines: ADP, UNDP, UNPF. https://asiapacific.unwomen.org/en/digital-library/publications/2016/09/gender-equality-and-womens-rights-in-myanmar.

Aung, Hsu Mon. 2018. "Reforming Municipal Elections in Myanmar". International IDEA. 18 May 2018. https://www.idea.int/news-media/news/reforming-municipal-elections-myanmar.

Aydogan, Abdullah, Melissa Marschall, and Marwa Shalaby. 2016. "Women's Representation across National and Local Office in Turkey". Contemporary Turkish Politics Workshop, Rice University Baker Institute, Houston, TX, US, 14 October 2016. https://pomeps.org/womens-representation-across-national-and-local-office-in-turkey.

Baldersheim, Harald, and Hellmut Wollmann. 2006. *The Comparative Study of Local Government and Politics: Overview and Synthesis*. Germany: Verlag Barbara Budrich.

Batcheler, Richard. 2018. "State and Region Governments in Myanmar". Yangon, Myanmar: The Asia Foundation. https://asiafoundation.org/publication/state-and-region-governments-in-myanmar-new-edition-2018/.

———. 2019. "Where Top-Down Meets Bottom-Up: Planning and Budgeting in Myanmar". Yangon, Myanmar: The Asia Foundation. https://asiafoundation.org/publication/where-top-down-meets-bottom-up-planning-and-budgeting-in-myanmar/.

BBC. 2015. "ရပ်ကျေးရွေးကောက်ပွဲ ဥပဒေနဲ့မညီ". *BBC News* မြန်မာ. 29 December 2015. https://www.bbc.com/burmese/burma/2015/12/151229_local_election.

Brodie, M. Janine. 1985. *Women and Politics in Canada*. Toronto, Canada: McGraw-Hill Ryerson.

Burnley, Jasmine, Poe Ei Phyu, and Melanie Hilton. 2016. "A Case for Gender Responsive Budgeting in Myanmar". London, UK: OXFAM GB, ActionAid, Care, Women's Organizations' Network.

Celis, Karen, and Silvia Erzeel. 2017. "Balanced Participation of Women and Men in Decision-Making". Council of Europe. https://rm.coe.int/analytical-report-data-2016-/1680751a3e.

Dovi, Suzanne. 2002. "Preferable Descriptive Representatives: Will Just Any Woman, Black, or Latino Do?" *American Political Science Review* 96, no. 4: 729–43.

Eder, Christina, Jessica Fortin-Rittberger, and Corinna Kroeber. 2016. "The Higher the Fewer? Patterns of Female Representation Across Levels of Government in Germany". *Parliamentary Affairs* 69: 366–86.
Gabriel, Oscar, Vincent Hoffmann-Martinot, and Hank V. Savitch, eds. 2000. *Urban Democracy*. Städte & Regionen in Europa. VS Verlag für Sozialwissenschaften. https://doi.org/10.1007/978-3-322-99969-6.
Gender Equality Network (GEN). 2017. "Gender and Politics in Myanmar: Women and Men Candidates in the 2015 Elections". Yangon, Myanmar: GEN.
Government of Myanmar. 2012. *The Ward or Village Tract Administration Law*.
Hansen, Henrik, John Rand, and Ngu Wah Win. 2020. "The Gender Wage Gap in Myanmar: Adding Insult to Injury?" SSRN Scholarly Paper ID 3740822. Rochester, NY: Social Science Research Network. https://doi.org/10.2139/ssrn.3740822.
Karen Women's Organization (KWO). 2010. "Walking amongst Sharp Knives: The Unsung Courage of Karen Women Village Chiefs in Conflict Areas of Eastern Burma". Mae Sariang, Thailand: KWO.
Kempel, Susanne, Chan Myawe Aung Sun Sun, and Aung Tun. 2015. "Myanmar Political Parties at a Time of Transition: Political Party Dynamics at the National and Local Level". Yangon, Myanmar: Pyoe Pin Programme.
Kempel, Susanne, and Aung Tun. 2016. "Myanmar Ward and Village Tract Administrator Elections 2016: An Overview of the Role, the Laws and the Procedures". Yangon, Myanmar: Norwegian People's Aid.
Khin Khin Mra and Deborah Livingstone. 2022. "When Heads of the Household become Heads of the Village: Gender and Institutional Change in Local Governance Settings in Myanmar". In *Waves of Upheaval in Myanmar: Gendered Transformations and Political Transitions*, edited by Jenny Hedström and Elisabeth Olivius. Copenhagen: NIAS Press.
Khin Mar Mar Kyi. 2018. "Gender". In *Routledge Handbook of Contemporary Myanmar*, edited by Adam Simpson, Nicholas A., Farrelly, N. and Ian Holliday, I. (eds), pp. 380–92. New York: Routledge.
Khosla, Prabha, and Bernhard Barth. 2008. *Gender in Local Government: A Sourcebook for Trainers*. Nairobi, Kenya: United Nations Human Settlements Programme. https://www.un.org/womenwatch/directory/pdf/Source_BK_9-May.pdf.
Kjaer, Ulrik. 2010. "Women in Politics: The Local-National Gender Gap in Comparative Perspective". *Politische Vierteljahresschrift*, January 2010.
Kyed, Helene Maria, Annika Pohl Harrisson, and Gerard McCarthy. 2016. "Local Democracy in Myanmar: Reflections on Ward and Village Tract Elections in 2016". Roundtable Summary. Copenhagen, Denmark: Danish Institute for International Studies. https://pure.au.dk/ws/files/108219871/Myanmar_Elections_WEB.pdf.

Latt, Shwe Shwe Sein, Kim N.B. Ninh, Mi Ki Kyaw Myint, and Susan Lee. 2017. "Women's Political Participation in Myanmar: Experiences of Women Parliamentarians 2011–2016". Yangon, Myanmar: The Asia Foundation. https://asiafoundation.org/publication/womens-political-participation-myanmar-experiences-women-parliamentarians-2011-2016/.

Löfving, Annami. 2011. "Women's Participation in Public Life in Myanmar". Yangon, Myanmar: ActionAid, CARE, OXFAM.

Lovenduski, Joni, and Pippa Norris. 1993. *Gender and Party Politics*. Thousand Oaks, Califorinia, USA: SAGE Publications.

Mansbridge, Jane. 1999. "Should Blacks Represent Blacks and Women Represent Women? A Contingent 'Yes'". *The Journal of Politics* 61, no. 3: 628–57. https://doi.org/10.2307/2647821.

Mariani, Mack D. 2008. "A Gendered Pipeline? The Advancement of State Legislators to Congress in Five States". *Politics & Gender* 4: 285–308.

McCarthy, Gerard. 2016. "Building on What is There: Insights on Social Protection and Public Goods Provision from Central East Myanmar". Yangon, Myanmar: International Growth Centre.

Minoletti, Paul. 2014. "Women's Participation in the Subnational Governance of Myanmar". San Francisco, United States: The Asia Foundation. http://asiafoundation.org/publications/pdf/1374.

———. 2016. "Gender (in)Equality in the Governance of Myanmar: Past, Present, and Potential Strategies for Change". Yangon, Myanmar: The Asia Foundation. https://asiafoundation.org/publication/gender-inequality-governance-myanmar-past-present-potential-strategies-change/.

———. 2019. "Gender Budgeting". Yangon, Myanmar: The Asia Foundation. https://asiafoundation.org/publication/myanmar-gender-budgeting/.

Minoletti, Paul, La Ring Pausa, and Elin Bjarnegård. 2020. "Gender and Political Participation in Myanmar". Yangon, Myanmar: EMReF/IDRC.

Mon, Ye. 2021. "Thankless Job: Local Administrators up for Election". *Frontier Myanmar* (blog). 26 January 2021. https://www.frontiermyanmar.net/en/thankless-job-local-administrators-up-for-election/.

My Justice. 2018. "Searching for Justice in the Law: Understanding Access to Justice in Myanmar". London, UK: My Justice Myanmar; British Council. https://www.myjusticemyanmar.org/sites/default/files/MJS percent20Report_FINAL_online.pdf.

Norris, Pippa. 2006. "The Impact of Electoral Reform on Women's Representation". *Acta Politica* 41, no. 2: 197–213. https://doi.org/10.1057/palgrave.ap.5500151.

Peace Support Fund. 2016. "The Women Are Ready: An Opportunity to Transform Peace in Myanmar". Yangon, Myanmar: The Peace Support Fund. https://reliefweb.int/sites/reliefweb.int/files/resources/the_women_are_ready_english__1.pdf.

Robertson, Bart, Cindy Joelene, and Laura Dunn. 2015. "Policy Dialogue Brief Series No. 9: Local Development Funds in Myanmar". *The Asia Foundation* (blog). https://asiafoundation.org/publication/policy-dialogue-brief-series-no-9-local-development-funds-myanmar/.

Röell, Emilie. 2015. "Women and Local Leadership". Yangon, Myanmar: UNDP, MIMU. https://themimu.info/sites/themimu.info/files/documents/Report_Women_and_Local_Leadership_UNDP_Nov2015.pdf.

Rule, Wilma. 1987. "Electoral Systems, Contextual Factors and Women's Opportunity for Election to Parliament in Twenty-Three Democracies". *Political Research Quarterly* 40, no. 3: 477–98.

Schreurs, Miranda A. 2008. "From the Bottom Up: Local and Subnational Climate Change Politics". *The Journal of Environment & Development* 17, no. 4: 343–55. https://doi.org/10.1177/1070496508326432.

Vengroff, Richard, Zsolt Nyiri, and Melissa Fugiero. 2003. "Electoral System and Gender Representation in Sub-National Legislatures: Is There a National—Sub-National Gender Gap?" *Political Research Quarterly* 56, no. 2: 163–73.

Williscroft, Caitlin. 2020. "Not Enough Time: Insight into Myanmar Women's Urban Experiences". Yangon, Myanmar: The Asia Foundation. https://asiafoundation.org/publication/not-enough-time-insight-into-myanmar-womens-urban-experiences/.

APPENDICES

APPENDIX ONE

Background of Selected Political Parties and Vote Shares

Arakan National Party (ANP)

GE Year	Total number of candidates in all parliaments	Vote share in the election (%)
2015	77	2.2%
2020	15	1.3%

The Arakan National Party (ANP) was the product of a merger between the Rakhine National Development Party (RNDP) and the Arakan League for Democracy (ALD) and was registered with the Union Election Commission (UEC) on 6 March 2014.[1] At the time of their founding, ANP's goals were "federalism", "democratisation", and "development", but in practice the party has had a strong focus on Rakhine nationalism.[2] Previously, the RNDP, led by Dr Aye Maung, was registered on 6 May 2010 and won a total of 32 seats in the 2010 elections.[3] The ALD was founded in 1989 and ran in the 1990 election, winning 11 seats.[4] The ALD re-registered with the UEC in 2012, before combining with the RNDP to form the ANP in 2014. The party claimed to have township executive committees (TECs) in 17 townships and more than 20,000 members in 2020.[5]

Kachin State Democracy Party (KSDP)

GE year	Total number of candidates in all parliaments	Vote share in the election (%)
2015	55	0.1%
2020	8	0.7%

Dr Manam Tu Ja, former vice president of the Kachin Independence Organization (KIO), attempted to register the Kachin State Progressive Party with the UEC for the 2010 elections. He was controversially prevented from doing so, like the other ethnic Kachin parties.[6] He then founded the Kachin State Democracy Party (KSDP) in 2013, and, at the second attempt, on 13 January 2014.[7] The KSDP claimed to have around 13,000 members in 2015.[8] The KSDP was merged with three other ethnic Kachin parties to form the Kachin State People's Party.[9]

Lisu National Development Party (LNDP)

GE Year	Total number of candidates in all parliaments	Vote share in the election (%)
2015	53	0.4%
2020	12	1%

The LNDP was registered with the UEC on 17 December 2013, with the aim of representing the Lisu people in Myanmar and promoting the development of that ethnicity.[10] The LNDP has a close cooperative relationship with the USDP.[11] The party claimed to have TECs in 18 townships and around 11,000 members in 2020.[12]

Mon National Party (MNP)

GE year	Total number of candidates in all parliaments	Vote share in the election (%)
2015	27	0.1%
2020	2	0.17%

The Mon Democratic Front was established in 1988 and ran in the 1990 elections, winning 5 seats.[13] The party re-registered with the UEC after the 2010 elections, using the name the Mon Democratic Party. In 2014, the party joined with a few MPs from the All Mon Region Democracy Party and changed its name to the Mon National Party.[14] In 2018 (overlapping the start of our field research) the MNP merged with other ethnic Mon parties to form the Mon Party.[15]

National League for Democracy (NLD)

General election year	Total number of candidates in all parliaments	Vote share in the election (%)
2015	1130	57.1%
2020	920	82%

The NLD was established in late 1988, in the wake of the popular uprising against the military government. Aung San Suu Kyi (known as Daw Suu) became the focal point of the protest movement and one of the party's founders.[16] The NLD won a landslide victory in the 1990 election, winning 80.8 per cent of the available seats, but the military government did not recognize the result of the election.[17] Daw Suu spent most of the 1990s and 2000s under house arrest; many other NLD leaders and ordinary members were also imprisoned during this period. NLD decided not to compete in the 2010 general election, believing that it was not free and fair, including objecting to the requirement that parties must expel all members who were imprisoned or under detention orders.[18] Aung San Suu Kyi was released from house arrest in 2010, and the party participated in the 2012 by-elections, winning 43 out of 44 of the seats it contested.[19] The party claimed to have TECs in around 300 townships and at least 3 million members in 2020.[20]

Pa-O National Organization (PNO)

GE year	Total number of candidates in all parliaments	Vote share in the election (%)
2015	22	1.0%
2020	11	1.0%

The PNO was established in 1949, and its armed wing—the Pa-O National Army (PNA)—fought against the central government for much of the next five decades. However, in 1991 the PNO/PNA made a ceasefire agreement with the military government, under which the PNA became a "People's Militia Force", meaning it was closely allied with the Tatmadaw.[21] The 2008 constitution established a Pa-O Self-Administered Zone (SAZ), consisting of three townships in southern Shan State: Hopong, Hsiseng, and Pinlaung. The PNO competed in the 2010 and 2015 elections. In both, it won all the seats for constituencies located in the Pa-O SAZ, meaning that it also occupied all of the elected seats on the SAZ leading body.[22] The party claimed to have TECs in 17 townships and more than 80,000 members in 2020.[23]

Shan Nationalities League for Democracy (SNLD)

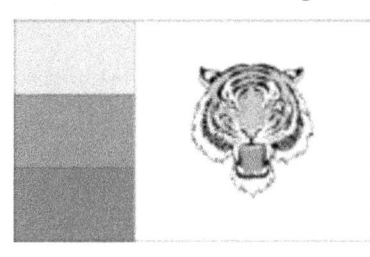

GE Year	Total number of candidates in all parliaments	Vote share in the election (%)
2015	1128	28.3%
2020	71	6.4%

The SNLD registered with the UEC in 1998 and ran in the 1990 election, winning 23 seats.[24] The party re-registered with the UEC on 12 June 2012.[25] At the time of the 2015 elections, the SNLD focused on appealing to ethnic Shan people, but in March 2019 the party announced that they "are trying to change into a state-oriented or policy-oriented party".[26] The party claimed to have TECs in more than 40 townships and around 60,000 members in 2020.[27]

Ta'ang National Party (TNP)

General election Year	Total number of candidates in all parliaments	Vote share in the election (%)
2015	27	0.4%
2020	12	1.0%

The Ta'ang National Party was registered with the UEC on 24 May 2010.[28] The TNP seeks to represent the Ta'ang ethnic group and to work with other ethnicities to establish a federal system of government in Myanmar.[29] In the 2010 election, the party won 6 seats,[30] increasing its tally to 12 in 2015.[31] The party claimed to have TECs in 12 townships and more than 30,000 members in 2020.[32]

Union Solidarity and Development Party (USDP)

GE year	Total number of candidates in all parliaments	Vote share in the election (%)
2015	158	1.6%
2020	42	3.8%

The Union Solidarity and Development Association (USDA) was founded in 1993. It claimed to be a mass social organization, but was led by Than Shwe—then chairman of the ruling military State Law and Order Restoration Council (SLORC) government—with other top positions filled by SLORC government ministers. Membership of the USDA "was essentially compulsory for civil servants and those who sought to do business with or receive services from the state".[33] In 2010 the USDA was reorganized into a political party, registering with the UEC as Union Solidarity and Development Party on 8 June.[34] In the 2010 general election, USDP won 883 out of 1,154 total available elected seats.[35] USDP fared much worse in 2015, taking only 117 seats.[36] The party claimed to have TECs in all of Myanmar's townships.[37]

APPENDIX TWO

Survey Questions

Section (3) Political and Social Attitudes

1. Please tell me how you feel about the following statements. Would you say you (1) strongly agree, (2) somewhat agree, (3) somewhat disagree, or (4) strongly disagree? (7) *Do not understand the question, (8) *Can't choose, (9) *Decline to answer
    1) In a group, we should sacrifice our individual interest for the sake of the group's collective interest.
    2) I think I have the ability to participate in politics.
    3) When a mother-in-law and daughter-in-law come into conflict, even if the mother-in-law is in the wrong, the husband should still persuade his wife to obey his mother.
    4) If one could have only one child, it is more preferable to have a boy than a girl.
    5) In politics, women should not be involved as much as men.
    6) If a woman earns more money than her husband, it's almost certain to cause problems.
    7) I would support my daughter to join parties and participate in politics if she so wished.
    8) When jobs are scarce, men should have more right to a job than women.

2. I prefer to have neighbours who are of the same religion than to have neighbours who are from a different religion.
    1) Strongly agree
    2) Agree
    3) Neither agree nor disagree
    4) Disagree
    5) Strongly disagree
    6) Refuse to answer

Section (4) Political Knowledge and Attitudes

1. I am going to name a number of institutions. For each one, please tell me how much trust do you have in them? Is it (1) a great deal of trust, (2) quite a lot of trust, (3) not very much trust, (4) none

at all? [For the enumerator: Mark 97 as "No answer/Don't know" and 98 as "Refuse to answer"]
1) The president
2) State/Region government
3) Political parties (not any specific party)
4) National Parliament
5) Civil service
6) The military
7) The police
8) Ward/Village/Tract Administrator
9) Health care administration
10) Education professionals (teachers, etc.)

2. Could you tell me for each whether you trust people from this group (1) completely, (2) somewhat, (3) not very much, (4) not at all? [For the enumerator: Mark 97 as "No answer/Don't know" and 98 as "Refuse to answer"]
   1) Your neighborhood
   2) People of another religion
   3) People of another nationality

3. Who elects the president in this country? [Note to enumerator: do not list options. Mark 97 as "No answer/Don't know" and 98 as "Refuse to answer"]
   1) Voters directly
   2) The party that gets most seats in Parliament
   3) The Pyidaungsu Hluttaw
   4) The military
   5) Others

4. On the whole, how satisfied or dissatisfied are you with the way democracy works today in Myanmar? Are you: [For the enumerator: Mark 97 as "No answer/Don't know" and 98 as "Refuse to answer"]
   1) Very satisfied
   2) Fairly satisfied
   3) Not very satisfied
   4) Not at all satisfied
   5) Do not understand the question

5. How important is it for you to live in a country that is governed democratically? [For the enumerator: Mark 97 as "No answer/Don't know" and 98 as "Refuse to answer"]
   1) Very important
   2) Somewhat important
   3) Little important
   4) Not at all important

6. How much influence do you think someone like you can have over the national government's decisions? [For the enumerator: Mark 97 as "No answer/Don't know" and 98 as "Refuse to answer"]
   1) A lot
   2) Some
   3) A little
   4) None at all

7. On the whole, how free and fair would you say the last national election was? [For the enumerator: Mark 97 as "No answer/Don't know" and 98 as "Refuse to answer"]
   1) Not free and fair/very dishonest
   2) Free and fair but with several major problems/somewhat dishonest
   3) Free and fair with some minor problems/somewhat honest
   4) Completely free and fair/very honest
   5) Do not understand the question

8. In your view, do you think the following sentences are accurate descriptions of Myanmar's last general elections? (1) YES (2) NO (7) Do not understand (97) Don't know/No Answer (98) Refuse to answer
   1) Votes are counted fairly.
   2) Opposition candidates are prevented from running.
   3) Voters are bribed.
   4) Election officials are fair.
   5) Rich people buy elections.
   6) Voters are offered a genuine choice in the elections.
   7) Voters are threatened with violence at the polls.

9. In the last national election, were opposition candidates/parties/campaign workers subjected to repression, intimidation, violence, or harassment by the government, the ruling party, or their agents? [For the enumerator: Mark 97 as "No answer/Don't know" and 98 as "Refuse to answer"]
    1) Yes
    2) No

10. Did you vote in the 2015 election? [For the enumerator: Mark 97 as "No answer/Don't know" and 98 as "Refuse to answer"]
    1) Yes
    2) No

11. Do you plan to vote in the 2020 election? [For the enumerator: Mark 97 as "No answer/Don't know" and 98 as "Refuse to answer"]
    1) Yes
    2) No

12. What was the nature of your household's participation in the most recent elections for Village Tract/Ward Administrator? (MULTIPLE ANSWERS POSSIBLE) [For the enumerator: Mark 97 as "No answer/Don't know" and 98 as "Refuse to answer"]
    1) No participation
    2) Voted for/nominated 10 Household
    3) Voted for/nominated 100 Household Head
    4) Voted for/nominated Village Tract/Ward Administrator
    5) Others (please specify)

13. Are you a member of a political party? [For the enumerator: Mark 97 as "No answer/Don't know" and 98 as "Refuse to answer"]
    1) Yes
    2) No

14. What is the most important reason for you in choosing a political candidate? Please choose one only [For the enumerator: Mark 97 as "No answer/Don't know" and 98 as "Refuse to answer"]
    1) Party Platform
    2) Party Leader
    3) Quality of candidate

Appendices 177

   4) Ethnicity
   5) Family ties
   6) Gender
   7) Others: _____

15. Have you ever voted for a female candidate? [For the enumerator: Mark 97 as "No answer/Don't know" and 98 as "Refuse to answer"]
    1) Yes
    2) No

16. What made you support her? [For the enumerator: Mark 97 as "No answer/Don't know" and 98 as "Refuse to answer"]
    1) Party she ran with
    2) Personal traits (likability)
    3) Proposals she made during campaign
    4) I know her personally
    5) The fact that she is a woman
    6) My relatives were voting for her
    7) Others: please (specify)

17. What is the most important reason for you in choosing a political candidate? [answer one only] [For the enumerator: Mark 97 as "No answer/Don't know" and 98 as "Refuse to answer"]
    1) Party platform
    2) Party leader
    3) Quality of candidate
    4) Ethnicity
    5) Family ties
    6) Gender
    7) Others: _____

18. What is the most important reason for you in choosing a political party? [answer one only] [For the enumerator: Mark 97 as "No answer/Don't know" and 98 as "Refuse to answer"]
    1) Party platform
    2) Party leader
    3) Quality of candidate
    4) Ethnicity

5) Family ties
6) Gender
7) Others: _____

19. What is the name of a member of parliament for this Township in the State/Region Pyithu Hluttaw? [Note to enumerator: if they say yes, please write down the name. Mark 97 as "No answer/Don't know" and 98 as "Refuse to answer"]
    1) Yes
    2) No

20. What is the name of a member of parliament for this Township in the Pyithu Hluttaw? [Note to enumerator, if they say yes, please write down the name. For the enumerator: Mark 97 as "No answer/Don't know" and 98 as "Refuse to answer"]
    1) Yes
    2) No

21. Whose decisions affect your life more? The national government in Nay Pyi Taw, the State/region government, the Township government, or your Village Tract/Ward administrator? [For the enumerator: Mark 97 as "No answer/Don't know" and 98 as "Refuse to answer"]
    1) National government in Nay Pyi Taw
    2) State/Region government
    3) Township authorities
    4) Village Tract/Ward administrator
    5) No one

Section (5) Gender Knowledge

1. In general, who do you think makes a better political leader? [For the enumerator: Mark 97 as "No answer/Don't know" and 98 as "Refuse to answer"]
    1) Men can be much better
    2) Same for men and women
    3) Women can be much better

2. In general, who do you think make a better business leader? [For the enumerator: Mark 97 as "No answer/Don't know" and 98 as "Refuse to answer"]
   1) Men can be much better
   2) Same for men and women
   3) Women can be much better

3. Is university education more important for men or for women? [For the enumerator: Mark 97 as "No answer/Don't know" and 98 as "Refuse to answer"]
   1) More important for men
   2) Equally important for men and women
   3) More important for women

4. Who should be the decision maker about important issues in the family? [For the enumerator: Mark 97 as "No answer/Don't know" and 98 as "Refuse to answer"]
   1) This household has a single parent.
   2) The husband
   3) Mutual decisions made by husband and wife together.
   4) The wife
   5) Not important
   6) Slightly important

5. How important is it that a wife obeys her husband even when she does not agree with him? [For the enumerator: Mark 97 as "No answer/Don't know" and 98 as "Refuse to answer"]
   1) Very important
   2) Somewhat important
   3) Not important at all

6. How often do women openly discuss political issues in public spaces? [For the enumerator: Mark 97 as "No answer/Don't know" and 98 as "Refuse to answer"]
   1) Always
   2) Often
   3) Rarely
   4) Never

7. Do you think there should be more, less, or roughly the same number of women representatives in politics? [For the enumerator: Mark 97 as "No answer/Don't know" and 98 as "Refuse to answer"]
   1) More
   2) Roughly the same
   3) Less
   4) Don't know

8. Do you think a woman should make her own choice for voting, or do you think men should advise her on her choice? [For the enumerator: Mark 97 as "No answer/Don't know" and 98 as "Refuse to answer"]
   1) Woman always make their own choice.
   2) Woman sometimes follow man's advice.
   3) Woman always follow man's advice.

9. How often should women tolerate violence in order to keep the family together (e.g. beating, spanking, hair pulling) [For the enumerator: Mark 97 as "No answer/Don't know" and 98 as "Refuse to answer"]
   1) Never
   2) Occasionally (once or twice a year at most)
   3) Sometimes
   4) Always when necessary

Section (6) Gender Base Violence and Actors

1. Before you turned 18 years old, how often have you ever seen or heard your mother being beaten by her husband or male friends? [For the enumerator: Mark 97 as "No answer/Don't know" and 98 as "Refuse to answer"]
   1) Often
   2) Occasionally
   3) Never

2. Before you turned 18 years old, were you ever been beaten at home? [For the enumerator: Mark 97 as "No answer/Don't know" and 98 as "Refuse to answer"]
   1) Often
   2) Occasionally
   3) Never

3. Before you turned 18 years old, were you ever been beaten at school by teachers/adults (NOT school friends)? [For the enumerator: Mark 97 as "No answer/Don't know" and 98 as "Refuse to answer"]
    1) Often
    2) Occasionally
    3) Never

Section (7) Security and Problem-Solving Actors

1. Do you feel safe to travel through your Township during the daytime? [For the enumerator: Mark 97 as "No answer/Don't know" and 98 as "Refuse to answer"]
    1) Yes
    2) No
    3) Somewhat
    4) Not sure

2. Do you feel safe to travel through your Township during the night time? [For the enumerator: Mark 97 as "No answer/Don't know" and 98 as "Refuse to answer"]
    1) Yes
    2) No
    3) Somewhat
    4) Not sure

3. In the last 30 days, how many times did you travel outside of your XX (for rural areas XX = village, for urban areas XX = Township)? If you live in a farm, how many times did you travel to a village that is not the closest one to the farm? [For the enumerator: Mark 97 as "No answer/Don't know" and 98 as "Refuse to answer"]
    1) Never
    2) Once
    3) A few times
    4) Nearly everyday/everyday

4. In the past 12 months, how often have you contacted any of the following people about an important problem, or to give them your views (for each person, options are: (1) once; (2) a few times

(4) once a week; (5) more than once a week; (6) never; (97) don't know; (98) refused to answer)
1) 10 Household Heads
2) 100 Household Heads/Village Heads
3) Ward/Village Tract Administrator
4) Ward/Village Elders
5) Local Religious Leaders
6) Township Administrator
7) Local MPs

Section (8) Media
1. How interested would you say you are in politics?
   1) Very interested
   2) Somewhat interested
   3) Not too interested
   4) Not at all interested

2. How often do you follow news about politics?
   1) Everyday
   2) Several times a week
   3) Once or twice a week
   4) Not even once a week
   5) Practically never

3. How do you normally get information about what is happening in the country? [then ask] Is there any other way you get information about what is happening in the country? (DO NOT READ OUT RESPONSES. RECORD TOP TWO RESPONSES FOR THE FOLLOWING).
   1) Television
   2) Radio
   3) Newspaper
   4) Internet/Facebook/Mobile Phone/Computer
   5) Religious Leader
   6) Friends
   7) Family and Neighbours
   8) Ward/Village Tract Leader
   9) 10 or 100 Household Heads
   10) Other (please specify)

4. How often do you discuss politics with friends?
   1) Everyday
   2) Several times a week
   3) Once or twice a week
   4) Not even once a week
   5) Practically never

5. Do you have a Facebook or Instagram account? [For the enumerator: Mark 97 as "No answer/Don't know" and 98 as "Refuse to answer"]
   1) Yes
   2) No

6. Do you ever see posts about ethnic or religious conflicts in Myanmar on Facebook/IG?
   1) Yes, frequently
   2) Sometimes
   3) Rarely
   4) Never
   5) Don't know

7. Do you ever see posts about sexual violence in Myanmar on Facebook/Instagram?
   1) Yes, frequently
   2) Sometimes
   3) Rarely
   4) Never
   5) Don't know

8. Have you asked a Facebook/IG/Reddit friend not to share graphic information related to ethnic or religious conflict?
   1) Yes, frequently
   2) Sometimes
   3) Rarely
   4) Never
   5) Don't know

9. Have you asked a Facebook/IG/Reddit friend not to share graphic information related to sexual violence?
   1) Yes, frequently
   2) Sometimes
   3) Rarely
   4) Never
   5) Don't know

10. When it comes to the content you see on Facebook, to what extent do you think it is true?
    1) Almost all of it is true.
    2) Most of it is true.
    3) Most of it is fake.
    4) All of it is false.
    5) Don't know

APPENDIX THREE
Focus Group Guide for Field Data Collection

1. Ice-breaking question: Please describe the changes you have seen in your ward/village over the last five years.
   (ရာမှာပြုန့်တဲ့ငါး၀ဲစ္စတြင့်၀း ဘယ်လို၊ေျပာင်းလဲမှုုုေြတရြှိခဲ့လဲ။)

2. Ice-breaking question: Please describe the festivals that you celebrate in your ward/village every year.
   (၀ဲစ္စ၃ ရြာ/ရပ်ကွက် မှာဘယ်လိုမီဘာသာေရးပဲြေြတလုပ်ပှုလှုရြှိလဲ)

3. Please describe how communal decisions are made in this ward/village. (*Note for facilitator—probe on which people have more and which people have less opportunity to participate in and influence decision-making.*)
   (ရပ်ကွက်/ရြာမှာ ရပ်ြာနှဲ့ ဆိုင့် ဆုံး၀ဲျဖတ်ကွဲ၊ေြတကွဲ့ ဘယ်လိုပုံစံ ခံမှုတ္ကသလဲ)
   (ပုံပြီးကူညီသူ မှုတွားရန် - ဆုံး၀ဲျဖတ်ကွဲ့တဲ့အခါ ဘယ်ျ၊ေြတက ပုံပြီးပါ၀င်းပုံ၀ြဲ၊ ဓနသ
   ဇာလမ့်မှုးမိုးပုံ၀ြဲပြီး၊ ဘယ်ျ၊ေြတေတ၊ ပါ၀င်နည်း၊ ဓနသဇာလမ့်မှုးမိုးနည်းသလဲဆိုတာ
   ေနာက်ထြပ် ေမး၀ျမနဲ့ရန်)

4. Can you, as a group, think of any ways to give more people opportunities to participate in village decision-making?
   (အခု အပ္ပုေအနနှဲ့ ရပ်ြာနှဲ့ ဆု၀ဲြ့ ဆုံး၀ဲျဖတ်ကွဲ့တဲ့ကိစ္စေြတမှာ လူအမား ပုံပြီး
   ပါ၀ွးပုံဝြ၊ ဘယ်ပိုနည်းလမ့်းေြတ သုံး၀ဲးသငွတ်ယ်နှဲ ေြတးမိသလဲ)

5. Please discuss what issues are most important for your ward/village? (*Note for facilitator—probe on whether they think everyone in the village agrees on what issues are most important, if not what differences are there e.g. between different wealth/income, age, occupation, religion etc.*)
   (ကုပ်ယ်ပုဲရပ်ြာမှာ ဘယ်ျစေြတဟာ အခိကေအရးအံကီးဆုံး၀း ေအးနာက၀း အ ရာလဲဆိုတာ
   ေြဆးေနွးြခင်းေစလုပ်ပါတယ်။ ပုံပြီးကူညီသူ မှုတွားရန် - ရပ်ြာမှာ ဘယ်ျစက ေအးအံကီး
   ဆုံး၀းလဲဆိုတာကို အားလုံး၀းက တညီတညြတ္ထည္းေြ သာဘာတူ၊ မတူ ေလ့လာပါ၊ မတူလှို့
   ဘာေြတ ြကြား ျျားသလဲဆိုတာ ဖနကညွှ၀ပါ။ ဥပမာ - ဆင့်းရဲခံမွ၀းသာ ၀င့်ေြြ၊ကြားမှု၊
   အသက်၊ အလုပ်ကိုင်၊ ဘာသာေရး၊ စသည်ဖြင် ြကာဟခက်က်)

6. Please work together as a group to describe what your Ward/Village Tract Administrator/Village Head/100 Household Head/10 Household Head do for your community.
(၁၀ အိမ်မှူး၊ ၁၀၀ အိမ်မှူး၊ ရပ်/ရွာပြကွက်/ကျေးရွာအုပ်စု အုပ်ချုပ်ရေးမှူး/ ရပ်ရွာခေါင်းဆောင်တို့ ကိုယ့်ရပ်ရွာ အတွက် ဘယ့်လိုကိစ္စတွေကိုဆောင်ရွက်ကူပေနေတယ်ဆိုတာ အဖွဲ့လိုက် ဆွေးနွေးပြောသပ်ပေးပါ။)
(ရာထူးတစ်ခုစီတိုင်းအတွက်ကျဲဲဲပြောမေးရန်)

7. Please discuss if there are other things that you think that it would be good if your Ward/Village Tract Administrator/Village Head/100 Household Head/10 Household Head did for your community.
(၁၀ အိမ်မှူး၊ ရပ်/ရွာပြကွက်/ကျေးရွာအုပ်စု အုပ်ချုပ်ရေးမှူး/ ရပ်ရွာခေါင်းဆောင်တို့ ရပ်ရွာအတွက် ဘာတွေထပ်ပြုပေးရရင်ပိုကောင်းမလဲ/ ထင်တွေရှိလား?)

8. Please discuss the characteristics of a good Ward/Village Tract Administrator.
(ရပ်ရွာခေါင်းဆောင်ကောင်းတစ်ယောက်မှာ ဘယ်လိုဝိသေသလဲဆိုတာ ဆွေးနွေးပါ။) (မေးခြင်းပါ ရပ်ရွာခေါင်းဆောင်ဆိုတာ ရပ်ကွက်/ကျေးရွာအုပ်စု အုပ်ချုပ်ရေးမှူးတို့ကို ဆိုလိုသည်)

9. a) Are there any women Ward/Village Tract Administrator/Village Head/100 Household Head/10 Household Head in your community?
ရွာမှာအမျိုးသမီး ၁၀ အိမ်မှူး၊ ၁၀၀ အိမ်မှူး၊ ရပ်/ရွာပြကွက်/ကျေးရွာအုပ်စု အုပ်ချုပ်ရေးမှူး ရှိလား။ ဘယ်နှစ်ဦးယောက်ရှိလဲ။

b) Please discuss if the current number of women in leadership positions in your 10 households/100 households/ward/village tract leadership positions is satisfactory? Why do you think it is/is not satisfactory?
(လက်ရှိ ၁၀ အိမ်မှူး၊ ရာအိမ်မှူး၊ ရပ်/ရွာကွက်/ကျေးရွာအုပ်စု အုပ်ချုပ်ရေးမှူး/ ရပ်ရွာခေါင်းဆောင်နေရာမှာ ရှိနေတဲ့အမျိုးသမီး အရေအတွက် အားရေကျနပ်ဖွယ် ကောင်းသလား။ ဘာကြောင့် အားရေနပ်/ အားမေနပ်ဖွယ်ပါလဲ?)

10. Please work together as a group to describe the most active women's group in your village/ward? What do they do? What do you think of their role in your village/ward?
(ကိုယ့်ရပ်ရွာထဲမှာ အတက်ကြွဆုံး အမျိုးသမီးအဖွဲ့ရှိဝ။ မရှိပါခင်းအေပ အစုအဖွဲ့အေနာနဲ့ စဉ်းစားပါပီ ပြောပြပေးပါ။ ရပ်ရွာမှာ သူတို့ရဲ့ အနေကဘာ ဘာတွေလဲ)

11. Do you think women and men have the same ability to be THE village/ward leader? Why is that? Please discuss. (*Note for facilitator — probe on: do women and men have the same opportunities/face the same challenges to become a leader? Please highlight leadership abilities mention by participants in your notes.*)

(ရပ်ကွက်/ကျေးရွာခေါင်းဆောင် ဖြစ်ဖို့ရာ အမျိုးသားနှင့် အမျိုးသမီး ဖြစ်မှုရသူတူညီတဲ့ အရည်အချင်း ရှိတယ်လို့ ထင်ပါသလား။ ဘာဖြစ်ကာင့်လဲ ထင့်/မထင့် ဆိုတာ ဆွေးနွေးပြောပြပေးပါ။ ပံ့ပိုးကူညီသူ မှတ်ထားရန် - ခေါင်းဆောင်တစ်ယောက် ဖြစ်ဖို့ရာ အမျိုးသားနှင့် အမျိုးသမီးတို့ အခွင့်အရေးအတူတူရနေပါသလား၊ ဖက်ကဲ့ရဲ့တဲ့ စိန်ခေါ်မှုများကို တူသလားဆိုတာ နောက်ထပ်ထပ်မေးမြန်းပါ။ ခေါင်းဆောင်အရည်အချင်းနှင့် ပတ်သက်ပြီး ပါဝင်ဆွေးနွေးသူတို့၏ အဓိကထားပြောဆိုကြကို မှတ်သားပေးပါ)

APPENDIX FOUR

Interview Guide Used for Field Data Collection

1. How many years have you held your current position?
   (အခုလက်ရှိရေနရာမှာတာဝန်မှုး ဆောင်နေတာ ဘယ်နှစ်နှစ်ရှိပြီလဲ)

   a. Did you hold any community leadership positions before that? If yes, please give dates and positions.
   (အရှေ့နှစ်ကာရော ရပ်ရွာဒေသရဲ့ ခေါင်းဆောင်ဖြစ်နေရာ တစုံတရာရာ တာဝန်ယူခဲ့တာမိုးရှိသလား၊ ရှိခဲ့ရင် ဘယ်ခုနှစ်ကလဲ၊ ဘယ်နေရာလဲဆိုတာ ဝေင်းဖူးပြီးပါပြီ ဖြေပေးပါ)

2. What is your current main occupation?
   လက်ရှိအဓိက အလုပ်ကဘာလဲ။ (တကယ်လို့ အလုပ်ကပိုရှိနေလျှင် အခန့်ညွှန်းပေးချပြီး၊ ဝင်ငွေအသည်းပို ရတဲ့အလုပ်ကိုဖြီကထားဖြေရန်။)

3. What is the highest level of education you have obtained?
   (အမြင့်ဆုံးတက်ရောက်ခဲ့တဲ့ ပညာအရည်အချင်းကို ဖြေပါ)

4. What were your main motivations for becoming a community leader?
   (ရပ်ရွာဒေသရဲ့ ခေါင်းဆောင်ဖြစ်ဖို့ လူထုကြီးမင်းကို အဓိကစဆောင်တုပ်ကြန်စဲ့ အခံကြောက်ဘာတွေလဲ)

5. Were there any role models that inspired you to engage in community affairs?
   (ရပ်ရွာဒေသ ကိစ္စတွေကို ဆောင်ရွက်ခွင့်အခါ ကိုယ့်လေးစားအားက် အတုယူခဲ့ရတဲ့ စံပုဂ္ဂိုလ်လို့ဘာ ဘယ်သူတွေလဲ)

6. Has anyone else in your family or relatives been involved in community affairs? If so, please give details. (*Note to interviewer — this includes all relatives e.g. cousins, uncles, grandparents etc., not just their immediate family*)
   (ကိုယ့်မိသားစုထဲ၊ ဒါမှမဟုတ် ဆွေမျိုးသီကြာထဲ မှာရော ရပရေးရွာရေးကိစ္စတွေမှာ ဝင်ပါနေတဲ့သူရှိသလား၊ ရှိရင် အေးစိတ် ဖြေပါပါပြီ။ အကယ်၍သာ ဆိုးဘွားသားရှုည်းထည့်ရန်၊ မေးမြန်းသူမှတ်ရန် - ဆွေမျိုးသီးခြားထဲတွင် ဥပမာ - ဝမ်းကြမ်း၊ ဦးလေးများ၊ အဖိုးအဖြားများ အစရှိသူတို့ ပါဝင်သည်၊ ဆွေးဆောင်းအရင်းအချာတညားမဟုတ်)

Appendices

7. When did you first stand for election as a 10 Household leader/Village head/100 Household Head/Ward/Village Tract Administrator?
(၁၀ အိမ်မှူး၊ ၁၀၀ အိမ်မှူး၊ ရြာ/ရပ်ကွက်/ဝေက်းရြာအုပ်ပူ့ အုပ်ပိုဝေရေးမှူးအျဖစ္ ဘယ္ျနုားက ပထမဆံုးအနုကီမှ ဝေရးဝေကာကြံဝင့်တာလဲ)

8. a. Did you need to use your own financial resources to become a 10 Household leader/Village head/100 Household Head/Ward/Village Tract Administrator/community leader?)
(၁၀ အိမ်မှူး၊ ၁၀၀ အိမ်မှူး၊ ရြာ/ရပ်ကွက်/ဝေက်းရြာအုပ်ပူ့ အုပ်ပိုဝေရေးမှူး/ ရပ်ရွာဝေခါင်းဝေဆာင္ ျဖစ္ဖို့၊ ကုိယ်ပိုင်ရဲ့ ဝေငြေဖျကးဝေငြသံုးပုးစဲြရန်ခဲ့တာ ရှိသလား)

b. Do you have to spend your own financial resources in your role as a 10 Household leader/Village head/100 Household Head/Ward/Village Tract Administrator/community leader?
ယခုလက်ရှိလုပ်ဝတာဝန္မႈးဝေဆာင္ဝေနတဲ့ဝေနရာကို ထိန္းသိမ္း ထားဖို့
ုုဝေငြေဖျကးသံုးပုးစဲြဝေနရတာရှိပါလား။

9. What skills and abilities helped you to become a 10 Household leader/Village head/100 Household Head/Ward/Village Tract Administrator/community leader?
(၁၀ အိမ်မှူး၊ ၁၀၀ အိမ်မှူး၊ ရြာ/ရပ်ကွက်/ဝေက်းရြာအုပ်ပူ့ အုပ်ပိုဝေရေးမှူး/ ရပ်ရွာဝေခါင်းဝေဆာင္ ျဖစ္ဖို့၊ ဘယ္လိုအ ရည္ခ္င်း ဝေတြက အေထာက္ကူျပဳပီသလဲ)

10. When you were running as a candidate for the village/10 Household leader/Tract Administrator position, what kind of response did you get from your community?
(၁၀ အိမ်မှူး၊ ရြာ/ရပ်ကွက်/ဝေက်းရြာအုပ်ပူ့ အုပ်ပိုဝေရေးမှူး/ ရပ်ရွာဝေခါင်းဝေဆာင္ အျဖစ္ ဝင်ဝေရာက္ အေရးခံယ္ဲတုန္းက ရပ်ရွာဝေဒသကလူဝေတြက ဘယ္လို တုန္ ့ျပန္ ကာသလဲ) (၁ဖနုက်မွထက်ဝင်ဝေရာဝေကြေရးခံယ္ဲခဲ့ လ့်ညႊး အနုကီမွ့်ရင်းအကြက် ဝေမးရန္)

11. Has your participation in community life resulted in any difficulties or challenges in your home life?
(ရပ်ရွာဝေဒသကိစၥဝေတြမွာ ပါဝင့်အကြက် ကုိယ်ပိုင်မီသားစုဘဝမွာ အခက္အခဲျဖစၥာဝေတြ၊ စိန္ဝေခနုမးဝေတြ ရွိလာတာဝေတြ ရွိသလား) (၁ ဖနုက်မွထက်ဝင်ဝေရာဝေကြေရးခံယ္ဲခဲ့လ့်ညႊး အနုကီမွ့်ရင်းအကြက် ဝေမး ရန္)

12. Did you face any harassment or intimidation or strong competition during your election? If so, please elaborate.

    (ရပွေးကေံရေးကောကြွဝဂ္ဂနွံးက ကုဝိယှ့်ကို ဝေစာ့ကား့ဝွိမ့်ခင်တာဝေတြ၊ သိကရှာခံ ဝေး့ဝွဘကွ္ဂတ္ထာ ဝေတြ ဖှကဝိခဲဖှူးသလား။ ဖှကဝိခဲဖှူးရင် အက်ယ့်ပဲ့ ဝေပျဟပျုပပါ)

Community Leadership and Governance
(ရပြွာဝေသ ဝေခါင့်းဝေဆာင်းှဝ့်ှ အုပ်ပိမိုး)

13. In your opinion, what kind of leader does your community prefer?

    (သ့်ှအျုမဏ္ဍရ၊ သ့်ှရဲ့ှ ရပြွာဝေသကလူဝေတြက ဘယ်ျုဝိဝေခါင်းဝေဆာင့်ကိုဝိ ပိုသေဘာက်တယျှိ/ ထွ့လဲ) (သူတို ဝ့ှိဆီကအေျှုဖပဲလိုခ်င့်ာ၊ ဉပမာအရ့်ဝေပးလို ဝ့မရ)

14. How do you make decisions for your community?

    (ရပြွာဝေသအတြက် ဆုံးျုဖတ်က့်ဝေတြကုဝိ ဘယျှိခံမှတ့်ှဝေလ့်ရှိသလဲ (၁၀ အိမ့်း၊ ၁၀၀ အိမ့်း ဝေတြဆိုရင္ဂီမိအပို့်ဝေတြကိုည္ဂနဲ့းျုပီးဝေမးသာရန))

15. What opportunities do your community have to participate in decision-making?

    (ရပြွာဝေသက လူထုကုဝိယွှ့ဂီဂ္ ဆုံးျုဖတ္ဂီက့်အပို့်းဝေတြမှာ ဝဂ္ဂိုးပုဝိ့်ှ ဘယ္ဂီအခြ့်ှအေရးမ်ီဝေတြ ရှိသလဲ)

16. Are community meetings held in your ward/village? If so, how regular are they? Who attends the meetings?

    (ကိုယှ့်ရပြွာက့်/ဝေက်းရြာမှာ လူထုအစည့်းအဝေးပြဝေတြ က်င်းပသလား၊ က်င်းပရင် ဘယ္ဂီပိုမှန္ဂ က်င်းပသလဲ။ ဘယ္ဂျူဝေတြ တက္ဂဝေရာက္ဂလဲ၊ ဘယ္ဂျူဝေတြကပိုျုပီးဝေဆြးဝေးျင်းဖှကောလ့်ရှိလဲ)

17. Do you do anything to promote a close relationship between village/household leaders and community?

    (ဝေက်းရြာဝေခါင်းဝေဆာင့်/အိမ္ဂီမ့်ထာရှုဝေခါင်းဝေဆာင့်ဝေတြနဲ့ /\ ရပြွာလူထုအဖှကား ရင်းးှဝီးတ့်ဲ ဆက္ဂီဆံရေးျုဖစ်ဝေအာင့် ဖှကဝိစားတည့်ဝေဆာက္ဂဝေပးတာမ်ီရှိလား (ဉပမာဝေပးလိုရ၊ သို ဝ့ေသာ့ အရဝေ့ေပးရ။ ဉပမာဝေပးခဲ့ရင်ဝေးမ့်ွထ္ထားရန))

Political Ambition of Community Leaders
(ရပ်ရွာလူထုခေါင်းဆောင်များ၏ နိုင်ငံရေးရည်မှန်းချက်)

18. As a community leader/village leader/10 Household leader/100 Household leader/Tract/Ward Administrator, what do you think is your most important role?
    (၁၀ အိမ်မှူး၊ ၁၀၀ အိမ်မှူး၊ ရပ်/ရပ်ကွက်/ကျေးရွာအုပ်စု အုပ်ချုပ်ရေးမှူး/ ရပ်ရွာခေါင်းဆောင်အဖြစ်နှင့် ကိုယ့်ရဲ့ အခမ်းအနားအဖွဲ့အဖွဲ့အကြီးဆုံး အခန်းကဏ္ဍက ဘာလို့ ထင်လဲ)

19. As a female village leader/10 Household leader/Tract Administrator, do you think you have a particular role to play?
    အမျိုးသမီး ၁၀ အိမ်မှူး၊ ရပ်/ရပ်ကွက်/ကျေးရွာအုပ်စု အုပ်ချုပ်ရေးမှူး/ ရပ်ရွာခေါင်းဆောင်အဖြစ်နှင့် သီးခြားလုပ်ရပ်ဆောင်ချက် အခန်းကဏ္ဍ ရှိပါသလား (ဥပမာဆိုသူကအမျိုးသမီး ဖျစ်စဉ် နေမှသာမေးရန်၊ အမျိုးသမီးထူးအသားကြောင်းတွင် ရှိမရှိကိုအသားပေးမေးရန်)

20. Do you think that women and men have the same opportunities and face the same challenges to become a community leader/village leader/10 Household leader/Tract Administrator?
    (အမျိုးသမီးနှင့် အမျိုးသားဟာ ၁၀ အိမ်မှူး၊ ရပ်/ရပ်ကွက်/ကျေးရွာအုပ်စု အုပ်ချုပ်ရေးမှူး/ ရပ်ရွာခေါင်းဆောင်ဖြစ်ဖို့ အခြေအနေအတူတူရှိလျှင်/ ထင်ပါသလား၊ ပြီးတော့ သူတို့ရှင်းဆုံ စိန်ခေါ်မှုတွေကရော အတူတူလို့ ထင်သလား)

21. In the future, would you be interested in joining a political party? What kind of position would you be interested in the party?
    (အနာဂတ်တွင် နိုင်ငံရေးပါတီတခုခုမှာ ပါဝင်ဖို့ စိတ်ဝင်စားပါသလား၊ ပါတီမှာ ဝင်ပြုလုပ်ရင် ဘယ်လိုနေရာ/ရာထူးတွေမှာ လုပ်ဖို့ စိတ်ဝင်စားပါသလဲ)

22. Can you imagine yourself ever becoming a member of parliament? Will you want to run for elections at the national level?
    (ကိုယ့်ကိုကိုယ် လွှတ်တော်ကိုယ်စားလှယ်စဉ်း ဖြစ်လာဖို့ စိတ်ကူးဖူးပါသလား။ နိုင်ငံအဆင့် ရွေးကောက်ပွဲတွေမှာ ပါဝင်ချင်ပါသလား)

23. On hindsight, what do you think is the best experience or accomplishment in your community leadership career?
    (နောက်ကြောင်းအနေနှင့် ကိုယ့်ရပ်ရွာဒေသအတွက် ခေါင်းဆောင်အဖြစ် ပေးခဲ့တဲ့နေရာမှာ အကောင်းဆုံးလုပ်ဆောင်နိုင်တဲ့ အတွေ့အကြုံနှင့် ပြီးမြောက်မှုကွဲတွဲအလုပ်တွေက ဘာတွေ ဖြစ်သလဲ)

APPENDIX FIVE

Samples of Elite Interview Questions

Party Recruitment, Candidate Selection and Attitudes Towards Political Leadership (Gatekeepers)

Personal Political Experiences

1. Please describe your occupational/educational background (*Icebreaking question*).
2. Did you have any experience participating in politics or public life before joining party?
3. What were your main motivations for becoming involved in politics/party?
4. Has anyone else in your family been involved in politics? If so, please give details.
5. How many years have you been an active member of _____ party? (*ask only if you cannot get the information publicly*)
6. Has your participation in politics resulted in any difficulties or improvements in your home life?
7. Did you face any harassment or intimidation being a party gatekeeper? (*Note to interviewer: this can be in the form of online, social media, verbal harassment, physical threats, attacks or exclusion from places to campaign*)

Intra Party Rules and Candidate Selection Procedures

8. Please tell me how people in your party get chosen to be members of central committee (CC) or central executive committee (CEC)?
9. Different levels of candidate selection:
    a. Did your Central Committee play an important role in selecting candidates?
    b. Did your Township Chairman play an important role in selecting candidates?
    c. Were there other individuals who played a key role in the candidate selection process? (*please identify gender*)
10. Experience in Party Positions:
    a. Have you held any position within your party? (e.g. *Central committee, township committee, Youth wing, Women's wing*)
    b. If so, how did you get chosen for that position?

11. How do people in your party get chosen to become members of the party's township committee? (*prompt to interviewer: please record separately the process for: i) chairperson, ii) secretary, and iii) other positions*)
12. Can you explain more of your party's rules, criteria and procedures in selecting candidates for the last general election? (Please check if there is an internal election process, check if ordinary party members have a chance to be nominated as candidates). Can you describe the process in more detail?
13. Can the ordinary party members decide who the party nominates as a candidate for a general election?
14. If you could change the rules and procedures used by your party for candidate selection, what would you change?
15. In your opinion, what kind of candidates does your party prefers? Are there specific criteria or skills your party is looking for? (Prompt to interviewer, please check for all the following: e.g. occupation, age, education, political background, gender, appearance, ethnic, family or religious background)
16. Do you think there was gender balance in your party's list of candidates in the 2015 election? Why do you think so?
17. Do you think that there was an appropriate amount of diversity in your party's list of candidates for the 2015 election? Why do you think so?
18. In the 2015 elections, did your party have policies to increase the number of female candidates? If so, how effective do you think these were?
19. Does your party have any plans or policies to try and increase the number of female candidates for 2020?

Attitudes Toward Candidates and Politicians

20. As a Township Chairman/CEC/CC member, what do you think is your most important role?
21. Do you think that women and men have the same opportunities and face the same challenges to become parliamentary candidates?
22. Do you think more ought to be done to improve women's political participation and ambition to become parliamentarians? (Prompts for interviewer, e.g. more political funding, training, mentorship, quotas etc.) Please elaborate.

Party Recruitment, Candidate Selection and Attitudes Towards Political Leadership (Candidates and MPs)

Personal Political Experiences

23. Please describe your occupational/educational background (Ice-breaking question).
24. Did you have any role model or leader who inspired you to join politics?
25. Did you have any experience participating in politics or public life before joining party?
26. What were your main motivations for becoming involved in politics/party?
27. Has anyone else in your family been involved in politics? If so, please give details.
28. How many years have you been an active member of _____ party? (ask only if you cannot get the information publicly)
29. When did you first become a candidate and stand for elections?
30. Did financial resources affect your decision to stand in election?
31. What skills and abilities do you think you have that were especially helpful for you to compete/win parliamentary elections?
32. Has your participation in politics resulted in any difficulties or improvements in your home life?
33. Did you face any difficulties travelling around your constituency during the campaign?
34. Did you face any harassment or intimidation during your campaign? (Note to interviewer: this can be in the form of online, social media, verbal harassment, physical threats, attacks or exclusion from places to campaign)

Intra Party Rules and Candidate Selection Procedures

35. Please tell me how people in your party get chosen to be members of central committee (CC) or central executive committee (CEC)?
36. Different levels of candidate selection:
    a. Did your Central Committee play an important role in selecting candidates?
    b. Did your Township Chairman play an important role in selecting candidates?
    c. Were there other individuals who played a key role in the candidate selection process? (please identify gender)

37. Experience in Party Positions:
    a. Have you held any position within your party? (e.g. Central committee, township committee, Youth wing, Women's wing)
    b. If so, how did you get chosen for that position?
38. How do people in your party get chosen to become members of the party's township committee? (prompt to interviewer: please record separately the process for: i) chairperson, ii) secretary, and iii) other positions)
39. Can you explain more of your party's rules, criteria and procedures in selecting candidates for the last general election? (Please check if there is an internal election process, check if ordinary party members have a chance to be nominated as candidates). Can you describe the process in more detail?
40. Can the ordinary party members decide who the party nominates as a candidate for a general election?
41. If you could change the rules and procedures used by your party for candidate selection, what would you change?
42. In your opinion, what kind of candidates does your party prefers? Are there specific criteria or skills your party is looking for? (Prompt to interviewer, please check for all the following: e.g. occupation, age, education, political background, gender, appearance, ethnic, family or religious background)
43. Do you think there was gender balance in your party's list of candidates in the 2015 election? Why do you think so?
44. Do you think that there was an appropriate amount of diversity in your party's list of candidates for the 2015 election? Why do you think so?
45. In the 2015 elections, did your party have policies to increase the number of female candidates? If so, how effective do you think these were?
46. Does your party have any plans or policies to try and increase the number of female candidates for 2020?

Attitudes Toward Candidates and Politicians
47. As a member of parliament, what do you think is your most important role?
48. What issues do you think ought to be raised or debated more in Parliament in Myanmar?

49. Do you think that women and men have the same opportunities and face the same challenges to become parliamentary candidates?
50. As a female/ethnic minority member of parliament, do you think you have a particular role to play for women/your ethnic community?
51. Do you think more ought to be done to improve women's political participation and ambition to become parliamentarians? (Prompts for interviewer, e.g. more political funding, training, mentorship, quotas etc.) Please elaborate.
52. On hindsight, what do you think is the best experience or accomplishment in your political career?

NOTES

1. Information on party registration taken from www.uec.gov.mm (accessed 17 February 2020).
2. Martin Smith, *Arakan (Rakhine State): A Land in Conflict on Myanmar's Western Frontier* (Amsterdam: Transnational Institute, December 2019), pp. 88–90.
3. Enlightened Myanmar Research, "Factbook of Political Parties in Myanmar, 2010–2012" (Yangon: Enlightened Myanmar Research, March 2014), p. 207.
4. Ibid., p. 95.
5. Telephone conversation with senior central party official, February 2020.
6. Martin Smith, "Reflections on the Kachin Ceasefire", in *War and Peace in the Borderlands of Myanmar*, edited by Mandy Sadan (Copenhagen: NIAS Press, 2016), pp. 87–88.
7. BNI Election Newsroom, "KSDP leader Dr. Tu Jar calls for peace in Kachin State during the election campaign", 14 October 2015, https://www.bnionline.net/en/2015-election/kachin-state/item/935-ksdp-leader-dr-tu-ja-calls-for-peace-in-kachin-state-during-election.html.
8. Telephone conversation with senior central party official, February 2020.
9. Kachin News Group, "Another Kachin Political Party Merges with KSPP", *BNI*, 23 December 2019, https://www.bnionline.net/en/news/another-kachin-political-party-merges-kspp.
10. www.uec.gov.mm (accessed 17 February 2020).
11. Emily Fishbein, "'The Blood Spoke': Lisu Deaths Stir Unrest in Kachin", *Frontier Myanmar*, 11 July 2019.
12. Telephone conversation with senior central party official, February 2020.
13. Derek Tonkin, "The 1990 Elections in Myanmar: Broken Promises or a Failure of Communication?", *Contemporary Southeast Asia: A Journal of International and Strategic Affairs* 29, no. 1 (2007): 35.

14. Susanne Kempel, Chan Myawe Aung Sun, and Aung Tun, "Myanmar Political Parties at a Time of Transition: Political Party Dynamics at the National and Local Level" (Yangon: Pyoe Pin, April 2015).
15. Naw Betty Han, "Three Political Parties Merge Under Mon Party Banner", *Myanmar Times*, 26 September 2018, https://www.mmtimes.com/news/three-political-parties-merge-under-mon-party-banner.html.
16. Bertil Lintner, *Aung San Suu Kyi and Burma's Struggle for Democracy* (Chiang Mai: Silkworm Books, 2011), p. 64.
17. Ibid., pp. 6–10.
18. Burma Fund UN Office, "Burma's 2010 Elections: A Comprehensive Report" (New York: Burma Fund UN Office, January 2011), p. 8.
19. Enlightened Myanmar Research, "Factbook of Political Parties in Myanmar, 2010–2012" (Yangon: Enlightened Myanmar Research, March 2014), p. 133.
20. Telephone conversation with senior central party official, February 2020.
21. Kim Jolliffe, *Ethnic Armed Conflict and Territorial Administration in Myanmar* (Yangon: The Asia Foundation, 2015), p. 61.
22. Kim Jolliffe, *Ethnic Armed Conflict and Territorial Administration in Myanmar*, p. 61.
23. Telephone conversation with senior central party official, February 2020.
24. Tonkin, "The 1990 Elections in Myanmar", p. 35.
25. www.uec.gov.mm (accessed 17 February 2020).
26. Myat Moe Thu, "SNLD to Change Focus from Ethnic- to Policy-Oriented Party", *The Myanmar Times*, 1 March 2019, https://www.mmtimes.com/news/snld-change-focus-ethnic-policy-oriented-party.html.
27. Telephone conversation with senior central party official, February 2020.
28. Union Election Committee's website: www.uec.gov.mm.
29. Ibid.
30. Kudo Toshihiro, "Results of the 2010 Elections in Myanmar: An Analysis" (The Institute of Developing Economies, January 2011), https://www.ide.go.jp/English/Research/Region/Asia/20110104.html.
31. See Table 1.
32. Telephone conversation with senior central party official, February 2020.
33. Robert H. Taylor, *The State in Myanmar* (Singapore: NUS Press, 2009), p. 446.
34. www.uec.gov.mm (accessed 17 February 2020).
35. Toshihiro, *Results of the 2010 Elections in Myanmar*.
36. See Table 1.
37. Telephone conversation with senior central party official, February 2020.

INDEX

A

adolescent experiences, 92, 112
Advisory Board, 154
Ahka National Development Party, 64
ALD (Arakan League for Democracy), 18, 65, 167
All Mon Regions Democracy Party, 64
Amyotha Hluttaw, 4, 13, 36, 75. *See also* Central Executive Committee (CEC); national level; township chairman (TC); Township Executive Committee (TEC)
ANP. *See* Arakan National Party (ANP)
appointment, 37. *See also* candidate selection
Arakan League for Democracy (ALD), 18, 65, 167
Arakan National Party (ANP)
   background of, 167
   candidate selection (*see* candidate selection)
   women's representation (*see* women's representation)
Arakan Patriot Party, 64

Asho Chin National Party, 64
Association for the Protection of Race and Religion, 130
Aung San Suu Kyi
   and NLD, 4, 33, 39, 40, 65, 169–70
   imprisonment of, 69
   public speech, 83n4
authoritarianism, 123
Aye Maung, 167
Ayeyarwady Region, 19, 94–95, 113, 134, 148

B

Bamar ethnic population, 13, 16, 17, 20, 21, 94. *See also* Ayeyarwady Region; Mandalay Region; non-Bamar ethnic population
barriers to political participation, 154–59. *See also* safety; security
Beijing Declaration and Platform for Action, 6
BSPP (Burmese Socialist Programme Party), 63, 65
Buddhism, 67, 91, 93
budgetary power, 25, 146
Burmese Socialist Programme Party (BSPP), 63, 65

Index

C
candidate selection
  intra-party process during, 33–35
  for Myanmar's 2015 GE, 36–38
  nomination process, 51n5
  non-party members in, 42–43
  recruitment process, 68
  traits preferred during, 43–45
  women's representation and, 71–74
  See also decision-making process; party institutionalization
catch-all parties
  ethnic parties vs., 61–63, 71–74, 74–77
  party institutionalization/age, 68
  See also National League for Democracy (NLD); Union Solidarity and Development Party (USDP)
Central Committee (CC), 38, 40
Central Executive Committee (CEC), 48–50, 73. *See also* Amyotha Hluttaw; gatekeepers; national level; township chairman (TC); Township Executive Committee (TEC)
China, 6
Chin League for Democracy, 64
Chin National Democratic Party, 64
Chin National League for Democracy, 65
Chin Progressive Party, 64
Christian minority, 16
citizens
  gender equality among, 6, 8, 10, 25
  violence, attitudes towards, 100, 124, 136, 137
  women's representation among, 145–47
civil war, 122

Committee Representing the Pyidaungsu Hluttaw (CRPH), 160
community level, 19
Constituency Development Fund, 150
constitution, 9–11, 13, 81, 148, 149, 154
corporal punishment, 125, 134–35. *See also* imprisonment; violence
COVID-19 pandemic, 23
CRPH (Committee Representing the Pyidaungsu Hluttaw), 160
cultural norms, 8, 22, 70–71, 147, 154. *See also* traditional norms

D
Danu National Democracy Party, 64
Danu National Organization Party, 64
Daw Suu. *See* Aung San Suu Kyi
decision-making process, 35, 42, 47, 146, 149, 151. *See also* candidate selection
democracy
  commitment to, 61, 77
  satisfaction with, 93, 98–100, 105
Democracy and Human Rights Party, 64
democratic institutions, 123, 126, 136
demographic characteristics, 89, 94, 103, 147
Development Affairs Organizations, 150
diversity policy, 43–44
dry zone, 19, 160
Dynet National Race Development Party, 64

E
EAO (ethnic armed organization), 161n7

East Shan State Development
    Democratic Party, 64
education
    candidate traits preferred, 43
    gender differences in, 8–9, 98, 103,
        105–8, 147, 153
    political efficacy and, 89
elderly members, 42–43. *See also*
    candidate selection
elections
    campaign, 25, 121, 123, 124, 128
    candidate selection for (*see*
        candidate selection)
    constituencies, 26n4
    integrity of, 123, 126
    for local leadership positions, 154
    for lower house, 36
    systems of, 11–13
    violence during, 128–29
electoral systems, 11–13
empowerment, 22, 74, 135
Enlightened Myanmar Research
    Foundation (EMReF), 2, 18, 23,
    34, 94
ethnic armed forces, 94, 122, 129
ethnic armed organization (EAO),
    161n7
ethnic conflict, 61–62
ethnic groups, 13, 49, 94
ethnic intolerance, 133
ethnic literature, 44
ethnic minority communities, 16,
    61–62, 67, 74, 122
ethnic parties
    catch-all parties vs., 61–63, 71–74,
        74–77
    differences among, 77–79
    establishment of, 63–65
    women's representation and, 58–59,
        65–74
ethnic revolutionary organizations,
    160

F
family violence, 92, 108–10, 112–13,
    125, 134–36
federalism, 61, 78, 81, 82, 167
female candidates
    candidate traits and, 43, 44
    harassment of, 130
    old boy's network and, 39
    proportion of, 15, 57, 76–77
focus group discussion (FGD), 19–21,
    27n10, 27n11, 148–49. *See also*
    interview

G
GAD (General Administrative
    Department), 149, 150
gatekeepers, 18, 33, 59, 133. *See also*
    Central Committee (CC); Central
    Executive Committee (CEC);
    political leadership; township
    chairman (TC); Township
    Executive Committee (TEC)
gender composition, 7, 13–16, 38
gendered attitude, 11, 108–110, 125.
    See also gender equality
gendered social roles, 91, 158
gendered violence, 98, 119, 122,
    124–26, 127, 130–32
gender equality
    attitudes towards, 89, 90, 91, 93,
        96–102, 103–106, 110
    and political participation, 48, 112,
        135
    rural–urban differences in, 114
    See also gendered attitude;
        gender inequality; male
        dominance; otherness; political
        efficacy; security; women's
        representation
Gender Equality Network (GEN), 9,
    82
gender gap, 9, 95

gender inequality
  attitudes towards, 93
  catch-all parties and, 58
  violence (*see* gendered violence)
  See also gendered attitude; gender equality
gender norms, 66–67, 93, 126, 129, 147, 153
gender quotas. *See* quotas
General Administrative Department (GAD), 149, 150
general elections (GE), 32, 34, 41, 57, 144

H

harassment, 121, 124, 128, 132–33, 136–37. *See also* violence
Hluttaw. *See* Amyotha Hluttaw; Pyidaungsu Hluttaw; Pyithu Hluttaw
household head (HH), 144–45, 150, 154. *See also* political leadership; village tract administrator (VTA)
household violence, 108–10, 112–13, 125, 134–36

I

IDRC (International Development Research Center), 127
imprisonment, 121, 129. *See also* corporal punishment
income-generating activities, 131
Inn Ethnic Party, 64
Inn National Development Party, 64
institutional barriers, 154–56, 159. *See also* structural barriers
internal elections, 41
International Development Research Center (IDRC), 127
interpersonal violence, 98. *See also* violence
interview, 17–21, 148–49, 151. *See also* focus group discussion (FGD)
intimidation. *See* harassment; violence
intrafamilial violence, 92, 108–10, 112–13, 125, 134–36
intra-party politics. *See* candidate selection; Central Executive Committee (CEC)

K

Kachin Democratic Party, 64
Kachin Independence Army (KIA), 129
Kachin Independence Organization (KIO), 168
Kachin National Congress Party, 63
Kachin National Democracy Congress Party, 64
Kachin State Democracy Party (KSDP)
  background of, 168
  candidate selection (*see* candidate selection)
  women's representation (*see* women's representation)
Kachin State Party (KSP), 50
Kachin State People's Party, 168
Kaman National Progressive Party, 64
Karen National Democratic Party (KNDP), 50
Karen National Party, 64
Karen National Union (KNU), 63
Karen Youth Organization (KYO), 63
Kayah State Democratic Party, 81
Kayah Unity Democracy Party, 64
Kayan National Party, 64
Kayin Democratic Party, 64
Kayin People's Party, 64
Kayin State Democracy and Development Party, 64

Khami National Development Party, 64
Khumi National Party, 64
KIA (Kachin Independence Army), 129
KIO (Kachin Independence Organization), 168
KNDP (Karen National Democratic Party), 50
KNU (Karen National Union), 63
Kokang Democracy and Unity Party, 64
KSDP. *See* Kachin State Democracy Party (KSDP)
KSP (Kachin State Party), 50
KYO (Karen Youth Organization), 63

L

Lahu National Development Party, 64
landslide victory, 169
Lhavo National Unity and Development Party, 64
life experiences, 96–102. *See also* gender equality; political efficacy; women's representation
Lisu National Development Party (LNDP)
  background of, 168
  candidate selection (*see* candidate selection)
  women's representation (*see* women's representation)
local administrator. *See* village tract administrator (VTA)
local level, 33, 128, 133. *See also* Pyithu Hluttaw; national level; township chairman (TC); Township Executive Committee (TEC)

M

Ma Ba Tha, 130
male candidates. *See* female candidates
male dominance, 39, 40. *See also* gender equality
Manam Tu Ja, 168. *See also* Kachin State Democracy Party (KSDP)
Mandalay Region, 19, 94–95, 113, 134, 148
member of parliament (MP)
  candidate selection and (*see* candidate selection)
  proportion of, 5, 15, 16, 88, 144
  stereotypes of female, 70, 71, 130
military-backed party. *See* Union Solidarity and Development Party (USDP)
military coup, 137, 138, 144, 160
militia, 94, 122, 129
Mon National Party (MNP)
  background of, 169
  candidate selection (*see* candidate selection)
  women's representation (*see* women's representation)
Mon Party, 50
Mon State, 5, 14–15, 19, 94, 148
Mon Unity Party, 81
Mon Women's Party, 64
Mro National Democracy Party, 64
Mro National Development Party, 64
Mro Nationalities Party, 64
Muslim, 16

N

National Community Driven Development Programme, 150, 151, 161n9
National League for Democracy (NLD)
  background of, 169–70

Index   **203**

candidate selection (*see* candidate
    selection)
  ethnic parties and, 65, 68
  violence and, 121, 122, 133
  women's representation (*see*
    women's representation)
  See also Union Solidarity and
    Development Party (USDP)
national level, 128, 129, 133. *See
    also* Amyotha Hluttaw; Central
    Executive Committee (CEC);
    local level
National Unity Consultative Council
    (NUCC), 160
National Unity Government (NUG),
    1, 51, 81, 160
NGO (non-governmental
    organization), 2, 133
NLD. *See* National League for
    Democracy (NLD)
non-Bamar ethnic population, 16, 21,
    81. *See also* Ayeyarwady Region;
    Bamar ethnic population;
    Mandalay Region
non-governmental organization
    (NGO), 2, 133
non-party members, 42–43
norms
  cultural norms, 8, 22, 70–71, 147,
    154
  gender norms, 66–67, 93, 126, 129,
    147, 153
  traditional norms, 131
NUCC (National Unity Consultative
    Council), 160
NUG (National Unity Government),
    1, 51, 81, 160

O
old boy's network, 39. *See also* female
    candidates

otherness, 135, 136. *See also* gender
    equality; violence

P
Pa-O National Army (PNA), 170
Pa-O National Organisation (PNO)
  background of, 170
  candidate selection (*see* candidate
    selection)
  proxy party, 76, 84n28
  women's representation (*see*
    women's representation)
party institutionalization, 58, 66, 68–
    69, 72, 77–79. *See also* candidate
    selection
party membership, 36, 45
party systems, 11–13
patriarchal values, 47, 50, 67, 112,
    113, 125, 126
personal characteristics, 89. *See also*
    political efficacy
Phlone-Sgaw Democracy Party, 64
physical violence, 124, 126, 128, 130,
    135, 138. *See also* harassment
PNA (Pa-O National Army), 170
PNO. *See* Pa-O National Organisation
    (PNO)
political ambition, 44, 47, 82, 135
political efficacy
  and education, 89
  by gender, 98–100
  internal, 91–93, 106–8, 113
  See also gender equality; life
    experiences; women's
    representation
political knowledge, 105, 108, 110–12,
    115n8
political leadership
  gatekeepers, 18, 33, 59, 133
  household head (HH), 144–45, 150,
    154
  local administrator, 144, 148

township chairman (TC), 36, 37, 40–42
VTA (*see* village tract administrator)
ward administrator, 131
political participation
 barriers to, 154–59
 by gender, 96–102, 112
 implications for women, 47–50
political representation. *See* women's representation
political violence
 during elections, 128–29
 gendered forms of, 98, 119, 124–26, 127, 130–32
 physical forms of, 124, 126, 128, 130, 135, 138
 violence in the family and, 134
post-coup era, 81–82
Poverty Reduction Fund, 150
power relations, 135
proportional representation (PR) systems, 58, 62, 66
"proxy party", 76, 84n28
public opinion, 137
public service provision, 146
Pyidaungsu Hluttaw, 13, 14, 15, 51, 78
Pyithu Hluttaw, 4, 10, 13, 33, 36, 75. *See also* local level; township chairman (TC); Township Executive Committee (TEC)

Q

quotas, 34, 47, 49–51, 58, 156. *See also* women's representation

R

Rakhine National Development Party (RNDP), 18, 167
Rakhine Patriotic Party, 64
Rakhine State National Force Party, 64
Red Shan (Tailai) and Northern Shan Ethnics Solidarity Party, 64
religious organizations, 42–43. *See also* candidate selection
resource constraints, 156, 157, 158. *See also* barriers to political participation
RNDP (Rakhine National Development Party), 18, 167
Rohingya crisis (2017), 122

S

safety, 98–100, 110. *See also* barriers to political participation; gender equality; security; violence
Saffron Revolution (2007), 44, 82
SAZ (self-administered zone), 13, 149, 170
security, 67, 150, 158–59. *See also* barriers to political participation; gender equality; safety; violence
self-administered zone (SAZ), 13, 149, 170
self-efficacy, 92. *See also* family violence
self-nomination, 37, 42. *See also* candidate selection
Shan Nationalities Democratic Party, 64
Shan Nationalities League for Democracy (SNLD)
 background of, 171
 candidate selection (*see* candidate selection)
 violence and, 129, 133
 women's representation (*see* women's representation)
Shan State, 19, 94–95, 113–14, 115n3, 148
Shan State Kokang Democracy Party, 64

single-member districts (SMD), 58, 66, 155
SLORC (State Law and Order Restoration Council), 65, 172
SNLD. *See* Shan Nationalities League for Democracy (SNLD)
social inequality, 92
social media, 124, 133, 137
State Administrative Council (SAC), 81
state and region
   Ayeyarwady/Mandalay Region, 19, 94–95, 113, 134, 148
   Mon State, 5, 14–15, 19, 94, 148
   Shan State, 19, 94–95, 113–14, 115n3, 148
State Law and Order Restoration Council (SLORC), 65, 172
stigma, 93. *See also* gender norms
structural barriers, 156–59. *See also* institutional barriers

T
Ta'ang National Party (TNP)
   background of, 171
   candidate selection (*see* candidate selection)
   violence and, 129, 130
   women's representation (*see* women's representation)
Tailai Nationalities Development Party, 64
Tatmadaw, 10, 16, 119, 122
TC. *See* township chairman (TC)
TDAC (Township Development Affairs Committee), 150, 151
TEC. *See* Township Executive Committee (TEC)
TNI (Transnational Institute), 83n1, 83n5
TNP. *See* Ta'ang National Party (TNP)

township chairman (TC), 36, 37, 40–42. *See also* Amyotha Hluttaw; Central Executive Committee (CEC); gatekeepers; local level; Township Executive Committee (TEC)
Township Development Affairs Committees (TDAC), 150, 151
Township Executive Committee (TEC)
   candidate selection (*see* candidate selection)
   parties and, 167–72
   roles of, 40–42
   See also Amyotha Hluttaw; Central Executive Committee (CEC); local level; township chairman (TC)
traditional norms, 131. *See also* cultural norms
Transnational Institute (TNI), 83n1, 83n5
trust, 98–100. *See also* democracy; safety

U
Union Election Commission (UEC), 27n7, 27n8, 71, 167, 171
Union Pa-O National Organization, 64
Union Solidarity and Development Party (USDP)
   background of, 172
   candidate selection (*see* candidate selection)
   women's representation (*see* women's representation)
   See also National League for Democracy (NLD)
United Kayin National Democratic Party, 64
Unity and Democracy Party, 64

V

village tract administrator (VTA)
  barriers to political participation, 154–59
  and FGDs, 20, 27n10, 27n11
  women's representation and, 144–45, 147, 148–51, 153
  See also household head (HH); political leadership

violence
  gendered form of, 98, 119, 122, 124–26, 127, 130–32
  intrafamilial form of, 92, 105, 108–10, 112–13, 125, 134–36
  normalization of, 129–30
  physical form of, 124, 126, 128, 130, 135, 138
  political form of (*see* political violence)
  See also corporal punishment; safety; security

W

Wa Democratic Party, 64
Wa National Unity Party, 64
ward administrator. *See* village tract administrator (VTA)
women's representation
  among citizens, 145–47
  attitudes related to, 89, 90–94, 100–102, 110–12
  ethnic parties and, 58–59, 65–74
  lack of, 4–6
  in local politics, 145–48, 151–54
  village tract administrator (VTA) and, 144–45, 147, 148–51, 153
  See also gender equality; political efficacy

Z

Zo Ethnic Regional Development Party, 64
Zomi Congress for Democracy Party, 64
Zomi League for Democracy, 5